THE DAY THE HOLOCAUST BEGAN

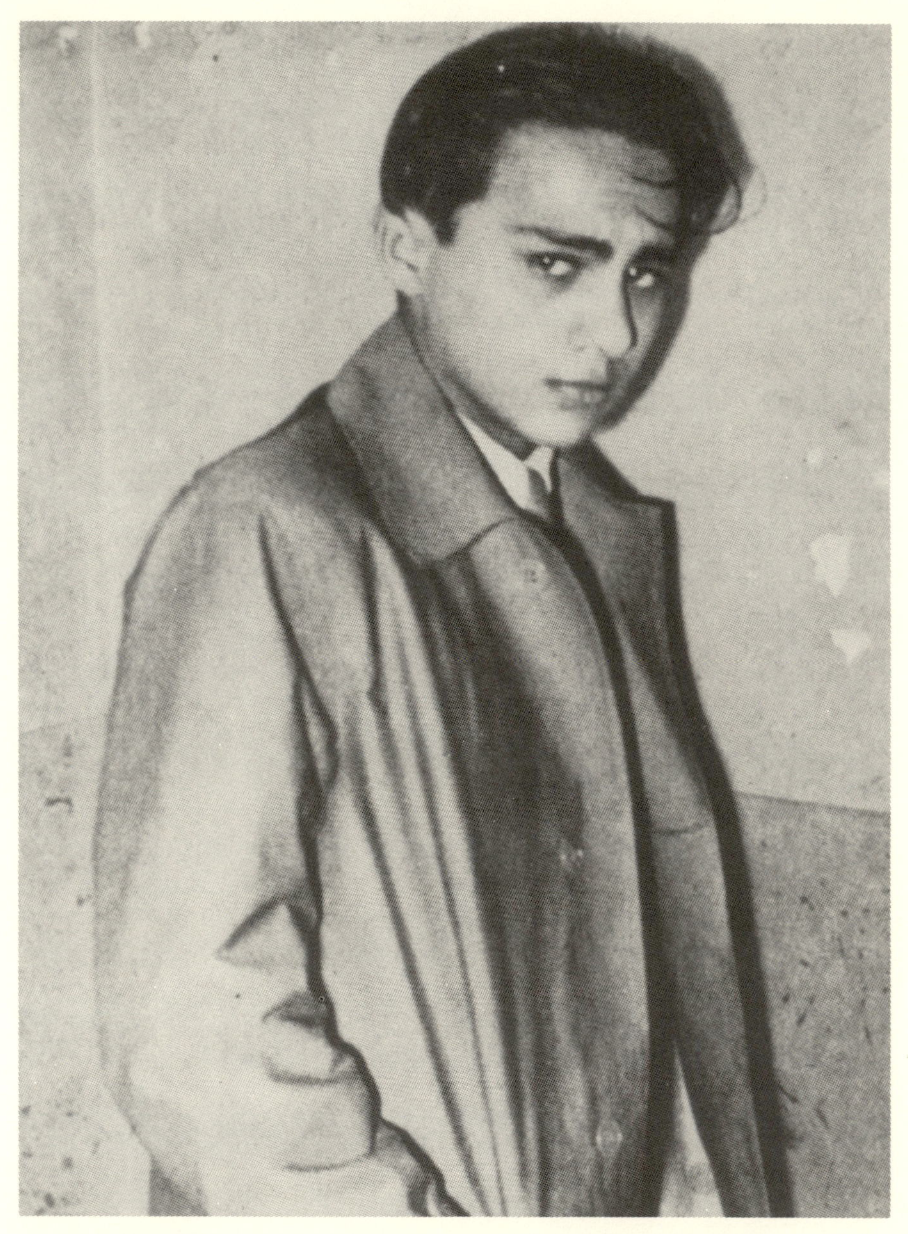

Herschel Grynszpan after his arrest. Courtesy of Archives du Centre de Documentation Juive Contemporaine.

THE DAY THE HOLOCAUST BEGAN

THE ODYSSEY OF HERSCHEL GRYNSZPAN

BY GERALD SCHWAB

PRAEGER

New York
Westport, Connecticut
London

Copyright Acknowledgment

The author and publisher are grateful for permission to reprint excerpts from LET THE RECORD SPEAK by Dorothy Thompson. Copyright 1939 by Dorothy Thompson Lewis. Copyright © renewed 1967 by Michael Lewis. Reprinted by permission of Houghton Mifflin Company.

Library of Congress Cataloging-in-Publication Data

Schwab, Gerald, 1925–
The day the Holocaust began : the odyssey of Herschel Grynszpan / Gerald Schwab.
p. cm.
Includes bibliographical references.
ISBN 0-275-93576-0 (alk. paper)
1. Grynszpan, Herschel Feibel, 1921–ca. 1943. 2. Germany—History—Kristallnacht, 1938. 3. Refugees, Jewish—France—Biography. I. Title.
DS135.G3315S37 1990
943.086′092—dc20
[B] 90-34289

British Library Cataloguing in Publication Data is available.

Library of Congress Catalog Card Number: 90-34289
ISBN: 0-275-93576-0

First published in 1990

Praeger Publishers, One Madison Avenue, New York, NY 10010
An imprint of Greenwood Publishing Group, Inc.

Printed in the United States of America

The paper used in this book complies with the Permanent Paper Standard issued by the National Information Standards Organization (Z39.48–1984).

10 9 8 7 6 5 4 3 2 1

To the memory of

Israel and Toni Nussbaum

on behalf of the millions of victims of the Holocaust,

to

David and Paula Schwab

on behalf of those who were able to flee the Nazi horror
and went on to become valued citizens in their adopted lands,

and to

Stefan Lux

on behalf of those brave souls who were prepared
to sacrifice their lives in order to alert the world
to the evils of Nazism.

It was Stefan Lux, a Czech journalist about whom I know very little else, who on the morning of July 3, 1936, during a meeting of the League of Nations, shot himself in full view of the delegates in the press section adjoining the podium. He left behind letters written the previous night to King Edward VIII of England, British Foreign Minister Anthony Eden, *The Times* of London, and the *Manchester Guardian*, calling attention to the plight of German Jews. In his letter to Foreign Secretary Eden, Lux had written, "I hope that this voluntary sacrifice of an unknown soldier of life will help bring a little clarity and truth. When a man dies deliberately after serious reflection he can ask to be heard." The forty-eight-year-old journalist, married and father of a twelve-year-old son, died that same evening in a Geneva hospital. His gesture was promptly forgotten.

Contents

Acknowledgments

As with any work of this sort, I am greatly obliged to a large number of people. First and foremost, I am indebted to the late Dr. Alain Cuénot, a physician of Arcachon, France, who over many years collected much material on the case of Herschel Grynszpan, especially on the period from September 1936 to June 1940, which the youth spent in France. Dr. Cuénot generously made available to me his unpublished French-language manuscript and his extensive files. I am also indebted to Mr. David Rome of Beverly Hills, California, for his inspiration and help. It was Mr. Rome who edited Dr. Cuénot's manuscript and arranged to have it translated (by Mrs. Joan Redmont) and reproduced, depositing copies in various institutions such as the Library of Congress and the Wiener Library. I have made extensive use of the materials collected by Dr. Cuénot, and both the original manuscript and the English translation.

Another important source of inspiration was Mr. Ron Roizen of the University of California, whose infectious interest and insights rekindled my own interest in the case. A major share of the credit for the book goes to my wife Joan for her encouragement, patience, counsel, and generous devotion of time (and typing skills) and to our daughters Susan and Teresa, whose support and help at times was so overwhelming that completing the manuscript almost became an act of self-defense.

In the course of my research I naturally utilized many sources of information, including The George Arents Research Library at Syracuse University (repository of the personal papers of Dorothy Thompson), the Leo Baeck Institute (New York), the Centre de Documentation Juive Contemporaine (Paris), the Library of Congress (Washington), the Hoover Institute and Library (Stanford), the Institut für Zeitgeschichte (Munich), the Political Archives of the Foreign Ministry of the Federal Republic of Germany (Bonn), the Wiener Library (London), the Central State Archives of the German Democratic Republic (Potsdam) and Yad Vashem (Jerusalem).

While all these individuals and organizations contributed much to the final product, I alone am responsible for the correctness of the information and the interpretation of the facts.

Introduction

It has been over fifty years, and yet these events remain clearly etched on my mind—the news of the shooting and, later, the death of Ernst vom Rath, the pogrom of November 1938 or *Kristallnacht*, as it has become known, and above all the arrest of my father and his return some five weeks later—a pale reflection of his former self, suffering severe frostbite—from the concentration camp at Dachau. A few months later, I found myself on a small Swiss farm, thanks to the efforts of a Swiss humanitarian organization and the generosity of a simple farm family. It was certainly a selfless act on their part, but a traumatic experience for this city-bred youngster who was aware that he might never see his parents again.

We were fortunate, able to emigrate to the United States in 1940. A mere six years later, after a stint as a combat infantry soldier in Italy, I found myself at Nuremberg's International Military Tribunal, translating the testimony of Max Juettner, the last head of the Nazi SA (storm troopers). He explained to the commission hearing evidence against various Nazi organizations that the SA's efforts during *Kristallnacht* were limited to trying to stop the wanton destruction of Jewish property by an enraged population. (The witness could not leave well enough alone; during a break in the proceedings, he came to compliment me on my knowledge of German. When I said that I had learned it in Germany, he pressed on, repeatedly asking for details. I finally told him that I had personally experienced *Kristallnacht* and had left Germany *after* the events of November 1938. That ended the conversation.)

After completion of the trial against Goering and cohorts, I transferred to the Berlin Document Center, reviewing files for possible use in subsequent trials of lesser Nazi war criminals. It was while going through the files of the Ministry of Justice that I first encountered the trail of Herschel Grynszpan. In one memorable occurrence, the German clerk who brought the files for review commented on my evident interest in Grynszpan and volunteered the information that he had worked at the German embassy in Paris during those fateful days in 1938. In front of me happened to be the tentative schedule for the youngster's show trial, due to take place in early 1942. The document listed two embassy clerks, Krueger and Nagorka, to be called as witnesses. I asked the gentleman whether he by any chance knew either person, only to have him identify himself as Nagorka. I was by then aware that Nagorka was a key witness, for reasons the reader will discover. It was at that point that I began my efforts to meet some of those directly involved, and was successful in interviewing Maître Vincent de Moro-Giafferri, Grynszpan's defense lawyer, the German prosecution psychiatrist, and after my return to the United States, journalist Dorothy Thompson.

Some years later I entered the U.S. Department of State and subsequently, the Foreign Service. While in Washington, I wrote a thesis on German plans to try Herschel Grynszpan and was pleased when in 1958 an English publisher expressed an interest in its publication. In keeping with Foreign Service regulations, I submitted it to the department's publications review panel and was informed that there was no objection to its publication, provided that I delete all negative references to Georges Bonnet, French foreign minister in 1938 and one of the leading proponents of Franco-German appeasement of his day. By 1958, he was a parliamentary deputy, while his namesake, Henri Bonnet, French ambassador to the United States from 1945 to 1955, was very active in organizations promoting Franco-American friendship. The matter ended there, and while I continued to collect materials on the case, I did not really focus on it again for another twenty years.

My continued interest in Herschel Grynszpan was not predicated on the assumption that the assassination of vom Rath in itself was either an exceptionally important act—it gained importance out of all proportion only because the Nazis chose to make it so—or that it was somehow a heroic or meaningful symbolic gesture, which it was not. In 1938, Herschel Grynszpan was an emotional, immature youngster. What attracted me to the case—aside from the obvious fact that I could identify with Herschel, having shared some of his experiences—and what makes it fascinating to this day, is what transpired after Herschel's arrest, especially after he was turned over to Nazi authorities. They decided to make him the subject of a major propaganda trial, designed to identify a scapegoat for the outbreak of the war and, more importantly, to justify the horror of the "Final Solution." By then, Herschel Grynszpan had become an entirely different individual, a twenty-one-year-old who decided to take on a huge and well-oiled propaganda machine that had been arrayed against him.

I believe that the story of Herschel Grynszpan deserves to be told. He was, after all, as composer Michael Tippett entitled his oratorio in honor of his memory, truly *A Child of Our Time.*[1]

1

November 7, 1938

The news came to the attention of a nervous world through newspapers and the radio on November 7, 1938. It recounted how at 9:45 that morning, a seventeen-year-old Jewish youth of Polish extraction had entered the German embassy in Paris and had shot and seriously wounded the twenty-nine-year-old *Legationssekretär* (Secretary of Legation) Ernst Eduard vom Rath.

Before long, additional details became available. They told how one Herschel Grynszpan, an illegal resident in France, had earlier that morning purchased a revolver from M. Carpe, a gunsmith, at his small store "À la Fine Lame" (The Sharp Blade), at 61 rue du Faubourg St. Martin.

Having made his purchase, young Grynszpan walked to the Metro station Strasbourg–St. Denis and took the subway to the Solférino station, from where it was only a short walk to his final destination, the German embassy at 78 rue de Lille. This was his first visit to the German embassy. He had previously visited only the German consulate on the rue Huysmans to make inquiries about his identity papers. He inquired of François Autret, a policeman on duty in front of the embassy, which entrance to use. Autret asked him for the reason of his visit and when told that the visitor wished to obtain a German visa, the policeman correctly informed him that he should address his request to the consulate instead.

But the youth was not to be deterred and once Autret pointed out the doorway, Grynszpan entered just as Count Johannes von Welczeck, the German ambassador, left the building for his morning constitutional. Once inside, Grynszpan encountered Mme Mathis, wife of the concierge. Her husband, who was also responsible for the building's heating plant, was just changing his clothing. Herschel asked in French to see an embassy official in order to submit some important papers to him. Mme Mathis, who saw nothing unusual in the request, in turn directed him one flight up to Herr Nagorka, the embassy clerk-receptionist on duty.

Grynszpan reported to Nagorka and repeated his request, saying that he had an important document he wanted to hand personally to "one of the embassy secretaries."[1] Nagorka volunteered to transmit the paper, but Grynszpan insisted that it was too important. Nagorka ushered the visitor into the waiting room on the ground floor and then went to ask vom Rath, the more junior of the two embassy officers in the building at the time, whether he would see the youth. Vom Rath agreed, and Nagorka led Grynszpan into his office, closed the door, and left.

Vom Rath, seated facing the window with his back to the door, asked his visitor to be seated in a leather chair to his left, then turned his chair a quarter turn in order to face Grynszpan and asked to be shown the document. According to the first deposition given French police after his arrest, Grynszpan exclaimed, "You're a filthy Kraut [*un sale boche*] and in the name of 12,000 persecuted Jews, here is the document."[2] With that, he whipped out the revolver from the inside left pocket of his jacket and blindly fired five shots at point blank range at vom Rath. (In later interrogations, Grynszpan gave somewhat different versions, specifically dropping any reference to the use of the term "un sale boche" and claiming to have made a somewhat longer statement outlining the plight of the Jews in Germany.)

Ernst vom Rath, struck by two bullets, stumbled into the hallway and called for help. Receptionist Nagorka, whose duty station was about thirty yards from vom Rath's office, rushed over and found the victim standing at the door of his office, clutching his abdomen with both hands, saying "I am wounded." The young attacker, his emptied weapon on the floor, remained in the room and readily permitted the unarmed Nagorka and his colleague Krueger to take him into custody, assuring them that he did not intend to escape. He did, however, ask to be turned over to the French police and his captors obliged, transferring him to François Autret, the policeman on duty outside the building.[3]

Once in the custody of Officer Autret, Grynszpan shouted "sales boches." Autret asked what had happened. Nagorka and Krueger quickly described what had transpired, adding that the victim was not dead. Krueger later would claim that at this point Grynszpan exclaimed, "It's a shame that he isn't dead." (Krueger was first questioned by French authorities in early December, and in January he asked to testify again, saying that the court reporter had failed to record Grynszpan's remark. Nagorka had no recollection of Grynszpan having made any such statement.)

Before taking him to the precinct station at 2 rue de Bourgogne, 500 yards away, Autret searched Grynszpan for weapons. Grynszpan appeared quite composed, reassuring the policeman "Don't worry, I will come with you." On the way to the precinct, he said, "I have just shot a man in his office. I do not regret it. I did it to avenge my parents who are miserable in Germany."

At the police station, Grynszpan was quickly brought before Police Commissioner M. J. Monneret, responsible for the precincts Invalides and École Militaire. The youth identified himself as Herschel Feibel Grynszpan, born on March 28, 1921, in Hanover, Germany, the son of Sendel and Rivka Grynszpan, both of Polish nationality.[4] The young man readily admitted the shooting and in response to a question about the motive declared, as he had already at the embassy when asked by *Botschaftsrat* (Embassy Counselor) Kurt Braeuer, that he wanted to avenge his fellow Jews.

The embassy was kept fully informed of what transpired at the police station. Within an hour of the shooting, Ambassador Welczeck had sent Herr Lorz, a mid-level embassy official, to ascertain what was happening. With Monneret's permission, he was allowed to pose a few questions to the prisoner.[5]

In his report to the Foreign Ministry, Lorz wrote that he queried the culprit concerning the reasons for his action, to which Grynszpan replied that he was Jewish and that he wanted to avenge the great wrong which had been visited on his fellow Jews in general and on his family in particular.

A quick search of the prisoner had revealed a wallet with 38 francs (about $1) in change and various papers, including a purchase declaration for the revolver which he was supposed to complete and submit to the responsible police precinct. There were also three invitations to a dance by the Sportsclub l'Aurore and two postcards, including one from his sister Esther dated October 31, 1938, from Zbaszyn, Poland, a frontier station on the German border on the main Berlin-Warsaw railroad, located forty miles southwest of Poznan.

> You undoubtedly heard of our great misfortune. I will describe to you what happened. On Thursday evening rumors circulated that all Polish Jews had been expelled from a city. But we didn't believe it. On Thursday evening at 9 o'clock a "Sipo" [*Sicherheitspolizei* or Security Police] came to us and informed us that we had to go to Police Headquarters and bring along our passports. As we were, we went together to Police Headquarters, accompanied by the "Sipo." Almost our entire quarter was already there. A police van brought all of us right away to the "Rusthaus." All were brought there. We were not told what it was all about, but we saw that everything was finished for us. Each of us had an extradition order pressed into his hand, and one had to leave Germany before the 29th [Saturday]. They didn't permit us to return home anymore. I asked to be allowed to go home to get at least a few things. I went, accompanied by a "Sipo," and packed the necessary clothes in a suitcase. And that is all I saved. We don't have a "Pfennig." [Note: There follows a sentence which is crossed out, but which appears to read: Could you send us something to Lodz.] More next time. Best regards and kisses from all of us. Berta.[6]

The other postcard had on the front a picture of Herschel, probably taken at a street fair or by an itinerant photographer, and on the reverse a message written the previous evening and addressed to Maison Albert, the residence and business address of his uncle, Abraham Grynszpan, with whom he lived.

> With God's help [written in Hebrew]
> My dear parents, I could not do otherwise, may God forgive me, the heart bleeds when I hear of your tragedy and that of the 12,000 Jews. I must protest so that the whole world hears my protest and that I will do. Forgive me. Hermann.[7]

Having obtained Herschel's confession, Commissioner Monneret arranged to have him confronted by the receptionist of the Hotel de Suez, M. Carpe, and Uncle Abraham. It was late afternoon when he set out with the young gunman to retrace his movements since the previous evening. Arriving at the embassy, Herschel refused to enter for fear of being trapped on German territory, so Monneret visited the scene of the crime by himself. There, in the corner to the right of the door to vom Rath's office, he found the pistol, the price tag still attached to the trigger by a red string. Five empty cartridges were in the chamber. Two bullet holes were clearly visible, one on the coat closet, the other on the wall, both about three feet from the floor.

It was already late evening when Grynszpan was brought to the Criminal Investigation Department which had in the meantime received Monneret's report. Police Inspector Badin proceeded to question the youth in greater detail.

Grynszpan told how he had been received by an attaché who had offered him a chair and asked after the reason for his visit.

> I said to him: "You are a filthy Kraut ["un sale boche"] and now I will give you the document in the name of 12,000 persecuted Jews." I pulled the revolver, which I had hidden in the inside pocket of my jacket, and fired; at the moment when I pulled the weapon, the attaché rose from his seat. However, I fired all bullets. I aimed at the middle of the body. My victim hit me with his fist and left the room, calling for help. I remained in the office, where I was arrested a few moments later. . . . I received the postcard which was in my wallet on Thursday [November 3] and at that moment I decided to kill a member of the embassy in protest. I knew of the subjugation of my fellow Jews from the press. That was the only reason which caused me to take the step I took.[8]

Later, Grynszpan—presumably on advice of counsel—sought to distance himself from the idea that the assassination had been premeditated, claiming that he had acted in a sort of trance. He specifically sought to withdraw the statement made to Inspector Badin, attributing it to stress and fatigue brought on by the late hour. But there still remained the postcard to his parents which the Nazi authorities later sought to use to attribute premeditation to the young man.

According to contemporary press accounts of the first day's interrogation, Grynszpan also said that he had decided to kill a member of the German embassy in order to create a stir so great that the world could not ignore it. Herschel Grynszpan succeeded in his endeavors, probably beyond his wildest expectations, but perhaps not quite in the manner that he had hoped.

Speculation started almost immediately, in a Europe rife with conspiracy theories, whether there was some other reason behind the shooting. Had the perpetrator acted independently? Why had the assassin selected this particular victim, and why had vom Rath, rather than another embassy official, received Grynszpan that fatal morning? The most obvious explanation was that vom Rath was the junior officer on duty at the moment. Ambassador Welczeck was quoted as saying that it was pure chance that vom Rath was attacked, not because he was the junior official present, but because he was the only functionary of importance who had already arrived at his desk.

Yet why should a "functionary of importance" be expected to receive a seventeen-year-old, Semitic-looking youth? According to Monneret's report on the initial interrogation, Herschel Grynszpan stated that he had told Nagorka that he wanted to see someone with knowledge of German "secrets" in order to give him an important and urgent document. Nagorka's initial statement, also as recorded by Monneret, quoted the young visitor as having "a confidential and very important document."[9] Was it possible that he had been directed to his victim because vom Rath was one of the embassy officials whose job involved the collection of "sensitive" information? According to one rumor circulating at the time, vom Rath was involved in intelligence activities. It was, however, only one of several rumors that made the rounds in those days. As it turned out, an entirely different story bruited about proved to have a profound effect on the case.

2

The Death of vom Rath

While Krueger and Nagorka went off with Grynszpan in tow to turn him over to the French police, the wounded vom Rath was helped by Embassy Attaché Ernst Achenbach, who had just arrived at his own office next door. Vom Rath managed to tell him that the assailant had fired almost immediately upon entering the office, saying that he wished to avenge the Jews. First aid was quickly organized by Achenbach and *Botschaftsrat* (Counselor of Embassy) Braeuer. An urgent call went out to Dr. Claas, one of the embassy's physicians, who had vom Rath transported to the Alma Clinic, a nearby hospital, at 166 rue de l'Université. Dr. Baumgartner, a surgeon accredited to the embassy, was called to vom Rath's bedside and took charge of the case.[1]

The initial examination showed that vom Rath had been hit by two bullets, one entering from the left side and lodging in the right shoulder, while the second also entered from the side but lower down. Consideration was given briefly to transferring the patient to the American Hospital in suburban Neuilly. But the doctors were faced with the need to cope urgently with a severe internal hemorrhage due to the rupture of the spleen. It was therefore decided to operate immediately without subjecting the patient to a further move. Dr. Baumgartner performed the complex operation. After removing the spleen, suturing the stomach, and removing the blood clots, vom Rath received a massive blood transfusion under the supervision of a renowned specialist, Dr. Jubé.

This was in the days before blood banks, when direct transfusions were required. The press made an instant celebrity of one blood donor, M. Thomas, a former Paris restaurant owner and decorated war veteran, who had given blood 108 times over the previous eight years. This time he gave it for a German. His "heroism" was hailed by German propagandists as the symbol of Franco-German friendship that, according to them, others were trying to destroy.

As soon as news of the shooting reached Berlin, Hitler sent to Paris Dr. Karl Brandt, his personal physician, and Dr. Magnus, director of the Surgical Clinic of the University of Munich. These prominent physicians were sent presumably to demonstrate the Fuehrer's personal interest and solicitude and, incidentally, to provide the German government with a reliable source of information on the condition of the victim. (After the war, Dr. Brandt was tried before the U.S. war crimes tribunal in Nuremberg and condemned to death because of the leading role he played in later years in the conduct of medical experiments on concentration camp inmates.)

The two doctors arrived in Paris at Le Bourget airport in the early hours of November 8. After checking into their hotel, they went to the Alma Clinic, arriving at 10:30 A.M., accompanied by Ambassador Welczeck and his deputy, Braeuer. After an examination of the young diplomat, the German doctors issued the following bulletin:

> The condition of Secretary of Legation vom Rath is extremely serious, especially because of the damage to the stomach. The consequences of the considerable loss of blood, caused by damage to the spleen, can probably be overcome by further blood transfusions. The excellent surgical efforts and treatment to date by Dr. Baumgartner, Paris, allows some optimism in regard to future developments.

The two doctors returned that evening for a further visit with their patient. This time their report was more ominous.

> The condition of Secretary of Legation vom Rath as of this evening has not improved. The situation is critical. The patient's [high] temperature remains. There are initial indications of circulatory problems.[2]

The same day, November 8, Gustav vom Rath, father of the victim, an industrialist and retired government official, arrived in Paris by train from Cologne with his second son, Guenter. They went directly to the Alma Clinic.

Vom Rath's condition had not improved by November 9. His father arrived at the clinic at about 10 A.M., accompanied by his wife. She carried a small valise, apparently intent on remaining at the clinic with her son. The young diplomat recognized his parents. They urged him not to talk in order to avoid any unnecessary exertion.

Dr. Baumgartner was interviewed by journalists as he left the clinic at 11:30 A.M. He limited his comments to noting that the condition of the young diplomat continued to be critical and that he remained on the danger list. When someone suggested that due to his age there might be more hope for his recovery, the doctor shrugged his shoulders, adding, "If there had been only one wound . . . but there are three!" (Dr. Baumgartner was mistaken. The autopsy later confirmed that there were only two wounds.)

Towards midday, Drs. Magnus and Brandt arrived. When they departed, they only declared, "We can say nothing except that the condition of the patient is still very grave and we will undoubtedly return during the course of the day."

They returned early in the afternoon. Shortly after 3 P.M., vom Rath went into a coma and died at 4:25 P.M. in the presence of his parents and the two German physicians. The swiftness of his death, the early appearance of fever, and the patient's state of shock seemed to indicate that the pancreatic injury was the immediate cause of death. At 5:25 P.M., the grieving parents left the clinic.

A communiqué was issued, signed by Drs. Magnus and Brandt:

> The *Legationsrat* [he had been promoted to counselor of legation by Hitler only a few hours earlier] and [National Socialist] party member vom Rath died of the wounds which he received on November 7. During the course of the morning the condition of Counselor of Legation vom Rath further worsened. A new blood transfusion was only temporarily effective. Blood circulation reacted insufficiently to medication. The fever remained high. Towards midday the effect of the stomach injury in conjunction with the damage to the spleen became more evident. The loss of the patient's strength could not be arrested; death occurred at 4:30 P.M.[3]

In the communiqué, the German doctors expressed their thanks to

Dr. Baumgartner, the French surgeon, as well as to the Alma Clinic and its staff.

An autopsy of vom Rath was carried out by Dr. Paul, a well-known forensic pathologist. His report confirmed that of the five bullets fired at point-blank range by Grynszpan, only two had hit the victim. One bullet had pierced the left side, passed through the thoracic cavity and lodged in the left shoulder. This wound did not effect any important organ. The other bullet, however, entered a bit lower on the left side, ruptured the spleen, perforated the stomach, and damaged the pancreas. It was this bullet which was finally the cause of death. The bullets were fired upward, presumably with vom Rath standing and Grynszpan seated.

The same evening, November 9, at 10:30 P.M., the body was removed to a mortuary chapel on the rue de Lille where an all-night vigil was kept by embassy personnel. A large swastika covered the coffin, as did wreaths contributed by the embassy and the French and Italian governments.

The death of vom Rath had come swiftly. The burial was to come more slowly, but then, state funerals require extensive preparations.

On Saturday, November 12, the coffin was taken to the German Lutheran Church at 5 rue Blanche for the religious ceremony in the presence of French government and diplomatic officials, including French Foreign Minister Georges Bonnet and personal representatives of Prime Minister Daladier and President Lebrun. Pastor Dahlgruen gave the funeral oration. The German delegation was led by State Secretary Freiherr Ernst von Weizsaecker, who in his funeral oration described vom Rath as the Foreign Ministry's first martyr to fall for the Third Reich. He concluded with, "Commence the journey to the homeland—all Germany awaits you." Wreaths from Hitler and Mussolini were laid at the bier. After the ceremony, the coffin was placed in the church vault to await transfer to Germany the following Tuesday for a state funeral.

The return of vom Rath's remains to Germany and the funeral services which followed were conducted with all the pomp and circumstance for which the Third Reich had become famous. The victim received honors worthy of royalty. The German people mourned the death of the young man and the well-oiled propaganda machine made the most of the opportunity.

On Tuesday evening, November 15, at 10:15 P.M., the body was quietly transferred from the German Lutheran Church of Paris to the Gare de l'Est, where a special French train was waiting. At 10:50 P.M., it left for Düsseldorf. Aboard were Ambassador Welczeck, State Secretary von Weizsaecker in his capacity as the personal representative of Hitler, Professor Friedrich Grimm (who had been asked by the Ministries of Propaganda and Foreign Affairs to ostensibly represent the vom Rath family), several journalists, and the family of the deceased.

The train entered German territory at dawn on Wednesday. In spite of the early hour and the heavy fog which hung over the countryside that November morning, a large number of people and Nazi party units lined the route. All stations were draped in black bunting and flags flew at half-mast. The speed of the train was reduced to twelve miles an hour and the slowness added to the solemnity of the procession. At Aachen (Aix-la-Chapelle), the coffin was transferred to a German train and vom Rath's remains were greeted with a short speech by the local party leader.

The trip ended in Düsseldorf. The coffin was placed on a caisson which slowly negotiated the two miles between the station and the Rheinhalle, a large indoor arena normally used for exhibitions, rallies, as well as sports and large cultural events. There, the body lay in state. A double line of people paid a last tribute to the young diplomat. All day Wednesday, silent crowds filed past the coffin. The next day, November 17, shortly before noon, Hitler arrived in Düsseldorf to participate in the ceremonies. He went directly to the Rheinhalle. Neither music nor acclamation met him, greatly enhancing the solemnity of the occasion. Accompanied by Foreign Minister Joachim von Ribbentrop, he paused briefly before the coffin and then seated himself in the front row between vom Rath's parents without saying a word.

After the playing of the Funeral March from Beethoven's Third Symphony (*Eroica*), *Gauleiter* Ernst Wilhelm Bohle, head of the Foreign Organization of the National Socialist German Workers' (Nazi) Party (NSDAP), spoke to the assembled. He described vom Rath as the eighth person to die for Germany in a foreign country, the others being Wilhelm Gustloff[4] and a number of party members who had died in Spain. "The shots fired in Davos [home of Gustloff in Switzerland], Barcelona, and Paris . . . are aimed at the Third Reich. . . . The death of these two men places a solemn obligation on each German abroad, whether he resides there for official or other reasons, always to faithfully serve this community and thereby the German people and its Fuehrer."

Foreign Minister Ribbentrop followed with the funeral oration, during which he called attention to yet another fateful November 9, that of 1923, when an attempted "putsch" by Hitler and his cohorts failed miserably in front of Munich's "Feldherrnhalle." He concluded his speech with the words which Hitler had pronounced at the grave of Gustloff: "We understand the challenge and we accept it."

After the national anthem, the Fuehrer, still silent, saluted the crowd, offered a few quick condolences, and departed for a meeting with local party leaders. In the presence of top SS and police officials, Hitler declared that an event such as this should reinforce their anti-Semitic policies and thus help launch a resolute struggle against all internal forces which opposed them, particularly the Protestant and Catholic churches.

Following Hitler's departure, the funeral procession formed once more and this time moved towards a wooded cemetery. Before a row of flags, a minister pronounced a few words at the family vault in stentorian tones. Amid tears, the mourners threw flowers on the coffin which, draped with a swastika flag, was slowly lowered into the grave. Thus ended in grandeur the short, and heretofore undistinguished, career of Ernst Eduard vom Rath.

3

The Victim

Ernst Eduard Adolf Max vom Rath was born June 3, 1909, in Frankfurt am Main, the oldest of three brothers—a sister, born in January 1912, died in infancy—into an old conservative German family. His father, Gustav Eduard vom Rath, born in Düsseldorf on February 21, 1879, studied law in Heidelberg, Geneva, and Bonn and in 1902 entered the civil service as a junior lawyer. Over the next eighteen years, with time out for military service, he served in East Prussia, Danzig (Gdansk), and from 1912, Cologne. In 1920 he left government service, moved to Breslau (Wroclaw), and took over the administration of the family's sugar factory.[1]

Ernst vom Rath attended primary and secondary schools in Frankfurt and Breslau. Upon graduation in March 1928, he studied law, first at the University of Bonn and then at the Universities of Munich and Königsberg in East Prussia (now Kaliningrad). After successfully passing his first law examination on March 30, 1932, he was apprenticed to the Magistrate's Court at Zinter near Königsberg and later to the Magistrate's Court in Berlin. It was at this point that he decided to embark on a diplomatic career, a decision probably influenced and helped by the fact that his uncle, Roland Koester, at the time served as the German ambassador in Paris.

Starting out as a junior civil servant at the Foreign Ministry in Berlin in 1934, Ernst vom Rath passed the required examinations and successfully completed a six-week training and observation period at the German embassy in Budapest. In preparation for the language part of the examination, he spent the summer of 1934 in Paris. On April 13, 1935, he formally entered the Foreign Ministry and was appointed, with the rank of attaché, to what he must have considered a very desirable assignment at the embassy in Paris. He spent the next year as personal secretary to his uncle, in charge of protocol matters, but was reassigned to Berlin on April 1, 1936, shortly after the death of his uncle in office.

After six months in Berlin, vom Rath was transferred to the consulate general in Calcutta. Before long, he contracted what was described as a severe case of dysentery, and was eventually ordered medically evacuated to Germany for treatment at the Berlin Institute of Radiology. Later he reportedly contracted a light case of pulmonary tuberculosis, for which he spent four months in a sanatorium in St. Blasien in the Black Forest. Once he had recovered his health, in July 1938, he was reassigned to Paris and placed in charge of cultural affairs, his third stay in the French capital in four years. On October 18, 1938, he was promoted to secretary of legation.

Throughout his professional career, the personnel evaluation reports on vom Rath were excellent. His superiors described him as a person of sound judgment, worthy of confidence, hard-working and energetic. They especially praised vom Rath's interest in the countries to which he was assigned and his ability to get along with people, both in and outside the office. All in all, the reports made him out to be a sympathetic individual and colleague.

Vom Rath's family, which in the postwar years repeatedly went to court to defend his name, has provided little additional information about him. As a result, other than the above basic facts, relatively little is known about the young vom Rath. Such information as became available from various sources after the assassination and in later years is not necessarily unbiased and, at least on the surface, at times is contradictory.

Following his assassination, for example, vom Rath's strong allegiance to the National Socialist cause was broadly publicized by the German propaganda machinery. For one thing, vom Rath joined the NSDAP (Nazi party) already on July 14, 1932, well before Hitler's ascent to power. He did so while still at the University of Königsberg, during this period a hotbed of German nationalism. In April 1933, he became a member of the party's *Sturmabteilung* (storm troopers), known by their initials SA.

However, it has also been reported that relatively soon after joining the party, vom Rath found himself in disagreement with Nazi aims and methods. Though not a regular churchgoer like his father, he was reportedly a devout Christian in outlook. The Foreign Ministry personnel reports make only marginal reference to his party membership, and the testimonials attesting to his party loyalty and devotion to Hitler and the Nazi movement were written after he had become a "martyr." Almost all photographs of vom Rath published at the time of his death showed him in civilian dress. One photograph in a Ministry of Propaganda booklet issued in 1939, showing him in Nazi uniform with his unit, had apparently been taken quite a few years earlier.

It is of course quite possible that vom Rath's perception of the Nazi movement underwent a change as a result of the events of the night of June 30, 1934. On that date, during the "night of the long knives," Hitler's cohorts decimated the storm troopers, eliminating the SA leadership (including his longtime associate and rival Ernst Roehm) and many of its members, thereby effectively transferring power from the SA to the *Schutzstaffeln* (SS) under the leadership of the more pliant Heinrich Himmler.

In any case, Ernst vom Rath, perhaps having lost his youthful illusions and enthusiasm, apparently put his party activities on hold. He remained a party member, which clearly was to his advantage, but may have used his foreign assignments to distance himself from its day-to-day activities.

The rumors of vom Rath's disenchantment with the Nazi regime might be attributable to reports of disagreements between vom Rath's father, a plaintiff in the French legal proceedings, and Nazi authorities. The Fuehrer's remoteness during his attendance at the funeral services was widely noted. Although Hitler conducted himself correctly in keeping with the circumstances, his attitude seemed perfunctory and lacking any warmth. As for vom Rath's deathbed promotion to counselor of legation, it was seen as a symbolic gesture of little consequence.

It was obviously felt necessary to deny these rumors of a rift and on January 7, 1939, Gustav vom Rath made a widely reported statement before the French examining magistrate. After affirming that civil suit had been brought on his behalf against Herschel Grynszpan and any accomplices who might be identified, he provided some details about his son. Finally, the elder vom Rath, in response to a series of questions by the examining magistrate, commented on certain reports about his son and his family.

> In order to reestablish the truth, in the light of certain press campaigns, and in order to prevent any false legends from arising, I consider it of importance to confirm that my son was a member of the National Socialist movement. He was a party member since 1932, that is, already since before the party came to power. He was in complete accord with his government and was fully devoted to the cause of National Socialism. As for myself, I have been a *Regierungsrat* [Government Counselor] since 1919 and am now in retirement.
>
> I was fully in accord with my son's politics. It is very painful for me to read in certain newspapers that I had difficulties with my government, and that on the occasion of my son's funeral, I even am supposed to have had differences with the Fuehrer. I declare that these are all lies.
>
> It also was rumored that I had been sent to a concentration camp. I trust that my presence in this courtroom, together with my second son, Guenter, is sufficient refutation of this new lie. Furthermore, I am at your disposal whenever you deem it appropriate to summon me.[2]

It is quite possible that the protestation of loyalty to the regime were not entirely Herr vom Rath's own idea. The pedestrian statement certainly seemed out of character. The family was too grieved, too moderate, and too discreet to indulge in that kind of public declaration concerning the death of their son.

Little also is known about Ernst vom Rath's attitude toward Jews. One of vom Rath's embassy colleagues testified after the war that "vom Rath came to regret these measures [taken by the German government against Jews] because of his humanitarian feelings, but, vom Rath did not vigorously oppose them since they appeared to be necessary for German national welfare."

Mlle Ebeling, his maid in Paris, said that even though he never expressed any opinions about Jews in her presence, she always had the impression that neither he nor his parents were anti-Semitic. She went on to say that vom Rath's "private life was quite proper. He received only a few personal friends, and in general led a very retiring life. As far as character was concerned, it would be difficult to find anyone kinder or more gracious than he was."

Vom Rath clearly was enamored with France. Initially his knowledge of the language was poor, but then he started taking lessons from Mlle Taulin, first during the summer of 1934 when he came to Paris to learn French. When he returned in August 1935, he resumed his lessons with Mlle Taulin, who described vom Rath as "a young man of great intelligence and perfect manners. His extreme reserve and calm disposition were outstanding. I never observed the slightest indication in his thought or expression that was either violent or vulgar." After leaving Paris, vom Rath continued to write to Mlle Taulin in French, asking her to correct and return his letters. When he returned to Paris once again in August 1938, he arranged with his former teacher to renew his lessons in late November.

He made it a point to get to know French families and was pleased to be invited to their homes. Otherwise, his social life apparently was quite circumscribed. The ambassador's private secretary, Herr Auer, was one of vom Rath's friends. According to Auer, they went out together occasionally, but rarely at night, primarily due to vom Rath's poor health. Auer went on to say that vom Rath's "private life was without incident. He was level-headed, not expansive, and he was always very moderate in the way he expressed himself."[3]

We may never know vom Rath's feelings at the time of his death about the regime he served. If indeed, as seems to be the case, he had by then certain reservations about its attitudes and policies—even if one makes allowances for youthful enthusiasm—one can only assume that he was extremely naive or immature at the time he joined the party.

The elder vom Rath was recalled into service during the war and became a top official of the Berlin police. He became responsible for Jewish affairs, but reportedly tried to be of some help to victims of Nazi policies and actions.[4]

4

The Aftermath—*Kristallnacht* (The Night of Broken Glass)

The death of Ernst vom Rath resulted in events which catapulted an act, which under normal circumstances would have been a regrettable, though quickly forgotten case of political assassination, into the forefront of the international stage. With the unintended assistance of Hitler's henchmen, Grynszpan succeeded, far beyond any reasonable expectations, in bringing the plight of Germany's Jews to the attention of the world.[1]

Vom Rath died on November 9, shortly after 4:00 P.M. That day almost the entire Nazi party leadership and most regional party officials were assembled in Munich for the annual commemoration of the (unsuccessful) *Bürgerbräukeller* (Beer Hall) putsch attempt of 1923.

On that day fifteen years earlier, Hitler and 3,000 storm troopers, accompanied by the legendary General Ludendorff of World War I fame, sought to seize power in Bavaria. They marched from the Bürgerbräukeller towards the War Ministry in the center of Munich, where other Brownshirts under SA leader Roehm were surrounded by troops of the *Reichswehr* (regular army). To reach their goal, the marchers had to pass through the narrow Residenzstrasse adjoining the *Feldherrnhalle*, a grandiose memorial from another era, and here a detachment of about 100 police, armed with carbines, blocked their way. Shooting erupted, the marchers flung themselves to the ground, and almost before it started, it was over. Sixteen marchers and three policemen were killed, and the other Nazis beat a hasty retreat, with Hitler reliably reported to have led the way. Only Ludendorff and his adjutant continued their march straight through the police lines, between the smoking carbines. Ludendorff would never again have anything to do with the World War corporal and future Chancellor of the Third Reich.

November 9, the "*Tag der Bewegung*" (Day of the Movement), an official holiday ever since Hitler came to power, traditionally was the single most important date for the party. It was the day on which party promotions and honors were announced and for the recipients it represented the first opportunity to strut about, showing off their new rank insignias and medals. Many party members who had participated in the putsch by now played an exalted role in the party, and this was their day to shine, to recall their early association with the Fuehrer. The 1938 celebration was especially significant since for the first time representatives from Austria and the Sudetenland officially were able to take part.

After the ceremonial parade from the *Bürgerbräukeller*, where it all started in 1923, to the laying of the wreaths at the *Feldherrnhalle*, where it had ended so ignobly, Hitler and his old comrades met in the early evening hours in the *Festsaal* of the Old City Hall. Shortly before dinner, between 7 and 8 P.M., a messenger arrived and in low tones informed the Fuehrer that vom Rath had died that afternoon. Hitler spoke for a while in an agitated manner with Josef Goebbels, but in such low tones that even those in the immediate vicinity were unable to hear the conversation, except that he was overheard to say that the SA "should have its fling." Immediately after the meal, to the general surprise of those present, he left the hall without making a speech.

Not long after Hitler's departure, Goebbels arose, announced the death of vom Rath and proceeded with a violently anti-Semitic speech. It was apparently a classic Goebbels performance. He described the recent events in such a manner and spoke so passionately about revenge that none of the SA and party leaders present had any doubts what was expected of them. They fully understood the exhortation that the party not organize demonstrations actually meant that the party was not to be identified as the organizer. To this end, while the November 9 festivities of previous years had been described in great detail in press accounts, including extensive quotations from speeches, the only report which appeared after the 1938 meeting was that it had taken place.

In early 1939, the Supreme Party Court was convened under SS *Obergruppenführer* (Major General) Walter Buch to investigate some of the "excesses" committed during *Kristallnacht* by members of the party and the SA, in order to remove the culprits from the reach of judicial authorities. In his final and secret report to Hermann Goering on February 13, 1939, Buch summarized the background of the riots:

> On the evening of November 9, 1938, Minister of Propaganda Goebbels informed the leaders assembled at a meeting of old comrades in the Old City Hall in Munich that anti-Jewish riots had taken place in [the regions of] Kurhessen and Magdeburg-Anhalt in the course of which Jewish stores had been destroyed and synagogues had been burned. [Rioting had taken place on November 8 and 9 in some isolated towns and villages, usually organized by local party or SA officials but without reference to or involvement of the middle and upper echelon party leadership.] The Fuehrer had decided at [Goebbels'] recommendation that such demonstrations were neither to be organized nor carried out by the party but once they started spontaneously were not to be quelled. . . .
>
> The verbal instructions of the minister of propaganda were apparently understood by all leaders present to mean that the party was not to appear to the outside as the originator of the demonstrations but in actuality was to organize and carry them out. Instructions to that effect were accordingly transmitted immediately—well before the transmission of the first teletype message—by telephone by a large part of the party members present to their regional offices.[2]

The report takes for granted that Goebbels meant his speech to be interpreted by those present as a call for action without the party seeming to be actively involved. After all, the report goes on, "the politically active groups which might undertake such demonstrations happen to be in the party and its units."

Goebbels' speech was unlikely to have been formulated spontaneously. It provided the necessary guidelines to local Nazi leaders about what was expected of them, without leaving a telltale paper trail of directives back to the party or the government. Goebbels also did not act behind Hitler's back. However, Hitler's absence permitted him to maintain the facade of respectability and statesmanship which he had acquired thanks to the Munich conference on the fate of Czechoslovakia of the previous September. Yet Hitler undoubtedly was fully informed of what was going on. If he did not know beforehand, the subject of his agitated conversation with Goebbels on hearing of vom Rath's death almost certainly concerned the actions which were to follow.

After Goebbels' speech, the party officials present rushed to telephone their units throughout the country, giving orders based on their understanding of Goebbels' purposely enigmatic speech. As events were to show, those perceptions differed markedly. There was not much confusion regarding *what* was to be done, but *how* it was to be carried out.

There had been a number of instances of destruction of Jewish businesses and synagogues and attacks on Jews since the shooting of vom Rath, almost all organized by SA units acting under the direction of eager local leaders. However, the wave of popular indignation which Goebbels evidently had hoped for did not materialize. Goebbels wanted to help things along, but he overestimated the perceptivity and finesse of his audience. As a result, his hope to isolate the party from the excesses was doomed to failure as the SA units enthusiastically proceeded to carry out their dirty work, many in full uniform, with flags flying.

The Supreme Party Court's secret report, by way of example, recounted the telephone orders which the chief of staff of the SA Group Nordsee, Roempagel, reported having received from his superior, the *Gruppenführer* of the SA Group Nordsee, from Munich during the night of November 9/10:

- All Jewish stores are to be destroyed immediately by SA men in uniform. After the destruction an SA guard is to be posted to assure that nothing of value can be taken. The responsible SA administrative officials are to safeguard all objects of value, including money.
- The press is to be called in.
- Jewish synagogues are to be set on fire immediately, Jewish symbols are to be safeguarded. The fire departments are not to interfere. The fire departments are to protect the houses of German Aryans. Adjacent Jewish houses are also to be protected by the fire department, but the Jews must vacate since Aryans will move in during the next days.
- The police must not intervene. The Fuehrer wishes that the police does not interfere.
- The identification of Jewish shops, depots and warehouses, as well as itinerant tradesmen, will take place by arrangement with the responsible chief mayors and mayors.
- All Jews are to be disarmed. In the event of resistance they are to be shot immediately.

- Signs with texts such as the following are to be affixed to Jewish shops, synagogues, etc.:

  Revenge for the murder of vom Rath
  Death to international Jewry
  No understanding with nations under the sway of Jews

Organized party units took the lead in the looting and faithfully followed such orders as to have synagogues "blown up or set on fire immediately."[3]

The events seem to have come as something of a surprise even to the leadership of the SS and the *Geheime Staatspolizei* (Secret State Police), better known as the *Gestapo*, who were not present at Goebbels' speech. Reinhard Heydrich, then chief of the SS *Sicherheitsdienst* or SD (Security Service)—and as such also superior to the head of the Gestapo—apparently first learned of the evening's events when a synagogue near the Hotel Vier Jahreszeiten, where he was staying in Munich, was set afire.

Heydrich's superior, Heinrich Himmler, was occupied with Hitler at the swearing in of new SS recruits, traditionally conducted at midnight on November 9/10. It was therefore not until about 1:20 A.M. on November 10 that Heydrich sent out a message from Munich to all Gestapo offices throughout Germany.[4]

Heydrich informed the Gestapo offices that as a result of the assassination of vom Rath, demonstrations against Jews were to be expected throughout Germany. The Gestapo offices were told, immediately upon receipt of the telex, to set up meetings with local and regional political authorities, to which local police officials were also to be invited, regarding the conduct of these demonstrations. During these meetings, the party officials were to be informed that the German police had received the following guidelines from Himmler in his capacity as chief of the SS and of the German Police:

- Measures are to be limited to such as will not jeopardize German life or property (e.g., synagogues to be burned only if there is no danger to the surrounding area).
- Jewish shops and houses are only to be destroyed, not to be plundered. The police are responsible for the prevention of looting and charged with the arrest of looters.
- Non-Jewish premises must be protected against any harm.
- Foreign citizens, even if Jews, are not to be molested.

- Provided the demonstrations follow the guidelines, the police are not to prevent them but should limit themselves to assuring the implementation of the guidelines.
- Immediately upon receipt of the telex, all historically valuable archival materials are to be confiscated from the synagogues and Jewish community offices to safeguard them.
- As soon as the events of the night permit the use of police officers for this purpose, as many Jews (especially those who are well-to-do) are to be arrested as can be accommodated in the available detention areas. For the time being "only healthy Jewish males who are not too old are to be arrested." The appropriate concentration camps are to be contacted regarding the housing of the Jews.

The message went on to caution the recipients that the Jews apprehended as a result of this action were not to be mistreated.

While this message apparently was the first official written communication on the subject to have emanated from Munich, it could not have come as much of a surprise to the recipients. The head of the Gestapo, *Standartenführer* Mueller, a Heydrich subordinate, had already more than an hour earlier (at 11:55 P.M. on November 9), dispatched a secret teletype from Berlin.[5] It informed Gestapo units throughout Germany that anti-Jewish demonstrations, especially aimed at synagogues, would take place in all parts of Germany and that these were not to be hindered, although important archival materials were to be safeguarded. Plundering and other similar activities were to be prevented. The message went on to alert the recipients of the planned arrest of 20,000–30,000 German Jews, promising further instructions in the course of the night. After noting that SS units could be utilized, Mueller's message cautioned the recipients to do everything necessary to assure that the Gestapo would be in charge of the conduct of the "action."

The Gestapo chief's telex differed in several important ways from the orders issued subsequently by Heydrich. It made no mention whatsoever of vom Rath or his death (as a justification for the demonstration), it was quite specific in the number of persons to be arrested (as opposed to the much less specific message from Heydrich), it did not mention Jewish businesses or homes and, most importantly, it stressed that the Gestapo was to be in charge.

It seems clear from Mueller's message that some such action had long been planned, and that the telex had been drafted earlier, just waiting for a suitable opportunity. This would explain why the concentration camps, after feverish activity during the preceding months, were able to accommodate the large sudden influx of prisoners.

Harry Naujoks, a longtime political prisoner in the Sachsenhausen concentration camp, in July 1938 was a foreman in the prisoner clothing supply unit. He recounted how at that time the unit received orders to increase at once the number of uniforms on hand, and also to produce several hundred uniforms for heavy-set individuals. The same month, the unit suddenly also received a large shipment of yellow marking cloth, the sort used to make patches identifying Jewish prisoners. When he had the cloth put in storage, he was reprimanded and told immediately to prepare the identifying patches. This, according to Mr. Naujoks, was totally contrary to previous experiences, since supplies were usually received long after they were needed and only after repeated requisitions.[6]

In the absence of his superiors from Berlin and after receiving reports of organized demonstrations from various parts of the country, Mueller apparently decided it was time to send the guidelines.

And thus began the pogrom of November 1938. While there had been many anti-Jewish demonstrations throughout Nazi Germany in the past, these had usually been local in nature. Two exceptions, the boycott of Jewish stores on April 1, 1933, and the burning of "subversive" books (by Jewish and non-Jewish authors) on May 10 of the same year, had by and large not been violent in nature. Now, for the first time, there was centrally orchestrated violence taking place at the same time all over Germany and Austria. The anti-Jewish outbursts had taken a grim new turn, one which would inexorably lead to the Holocaust.

During the twenty-four hours after the death of vom Rath, thousands of Jewish males were arrested and sent to concentration camps for "protective custody." Jewish property and places of worship were pillaged and burned, causing damage in the millions, while scores of Jews died in a violent fashion, through murder, suicide or other causes directly attributable to the riots. While the following figures testify to the violence of *Kristallnacht*, they obviously cannot adequately reflect the horror, violence, and human suffering visited on a hapless people:

- Total number of Jews under Nazi domination: approx. 550,000
- Number arrested: approx. 30,000 Jewish males, ages 16–80

Those apprehended were transported to the following concentration camps:

- Buchenwald: 9,815 (mainly from Central Germany)
- Dachau: 10,911 (Austria, Southern Germany)
- Sachsenhausen: 9,000 (est.) (Prussia, Baltic Coast)

The camps at Dachau and Sachsenhausen had been created by the Nazis almost immediately after coming to power, while Buchenwald was built in 1937. They were established to "silence by terror" adversaries of Nazism, Jews, and "anti-social types," but at the time were not the "death factories" which Treblinka, Auschwitz, and others were to become later.

- Murdered during *Kristallnacht* disturbances: at least 91 persons

The life of concentration camp inmates was harsh. Hundreds of those incarcerated during and immediately after *Kristallnacht* perished as a direct result, either from mistreatment, illness, suicide, or murder (such as those who ventured too close to the electric fences surrounding the camps and were shot during "attempts to escape"). In Dachau alone, 185 Jews died in the nine months between November 1938 and August 1939, while in Buchenwald, 231 died between November 10, 1938, and January 1, 1939. All in all, it has been estimated that 2,000–2,500 deaths were directly or indirectly attributable to the November pogrom:

- Seriously injured: 36
- Suicides: numerous, including entire families
- Rapes: Several. The Supreme Party Court ruled that a number of them were violations of the "Nuremberg Racial Laws" of 1935 and transferred them to civilian authorities for trial. (Thus they were not tried as crimes of violence against individuals but as crimes because they resulted in sexual relations with Jews.)
- Synagogues destroyed/burned: at least 267
- Stores destroyed and/or looted: 7,500
- Jewish cemeteries desecrated: almost all
- Private houses destroyed/burned: at least 177

- Windows broken: tens of thousands (hence, *Kristallnacht* or "Crystal Night")
- Glass damage: 6 million *Reichsmark* (RM), ($2.4 million), about half the annual production of the Belgian glass industry, which largely supplied Germany
- Total damage: Estimated at 1 billion RM ($400 million).[7]

The "excesses" that caused the Supreme Party Court to be convened included at least ninety-one murders. Major Buch's final report covers sixteen incidents, three sex offenses and thirteen cases of single and multiple murders, for which individual SA members were the subject of judicial proceedings. The report proposed that the Fuehrer cancel all but two indictments for rape since all other crimes committed were on the order of superiors or were the result of unclear or misunderstood directives. Another seventy-eight murder cases were still pending at the time the report was prepared but were eventually "resolved" in the same manner. The report notes that many of the men had to overcome serious scruples to carry out the murders they thought they were ordered to commit. In fact, the SA units were by and large much more brutal in their treatment of the Jews than the NSDAP (Party) units or other organizations, in part probably attributable to the SA's sense of frustration and emasculation which can be traced back to the 1934 "Night of Long Knives."

Finally, Buch's report noted that when the official reporting the first killing of a Jew—a Polish citizen—to Goebbels at 2 A.M. on November 10 expressed the belief that something needed to be done to prevent the entire operation from getting out of hand, Goebbels told the messenger not to become so excited over the death of one Jew since thousands of Jews were likely to suffer the same fate in the coming days. The report concluded that it would, at that point, still have been possible to stop most murders through the issuance of appropriate orders, but when that did not happen, one had to draw the conclusion that such actions were desired or at least condoned.

The odious activities of the SA failed to ignite the "righteous wrath" of the German people. While they received support from segments of the population, the demonstrations often were met with silence, apathy, and occasionally embarrassment on the part of the population in general. Many of the victims tell of signs of compassion and individual friendly gestures, large and small, by neighbors, the general public, and government officials. The Evangelical Confessional Church had the courage to call for prayers throughout the country "for all those who are suffering." Julius Streicher, *Gauleiter* of Franconia and publisher of the anti-Semitic *Der Stürmer*, felt constrained to warn the population against showing too much compassion for the Jews.

The U.S. consul general in Stuttgart reported to the American ambassador in Berlin on November 12 that "the vast majority of the non-Jewish German population, perhaps as much as 80 per cent, has given evidence of complete disagreement with these violent demonstrations against the Jews. Many people, in fact, are hanging their heads with shame."

Goebbels, the instigator of this well orchestrated outburst, did not even have the satisfaction of applause from his peers. Minister of Economy Walter Funk expressed indignation, though certainly not for reasons of compassion:

> Have you lost your head, Goebbels? How can you commit such base acts! It is a disgrace to be a German today! I knock myself out day and night to preserve the economic stability of the nation, and you throw millions out of windows. If you don't put a stop to this immediately, I will resign!

Goering also was furious, but not because he had suddenly been stricken with pangs of conscience. As he recounted at the Nuremberg trial with disconcerting candor:

> I had found out that Goebbels was responsible for the events of that night. I told Hitler that I wanted no part of those methods. As the person responsible for the Four-Year Plan, I was striving mightily to obtain maximum results.
>
> In several speeches, I had asked the people to save even empty toothpaste tubes, and rusty bent screws, and to turn them over to the recycling centers. And in the space of only one night, millions and millions of marks worth of merchandise were stupidly destroyed. Goebbels didn't care a fig for the economics of the situation.

Given his shrewd sense of timing and total lack of scruples, Goebbels deemed it appropriate to pose as a defender of law and order. On the afternoon of November 10, the DNB (German Press Agency) published a communiqué from the Ministry of Public Enlightenment and Propaganda, announcing legislative measures following the assassination in Paris of vom Rath. It read, in part:

> The justifiable and understandable indignation of the German people following the odious Jewish assassination in Paris was expressed last night by measures of reprisal against Jewish stores and establishments. I now address an urgent appeal to the entire population, asking them to cease at once all demonstrations and anti-Jewish acts. The definitive reply to the assassination in Paris will now be given through legislative means.[8]

And so the events of *Kristallnacht* entered an entirely new phase. In Nuremberg, Goering described what happened next:

> During the course of the afternoon, I went again to the Chancellery. I was talking with the Fuehrer when Goebbels joined us. A while before, I had told him on the telephone what I thought of his wretched deed. He was not in the least contrite and exploded into his usual anti-Semitic tirade. He had an interesting suggestion, however. He suggested that a collective tax be imposed on the whole of German Jewry. Of course, he at first proposed a ridiculously high figure. After a brief discussion, we agreed on a sum of a billion marks. Hitler took advantage of the occasion to express his desire to find a definitive solution to the Jewish question "in one way or another."

In order to expound his ideas, Goering in his capacity as plenipotentiary for the Four-Year Plan, called a conference on November 12. A copy of the proceedings was discovered by American investigators after the war and introduced at the Nuremberg trial.[9] Among the participants, besides Goebbels, were the ministers of the interior, justice, industry, finance and religious affairs, the chief of the SD (Heydrich) as well as the head of the regular police, the *Gauleiter* of Vienna, an under state secretary in the Ministry of Foreign Affairs, a director of the Reichsbank and a spokesman for German insurance companies. The presence of the ministers of finance and industry and the representative of the Reichsbank, men who would not ordinarily deign to soil their hands with such mundane matters as the excesses of party goons or the "fling" of the SA, pointed up that the aftermath of the pogrom had moved into a new phase. The German exchequer was nearly empty, the lack of foreign exchange had begun to seriously hamper German military preparations; something needed to be done.

The meeting, which was to last four hours, started with Goering pointing out that it was not called to discuss what was to happen in regard to Jews but rather to make it happen. And make it happen they did. The discussions were wide-ranging. It was estimated that at least half of the damages inflicted on Jewish homes and businesses were covered by ordinary fire, theft, and glass insurance. The plate glass damage was especially galling to Goering. Since many of the Jewish enterprises were located in premises owned by "Aryans," they had to be reimbursed. But much more frustrating to Goering (in his role as Germany's economic czar) was that it would be necessary to import from Belgium much of the plate glass, and of course pay for it in scarce foreign currency.

Goering didn't want the German insurance companies to bear the cost, but argued that if reinsured abroad, the foreign firms should be made to pay. Mr. Hilgard, on behalf of the German insurance companies, pointed out that little was covered by reinsurance abroad, so that the loss had to be borne by the German firms. Yet even though faced with major losses, the firms could not afford to renege on their debt (even with the approval of the Third Reich), lest they be judged unreliable abroad. How then to reconcile the conflicting demands, that is, having the insurance firms pay and not have the Jewish shop owners benefit? Heydrich came up with the solution—the insurance firms would pay, and the Reich would then confiscate the money. Thus the Jewish owners would not benefit, but the "honor" of the German insurance companies would be maintained in the eyes of the world's business community.

The main result of the meeting was a series of decrees which excluded Jews from the economic life in Germany by the "Aryanization" of all parts of the economy, followed by a series of other directives which sharply curtailed the already greatly limited social and cultural activities of the Jewish population. Jews were to repair the premises which had been sacked, and turn over all property to the Reich. The Reich would subtract the sums due it, including the cost of cleaning the streets after the destruction and the expenses for those who had been interned. From the remainder, Jews would be given a living allowance, supposedly sufficient for their needs. The allowance was never distributed.

On November 14, the *Reichsgesetzblatt* (Law Gazette) formally reflected the three most important decisions reached by the meeting. Accordingly, Jews were:

- required to pay the German Reich a collective "contribution" of 1 billion RM ($400 million);
- obliged to make, at their expense, repairs to all business establishments and private residences, with any insurance reimbursements to be confiscated by the Reich;
- prohibited from operating any wholesale or retail business or from practicing any craft or carrying out any independent trade.

On December 3, there appeared the law requiring the dissolution of all Jewish-owned enterprises and their eventual transfer to German ownership. Soon, most businesses were "sold" to suitable Aryans, usually for a fraction of their true value.

In the weeks that followed literally dozens of decrees were issued, designed to deprive Jews of their worldly goods. They were required to give up any stocks they held. Jewelry, precious stones, and metals, as well as art objects, had to be sold to state purchasing offices. Special tax rates for Jews were introduced.

Equally devastating were the decrees depriving the Jewish population of any sort of public social life. Goebbels, in his capacity as president of the Reich Chamber of Culture, prohibited theaters, concert halls, movie houses, and other places of amusement from admitting Jews as spectators. Jewish newspapers and Jewish schools were closed. The *Jüdische Rundschau*, the most important publication and means of communication among German Jews, was forced to close down. No advertisements from Jews could be published in the press. Jewish children who had retained permission to attend "Aryan" schools were expelled; only those of mixed blood could, by special authorization, continue their studies.

Everything was meticulously dealt with—the conditions under which Jews could visit a public park or a forest or sit on a public bench, the utilization of land on which a synagogue stood, access of Jews to trains and the creation of special railroad compartments (which had been the subject of a lengthy discussion between Goering and Goebbels at the November 12 meeting), the housing of Jews in ghettos, and so on. Drivers' licenses were withdrawn, ownership of automobiles was prohibited, and the use of public transport greatly limited. The restrictions not only deprived Jews of all means of cultural activities and self-expression, but of all means of existence.

Goering made it clear that worse was yet to come. "If the German Reich in the foreseeable future becomes involved in a foreign political conflict, it is certain that we in Germany will immediately settle accounts with the Jews."

Most of the tens of thousands of Jewish males who had been sent to concentration camps in the aftermath of *Kristallnacht* were released in the weeks and months that followed, provided, of course, that they survived the experience. Many suffered from the effects of frostbite and hundreds required the amputation of limbs. The average period of detention was about four to six weeks for the older internees, and longer for some of the younger ones.

The death of vom Rath offered the opportunity to carry out long-prepared steps to further intimidate Germany's Jewish population, and the Nazi authorities made the most of it. Even without the death of vom Rath, it is probable that German Jews would have experienced some sort of dramatic repression, probably not later than the summer of 1939. While it may never be known for certain to what extent the occurrences of the pogrom were in fact preplanned, its timing certainly influenced the course of events. They could not have come about in this form on any other day of the year, since that would have required the party to issue formal orders, something which at that point in history it wanted to avoid. The presence in Munich of most top local party officials almost made it possible to instigate a pogrom without attribution. The fact that it did not succeed was due largely to a lack of political savvy at the local leadership level.

As it was, the death of vom Rath provided a welcome opportunity not only for the party, but also for Germany's exchequer. In much the same manner as the 1933 *Reichstag* fire was used to eliminate the Nazis' political opposition, so the shooting of vom Rath was utilized to provide much needed support for an economy burdened by the heavy demands of the rearmament program. It was not a new idea. A special tax for Jews had already been contemplated in 1937 to coincide with the sentencing of David Frankfurter. Also, in the early 1900s, Heinrich Class, head of the *Alldeutscher Verband*, a small radical rightist organization with a strong anti-Semitic orientation, had proposed that Jews be taxed much more heavily than Aryans in order to finance Germany's drive to greatness.

Herschel Grynszpan provided the necessary excuse.

5

World Reaction

In the days that followed *Kristallnacht*, much of the free world's press and airwaves were filled with reports and editorials giving vent to expressions of horror at what had transpired. The German ambassador in London, von Dirksen, wrote after the war that "Hitler's Jewish pogrom let loose a cry of horror and of anger throughout the entire world."[1] However, this revulsion did not manifest itself in action by the major powers. The British government, after all, was still under the euphoria of Neville Chamberlain's "peace in our time" at Munich, and France was looking forward to a visit by Foreign Minister Ribbentrop to sign a "Franco-German Friendship Declaration." As a result, except in the United States, government reactions were muted; in France it was virtually nonexistent. The world's press, however, reacted forcefully. For the first time, foreign correspondents in Germany and Austria were basing their stories not on rumors of maltreatment in concentration camps or the application of repugnant laws to faceless individuals, but were filing eyewitness accounts of mob action and destruction while the police stood by.

Typical was the lead paragraph of an article in *The Washington Post* on November 11:

> Probably not since the evening of August 24, 1572, and the bloody days and nights that followed, had the European world seen anything quite

> comparable to what took place Thursday throughout Greater Germany. It is plain that, like the St. Bartholomew's Day massacre, the recent ferocious reprisals against the German Jews were officially sponsored.

The *Chicago Tribune* headlined its piece "Chaos Rather than Government" while the *St. Paul Dispatch* referred to "A Throwback to Barbarity." The *Boston Herald* used the headline "Germany Sanctions Lynch Law" and the *Buffalo Courier-Express* spoke of "Officials as Provocateurs." "Nazi Poison is Spreading" was how the *Gloversville* (N.Y.) *Morning Herald* topped its comments, and the *Springfield Republican* was no less negative in its assessment, referring to the "Morals of a Lynch Party." *The Omaha World Herald* sarcastically referred to "A Land of Law and Order," and the *Syracuse Post Standard* spoke of "Humanity Aghast and Ashamed." Strong editorial comments appeared in papers from coast to coast, from the *Los Angeles Times* to the *Baltimore Sun*.

The editorials reflected the general mood of a significant segment of the population. Protest demonstrations and meetings were the order of the day. The Georgia Baptist Convention, on behalf of its 418,000 members, petitioned Secretary of State Cordell Hull "to take urgent measures" to protest "the intolerant, brutal and inhuman treatment of Jews in Germany. Such treatment," said a resolution unanimously adopted, "is a denial of the ideals of decency, of justice and of Christianity."

Some 20,000 people packed into Madison Square Garden for a protest demonstration and public figures such as former President Herbert Hoover, former New York Governor (and 1928 Democratic presidential candidate) Alfred E. Smith, and New York District Attorney (and future Republican presidential candidate) Thomas E. Dewey made radio broadcasts. Union workers decided to show their solidarity by agreeing to contribute part of their earnings to the unfortunate victims, while schoolchildren started collections on their behalf.

During this period, U.S. restrictive immigration policies were relaxed somewhat. After the annexation of Austria, some restrictions on the use of the German and Austrian quotas were eliminated, and, in reaction to *Kristallnacht*, President Roosevelt announced that persons on "visitors" visas would not be forced to return to Germany. In fact, between the Austrian *Anschluss* and the invasion of Poland, U.S. immigration policy was more liberal than at any other time between 1919 and 1946. But in this context, "liberal" is a relative term. With the U.S.

population around 130 million, fewer than 85,000 refugees were admitted during this eighteen-month period.[2]

If German press reaction was any indication, they were clearly upset by a measure agreed upon between New York Mayor Fiorello H. LaGuardia (affectionately known as "The Little Flower") and Police Commissioner Lewis J. Valentine. Having been asked by the U.S. Department of State to arrange for the protection of the German Consulate General, they created a special squad of New York City policemen under the command of Captain Max Finkelstein, made up entirely of Jewish officers and patrolmen, to guard the consulate, to escort distinguished Nazi visitors, and to perform general police duty on all occasions requiring protection for Nazi sympathizers.[3]

LaGuardia's ploy was not an entirely new idea. Theodore Roosevelt recounted in his 1920 autobiography that, as police commissioner of New York (1895–97), he was called upon to silence a Rector Ahlwardt, a German preacher who had come to New York to preach a crusade against the Jewish people. Arguing that he did not want to make him a martyr, the future president instead assigned forty Jewish policemen to escort the preacher everywhere in the city. When he spoke he did so behind a phalanx of Jewish bluecoats and not surprisingly, his hate crusade was laughed into oblivion.

One of the most prominent and, as it turned out, most effective protests came in the form of a broadcast by Dorothy Thompson. Miss Thompson was one of America's most able and respected journalists of her generation, having established her reputation as a foreign correspondent in Germany, Vienna, and Moscow in the 1920s and 1930s. As the first female foreign correspondent in Berlin and the first woman to head a major American news bureau abroad, she had by 1938 become the First Lady of American Journalism. *Time* magazine in a 1939 cover story said of her: "She and Eleanor Roosevelt are undoubtedly the most influential women in the U.S."

Miss Thompson was well acquainted with the onslaught of Nazism in Europe. She had interviewed Hitler in 1931 and had written a book critical of him shortly thereafter. In 1934 she was unceremoniously expelled from Germany.

At 9 P.M. on Monday, November 14, 1938, Miss Thompson made one of her regular radio broadcasts on the "General Electric Hour," to which an estimated five million radio sets across the country were tuned. The subject of her talk was Herschel Grynszpan.

A week ago today an anaemic-looking boy with brooding black eyes walked quietly into the German embassy in the rue de Lille in Paris, asked to see the ambassador, was shown into the office of the third secretary, Herr vom Rath, and shot him. Herr vom Rath died on Wednesday.

I want to talk about that boy. I feel as though I knew him, for in the past five years I have met so many whose story is the same—the same except for this unique desperate act. Herschel Grynszpan was one of the hundreds of thousands of refugees whom the terror east of the Rhine has turned loose in the world. His permit to stay in Paris had expired. He could not leave France, for no country would take him in. He could not work because no country would give him a work permit. So he moved about, hoping he would not be picked up and deported, only to be deported again, and yet again. Sometimes he found a bed with another refugee. Sometimes he huddled away from the wind under the bridges of the Seine. He got letters from his father, who was in Hanover, in Germany. His father was all right. He still had a little tailoring shop and managed honorably to earn enough for food and shelter. Maybe he would have sent his son money, but he was not allowed to send any out of Germany. Herschel read the newspapers, and all that he could read filled him with dark anxiety and wild despair. He read how men, women and children, driven out of the Sudetenland by a conquering army—conquering with the consent of Great Britain and France—had been forced to cross the border into Czechoslovakia on their hands and knees—and then had been ordered out of that dismembered country, that, shorn of her richest lands and factories, did not know how to feed the mouths that were left.

He read that Jewish children had been stood on platforms in front of classes of German children and had had their features pointed to and described by the teacher as marks of a criminal race. He read that men and women of his race, amongst them scholars and a general decorated for his bravery, had been forced to wash the streets, while the mob laughed. There were men of his race whom he had been taught to venerate—scientists and educators and scholars who once had been honored by their country. He read that they had been driven from their posts. He heard that the Nazi government had started all this because they said the Jews had made them lose the World War. But Herschel had not even been born when the World War ended. He was seventeen years old.

Herschel had a pistol. I don't know why he had it. Maybe he had bought it somewhere thinking to use it on himself, if the worst came to the worst. Thousands of men and women of his race had killed themselves in the last years, rather than live like hunted animals. Still, he lived on. Then, a few days ago, he got a letter from his father. His father told him that he had been summoned from his bed, and herded with thousands of others into a train of box cars, and shipped over the border, into Poland. He had not been allowed to take any of his meager savings with him. Just fifty cents. "I am penniless," he wrote to his son.

This was the end. Herschel fingered his pistol and thought: "Why doesn't someone do something! Why must we be chased around the earth like animals!" Herschel was wrong. Animals are not chased around the world like this. In every country there are societies for the prevention of cruelty to animals. But there are none for the prevention of cruelty to people. Herschel thought of the people responsible for this terror. Right in Paris were some, who were the official representatives of these responsible people. Maybe he thought that assassination is an honorable profession in these days. He knew, no doubt, that the youths who murdered the Austrian Chancellor Dollfuss are heroes in Nazi Germany, as are the murderers of Rathenau. Maybe he remembered that only four years ago the Nazi Leader himself had caused scores of men to be assassinated without a trial, and had justified it simply by saying that he was the law. And so Herschel walked into the German embassy and shot Herr vom Rath. Herschel made no attempt to escape. Escape was out of the question anyhow.

Herr vom Rath died on Wednesday. And on Thursday every Jew in Germany was held responsible for this boy's deed. In every city an organized and methodical mob was turned loose on the Jewish population. Synagogues were burned; shops were gutted and sometimes looted. At least four people were done to death. Many, many more were beaten. Scores killed themselves. In cold blood, the German government imposed a fine of four hundred million dollars on the entire Jewish community, and followed it by decrees which mean total ruin for all of them. A horrified world was stunned. In the United States nearly every newspaper protested. A former governor, Alfred Smith, and the recent Republican candidate for New York State governor, Thomas Dewey, protested with unusual eloquence.

But in Paris, a boy who had hoped to make some gesture of protest which would call attention to the wrongs done his race burst into hysterical sobs. Up to then he had been apathetic. He had been prepared to pay for his deed with his own life. Now he realized that half a million of his fellows had been sentenced to extinction on the excuse of his deed.

I am speaking of this boy. Soon he will go on trial. The news is that on top of all this terror, this horror, one more must pay. They say he will go to the guillotine, without a trial by jury, without the rights that any common murderer has.

The world has endured for five years unheard-of things. The fortunes of American citizens have been all but confiscated in Germany. We have protested, and no attention has been paid. What could we do? Some weeks ago two hundred American citizens of Jewish blood were ordered to close their businesses and depart from Italy as undesirable aliens. Our State Department protested, but the protest has been all but ignored. What could we do? Every country in the world has had a refugee problem to add to all its others, as a result of a system which cares nothing for what happens to other countries, and we among them. What could we do?

We could, of course, do many things. There are half a million non-naturalized Germans in the United States, and as many Italians. We might have loaded them on boats, confiscated their property and shipped them home. There are hundreds of thousands of dollars in German and Italian fortunes in this country. We might have confiscated them as reprisals for the confiscated fortunes of American citizens and for unpaid debts. Why don't we do it? We don't do it because it isn't, according to our standards, decent. We don't do it because we refuse to hold people responsible for crimes that others commit. We don't do it because our sense of justice is still too strong to answer terror with terror. We don't do it because we do not want to add to the hatred and chaos which are already making this world intolerable. We fear that violence breeding violence will destroy us all in the long run.

When the dictators commit what to the rest of the world are crimes, they say there is a higher justice—they claim the justification of national necessity and emergency. We do not think that such justice is higher. We think it low and cannot therefore answer it in its own language.

But is there not a higher justice in the case of Herschel Grynszpan, seventeen years old? Is there not a higher justice that says that this deed has been expiated with four hundred million dollars and half a million existences, with beatings, and burnings, and deaths, and suicides? Must the nation, whose Zola defended Dreyfus until the world rang with it, cut off the head of one more Jew without giving him an open trial?

Who is on trial in this case? I say we are all on trial. I say the Christian world is on trial. I say the men of Munich are on trial, who signed a pact without one word of protection for helpless minorities. Whether Herschel Grynszpan lives or not won't matter much to Herschel. He was prepared to die when he fired those shots. His young life was already ruined. Since then his heart has been broken into bits by the results of his deed.

They say a man is entitled to trial by a jury of his peers, and a man's kinsmen rally around him, when he is in trouble. But no kinsman of Herschel's can defend him. No man of his race, anywhere in the world, can defend him. The Nazi government has announced that if any Jews, anywhere in the world, protest at anything that is happening, further

> oppressive measures will be taken. They are holding every Jew in Germany as a hostage.
>
> Therefore, we who are not Jews must speak, speak our sorrow and indignation and disgust in so many voices that they will be heard. This boy has become a symbol, and the responsibility for his deed must be shared by those who caused it.[4]

In addition to her emotional radio appeal, Dorothy Thompson devoted two "On the Record" columns in the *New York Herald Tribune* to Herschel Grynszpan, one on November 14 entitled "To a Jewish Friend," the other on November 16 headed "Give a Man a Chance." In her November 16 article she recounted:

> The response [to the broadcast] was flabbergasting. I am in receipt of 3,000 telegrams, still uncounted letters, and several hundred dollars in checks, although I did not ask for money and was speaking solely for myself. The telegrams came from forty-six states. Almost all of them gave their addresses and asked what they could do.

Given the unexpected response, on November 15 Miss Thompson announced the organization of the Journalists' Defense Fund to raise money for the defense of Herschel Grynszpan, stressing that it would appeal only to non-Jews for contributions "so that the Nazis can't say this is another Jewish plot." The first objective of the committee was to find a strong non-Jewish defender for the accused, one who would be capable of handling this difficult and complicated case. It was hoped that he would in the process make the trial a major forum for charging the Nazi regime with anti-Semitic policies but without, however, exposing the Jewish community still living in Germany to any new dangers and, incidentally, to defend the accused.[5]

In addition, Miss Thompson expressed the hope that the response to the appeal would help stiffen the backbone of the French and British peoples against "Nazi terrorism."

Among the prominent writers who became associated with the Journalists' Defense Fund from the very outset were such well known figures as Hamilton Fish Armstrong, editor of *Foreign Affairs*; columnist Heywood Broun; writer John Gunther; Brigadier General Hugh S. Johnson, columnist for *The New York World-Telegram*; Leland Stowe, staff writer and former Paris correspondent of the *New York Herald Tribune*; Raymond Gram Swing, writer and political commentator; and

William Allen White, editor of *The Emporia* (KS) *Gazette*. Others who subsequently became associated with the group included Louis Bromfield, Edward G. Robinson, F. Scott Fitzgerald, Westbrook Pegler, Alexander Woollcott, and Alice Roosevelt Longworth.

By November 18 it was announced that more than 25,000 letters had been received in support of the undertaking. In all, $40,203 were collected.[6] The Fund asked Edgar Ansel Mowrer, head of the European Bureau of the *Chicago Daily News* in Paris and André Geraud, editor of *L'Europe Nouvelle*, to represent it in France, thereby keeping the conduct of the affairs of the Fund in the hands of journalists.

Meanwhile, the German ambassador to Great Britain, von Dirksen, reported on November 17, 1938, in a dispatch to the Foreign Ministry in Berlin that "the political repercussions of the intensification of the anti-Jewish movement in Germany made impossible for the time being the intended British rapprochement through talks with Germany. For the anti-German circles in Britain, the excesses against the Jews and new legal measures were only grist to the mill; whereas for pro-German circles, yielding to the atmosphere here and to press propaganda, it was a severe shock. Their confidence in the possibility of an Anglo-German understanding is shaken; their effectiveness crippled."[7]

The reports from Ambassador Dieckhoff in Washington were equally discouraging. On November 14, he telegraphed the Foreign Ministry in Berlin that "any expression of public opinion (about the anti-Jewish demonstrations in Germany) is without exception irate vis-à-vis Germany and hostile toward her. And the outcry in this connection comes not only from Jews but in equal measure from all camps and classes, including the German-American camp."[8]

Contrary to pronouncements of Nazi propagandists, Jews as a group almost without exception deplored Grynszpan's crime right from the outset. They did not look on the act as heroic and generally disapproved of it as useless, dangerous, and a great disservice to Jews everywhere. German and Austrian Jews, trying to survive in a hostile environment, feared that they would have to bear the brunt of the retribution, and of course events quickly proved them right. Those elsewhere, while perhaps appreciating Herschel's motives, were fearful that this act by an immature Jewish boy would contribute to a further deterioration of the explosive political situation in which Europe found itself. They were most intent on maintaining the status quo, no matter how tenuous, hoping that things would improve with time, hoping that Hitler and his Nazis would go away. They almost unanimously disavowed Herschel, and probably none more so than French Jews.

The World Jewish Congress with headquarters in Geneva published this statement on the evening of November 10:

> Though the Congress deplores the fatal shooting of an official of the German embassy in Paris by a young Polish Jew of seventeen, it is obliged to protest energetically against the violent attacks in the German press against the whole of Judaism because of this act and, especially, to protest against the reprisals taken against the German Jews after the crime.[9]

The French Alliance Israélite stated:

> We remain faithful to the inalienable integrity of the human person and reject once again all forms of violence, regardless of author or victim of such an act. We condemn the act of homicide which resulted in the loss of a German official and indignantly protest the barbarous treatment inflicted on an entire innocent population which was made the scapegoat for the crime of an individual.

What was in the minds of many was expressed by *Le Droit de Vivre* (*The Right to Live*), the magazine of the French *Ligue internationale contre l'antisémitisme* (LICA), which published an article on "The truth behind the assassination." The article describes the act as that of a lone individual under Nazi influence. The article refers to the 3,000 francs that Grynszpan had mentioned at the time of his first interrogation and insinuated that, if this money came from Germany, this would only have been possible with official authorization and was therefore highly suspect. It also argued that the assassin was able to penetrate the German embassy only because he was known there. The article contributed little of substance, but it certainly represented a disavowal of Herschel Grynszpan by an influential publication.

6

Growing Up Jewish in Hitler's Germany

Herschel Feibel Grynszpan was the sixth child of Sendel and Rivka Grynszpan (née Silberberg). Both parents were born in western Russia, which had once been Poland, Sendel in 1886 in Dmenin and Rivka in Novo-Radomsk in 1887. In April 1910, not long after completing his Russian military service, Sendel and Rivka were married in Radomsk and emigrated to Hanover (Germany) in April 1911. When Poland regained its independence from Russia after World War I, the two acquired Polish citizenship.[1]

Herschel was one of six children of whom only three survived childhood. The first child was born dead in 1912. The second child, daughter Sophie Helena, born in 1914, died in 1928 of scarlet fever. Daughter Esther was born on January 31, 1916, and a son, Mordechai, on August 29, 1919. A fifth child, son Salomon, was born in 1920 and died in 1931 as a result of a traffic accident. On March 28, 1921, Herschel was born.

Sendel first worked as a plumber, but in June 1918 he opened a small tailor shop which provided an adequate living until the late 1920s. By then, however, the effects of the economic slump caused his business to fail, and from 1929 to 1934 he tried to eke out a living as a junk dealer, but that too proved unsuccessful. According to German records he received unemployment benefits totaling 1,028 Reichsmark ($360) between July 10, 1933, and October 15, 1934, when he once again took up tailoring.

The general health of Herschel's family was rather poor. Sendel himself was frail in stature and reportedly suffered from malaria. He was, however, able to work as long as he lived in Germany, though he apparently never earned a great deal, as evidenced by the fact that his name does not appear on the German tax rolls. Whatever ordeals life may have had in store for him, thanks to hard work, thrift, and a certain amount of luck in his later years, he survived. At the time of his testimony in Israel at the Eichmann trial in 1961, when he was seventy-five, he gave the impression of being a vigorous old man.

The Grynszpans lived at 36 Burgstrasse in the old city, not far from the central railroad station and the Church of the Cross, where the renowned philosopher Leibnitz is buried. In 1927, at age six, Herschel was enrolled in Hanover's *Volksschule* (Primary School) No. 1, a few steps from home. There he remained a student until Easter 1935, when, at fourteen, school attendance was no longer obligatory.

Herschel's teachers characterized the youth as a quick study and of above-average intelligence, but rather lazy. His report cards repeatedly judged his homework as unsatisfactory. Herschel had to repeat the sixth grade and on four occasions his promotion to the next grade was apparently granted only reluctantly or with reservations. When he left school in 1935, having completed the mandatory school attendance requirements, Grynszpan received an *Abgangszeugnis*, a school-leaving certificate, one year short of completing the eight-year elementary school program.

The Ministry of Propaganda collected copies of Herschel's report cards for the years 1927 to 1935. His course grades usually ranged between satisfactory and less than satisfactory, with *Drawing* occasionally judged "good" and *German* rated "fair" or "satisfactory." *Behavior* between 1927 and 1930 was generally rated "satisfactory" or "good," and mostly "good" thereafter, while *Attentiveness* was usually "satisfactory" but occasionally dropped to "deficient." In the category *Industry*, the teachers in the lower grades judged the youngster's work deficient but, starting in 1931, he was always rated "satisfactory." When it came to *Orderliness*, Herschel did not distinguish himself in the eyes of his teachers, with early efforts (1928 and 1929) judged "unsatisfactory" and later fluctuating between "satisfactory" and "deficient."

In his last appearance before Judge Tesnière on July 26, 1939, Herschel attributed leaving school to the teachers who no longer took an interest in Jewish students and relegated them to the back of the classroom. They were, he reported, treated as outcasts and hardly ever asked to participate in classroom exercises. While there is no reason to doubt Herschel's description, he almost certainly was not a diligent student and the German report to the French court after his arrest correctly noted, with obvious satisfaction, that his pre-1933 report cards were worse than those afterwards.

In marked contrast to the school's judgment of Herschel's behavior (satisfactory to good) was that of Klara Dessau, first the assistant director, and then the director, of the Jewish Community day-care center in Hanover. The center was attended by children aged 6–14 after school and Herschel was registered there for a number of years. During her interrogation by the Gestapo on March 28, 1939, Miss Dessau described Herschel as a very difficult child who was repeatedly ejected from the day-care center due to bad behavior. According to Miss Dessau, Herschel was the only child whom she ever had occasion to slap, when other means failed, in all the time she headed the day-care center. Miss Dessau, who described Herschel's siblings as model children, also reported that Herschel's mother often complained about her son.[2]

In response to a request by the French judicial authorities, the German Ministry of Justice provided a report on the person of Herschel Grynszpan. Like his teachers, it characterized the youth as intelligent, an easy learner with a good memory, but lazy. He was described as someone who had relationships with other Jews only, but was without comrades. The report described him a fighter who outside of school made use of his fists. It generally made him out to be mean-spirited, ill-tempered, sullen, and taciturn. In order to explain the discrepancy between this unflattering description and the positive comments on his behavior in his report cards, the report surmised that Herschel "internally" rejected school discipline while avoiding basic infractions.[3]

Herschel's early youth was relatively untroubled. His close, traditional family pampered their youngest. He was a member of the Jewish Sportsclub "Bar-Kochba Hannover," where he acquired the nickname "Etzel" (the Hun King) because, as a former friend recalls, "he was not too tall, dark complected and very hot tempered."[4] But the rise of Nazism cast its ominous shadow, and when Herschel left school, Sendel recognized that his son had no future in Germany. Sending Herschel to Poland, where he had never lived, was not the answer. Esther, a secretary, and Mordechai, a plumber by trade, both still lived at home. It, therefore, seemed best to send the fourteen-year-old to Palestine.

Sendel registered his son with the Palestine Service in Berlin, and had him enroll with the Mizrachi Youth Organization, which sought to prepare future immigrants for Palestine by providing them with spiritual training, the study of Hebrew, and physical training in an agricultural establishment.

With the assistance of the Jewish Community of Hanover, which contributed 15 RM a month toward the costs, the young recruit was sent to the Yeshiva in Frankfurt am Main, a rabbinical seminary directed at the time by a Dr. Hoffmann. There he studied Hebrew and the Torah, beginning on May 9, 1935, with a six-week break spent with his parents in Hanover. His teachers deemed him a student of average aptitude and intelligence, although he once more gained the reputation as something of a fighter, earning him the nickname "Maccabee."[5]

The entire course of study at the Yeshiva—designed to prepare students for professions such as rabbi, teacher of religion, or for employment by Jewish community organizations—normally was five years, but Herschel returned to Hanover on April 15, 1936, having spent only eleven months at the school. Herschel recounted to the French examining magistrate that he returned to Hanover when he was fifteen, hoping to obtain the necessary visa to leave for Palestine. When he was told to wait a year, probably because of his age and slight physical development, he said that he tried in vain to find work as an apprentice plumber or mechanic, but instead encountered taunts of "dirty Jew" and physical abuse by German children. Like those ubiquitous signs "Juden Unerwünscht" (Jews Not Wanted Here), which he almost certainly would have encountered, such experiences were familiar to anyone growing up Jewish in Germany during that period. However, Herschel apparently brought one other handicap to his job search. His profound religious beliefs did not allow him to work on Saturday, and according to one report, even most potential Jewish employers were unwilling to employ the youth under those circumstances. Herschel's brother Mordechai apparently encountered the same problems.

A one-year wait seemed a very long time under such conditions and so Herschel's family made an important decision. As Grynszpan recounted to the panel of French medical-legal experts who interviewed him after his arrest, one day at the synagogue he met "old Katz, the watchmaker" who told him not to stay in Germany.

He said to me, "A boy like you can't stay here under such conditions. In

> Germany, a Jew is not a man, but is treated like a dog." I told him that all the governments [*sic*] were closed to me. He advised me to go to France. He spoke of this to my father who accepted on condition that Uncle Abraham [brother of Sendel], who had been living in Paris since 1923, agreed to receive me. I myself wanted to go to Palestine. My father wrote to my uncle who not only agreed to receive me but wanted to adopt me.[6]

It was a wise decision to leave, for the atmosphere in Germany was becoming increasingly difficult for Jews. First came the infamous Nuremberg Decrees of September 15, 1935, which deprived Jews of German citizenship, reducing them to the status of "subjects," forbade marriage or extramarital relations between Jews and Aryans, and prohibited Jews from employing female Aryan servants under age thirty-five. These were followed by the laws of November 14, 1935, which deprived Jews of their voting rights and decreed the dismissal of all Jewish public employees—omens of things to come.

7

Grynszpan's Emigration—Life in Paris

While Herschel was studying at the Yeshiva, he obtained from the Polish consulate in Hamburg passport no. 1585/35, dated June 3, 1935, and valid for two years. When he returned to Hanover in April 1936, he requested the required German residence permit. This was issued on May 5, 1936, also valid until June 3, 1937, the expiration date of his Polish passport. For the time being and until mid-1937, his German papers were in order.

On July 9, 1936, not quite three months after his return from Frankfurt, Herschel requested an exit visa to Belgium from the Hanover police. According to his application, he wished to stay with his father's brother, Wolf Grynszpan, also a tailor, who had emigrated to Belgium three years earlier. Grynszpan wrote in his application that he wanted to go to Belgium to await permission to emigrate to Palestine, but that in order to obtain an entry visa for Belgium, he also needed a permit to return to Germany. The German authorities issued the reentry permit on July 16, 1936, valid until April 1, 1937.

Herschel first went to Essen, a steel town in the heart of Germany's Ruhr region, where he stayed with Isaac Grynszpan, yet another brother of Sendel. Two weeks later, the end of July 1936, he arrived in Brussels at the home of Wolf Grynszpan. In his initial declarations to the French examining magistrate, he had claimed to have come directly to France by way of Belgium. It was only during an interrogation on

February 17, 1939, that Herschel recounted the true story of his trip to Paris.

> Due to the ban on the export of money, it was impossible for me to take more than 10 marks ($4) so that I had almost no money with me on arrival in Brussels. I went directly to my uncle's and aunt's house. . . . They welcomed me rather coldly because I had come without funds and my arrival imposed additional expenses on them. I therefore moved to the house of a neighbor named Zaslawsky who is vaguely related to my family. He agreed to allow me to stay with him for several days, making it clear at the same time that I was not to overstay my welcome there.[1]

Herschel roomed with the Zaslawskys and ate some of his meals at his uncle's. But the fifteen-year-old was miserable in the strange environment where he felt unwanted. So even though his papers were in order and there were no other complications, he remained in Belgium for only a short time. At a very tender age, Herschel was beginning to feel like the proverbial wandering Jew.

Herschel's next destination was Paris, where Abraham Grynszpan, a third brother of Sendel, and his wife Chawa had volunteered to take the youngster under their wing. Without money or visa, it was decided to smuggle Herschel into France. (He later would claim that the 50 francs for a visa were stolen from him.) It was to prove a costly decision, the start of his subsequent difficulties. The actual event which triggered Herschel's move was the visit to Brussels of Mrs. Rosenthal, Mr. Zaslawsky's sister, who lived in Paris. She had been to Ostend on vacation and on her return journey visited Brussels. She agreed with Wolf Grynszpan, who probably was happy to see his nephew move on, to take charge of the inexperienced youth and to help him slip clandestinely over the frontier. It was a relatively simple task.

Herschel and Mrs. Rosenthal traveled to Quiévrain on the Franco-Belgian border. There she had him cross the frontier by taking the Quiévrain-Valenciennes tramway routinely used by workers living in the frontier area. The passports of passengers without baggage were rarely checked during rush hours. Mrs. Rosenthal returned alone to Paris. Though Herschel's uncle Abraham would later deny it when questioned by French police, he may have gone to Valenciennes to bring Herschel to Paris.[2]

Both uncle and nephew were to pay dearly for this illegal passage over the Franco-Belgian frontier. Young Grynszpan steadfastly maintained that Mrs. Rosenthal was ignorant of the fact that his passport was not in order, and Abraham would claim that Herschel had arrived in Paris on his own. Whatever the facts, Abraham was genuinely pleased to welcome his nephew to Paris in late September 1936 and presumably did everything to make the journey a relatively easy one.

When Herschel was asked, after his arrest, why he had gone to Belgium before coming to France, he claimed having heard that German frontier officials were systematically refusing to permit the departure of those with French visas. He did say, though, that he remained with his uncle in Brussels only in order to save up the money needed to acquire a visa for France.[3]

Herschel's argument on this point does not ring true. German authorities during this period actively "promoted" the exit of Jews and were unlikely to object to the departure to France of a fifteen-year-old Polish youngster. However, Germany did not permit the export of currency or other resources, while France was reluctant to admit immigrants without visible means of support. So while the reason Herschel put forward for not proceeding directly to France probably was incorrect, he was correct in contending that it was difficult for him to enter France legally.

France certainly was not alone in imposing limits on the immigration of refugees. A number of countries who considered themselves champions of the oppressed, including France, Great Britain, and the United States, solemnly assured German and Austrian Jews of their sympathy and condemned the inhumanity of Nazi anti-Semitism. At the same time, for reasons that seemed appropriate to them at the time, they restricted access to their countries to those who wanted to leave the Third Reich, using a variety of pretexts. Like so many other countries, France turned away newcomers who were considered undesirable (i.e., poor). Zionist organizations, for their part, felt it necessary to restrict emigration to Palestine to those who were physically able to contribute to the heavy work of building up the Jewish national homeland while limiting the influx of refugees who were sick, poor, too young, or too old.

In 1936, Abraham Grynszpan was forty-three years old. He was a hard worker, affable though taciturn. He enjoyed a good reputation and impressed acquaintances as an excellent man, reserved, rarely confiding in others. Like his older brother Sendel, he was a tailor, running his business from home. On the door of his apartment-workshop there was a plaque that read "Maison Albert," where he made clothes for several large stores.[4]

He earned 500–600 francs ($15) a week, not a princely sum, but enough for a modest living. His yearly rent of 5,000 francs ($140) consumed a substantial part of his budget. But being thrifty and with no children of their own, he and his wife Chawa could support Herschel. He provided Herschel 30 to 40 francs ($1) pocket money a week, enough to satisfy the young man's needs, which were far from extravagant. Abraham and Chawa treated their nephew as if he were their own child. This was in keeping with the wishes of Sendel, who had delegated legal paternal responsibility for Herschel to his brother through a legal document dated October 19, 1936. Herschel took up residence with his uncle and aunt in their little two-room apartment at 23 boulevard Richard Lenoir. They had to put a bed in the dining room for Herschel. Before long, all moved to 8 rue Martel.

The environment in which Herschel now found himself must have seemed quite familiar to the youngster, for it bore considerable resemblance to that which he had left behind. The population was predominantly Jewish and followed many of the customs to which he had been accustomed in Hanover. Yiddish, his mother tongue, was the primary language in use, and German, which he had spoken in school, was used extensively.

Abraham and Chawa saw few people outside their own immediate family. They worked hard and lived a rather secluded existence. They maintained a close relationship with Chawa's sister, Basila, who lived at 9 rue Ernestine. She was married to Jacques Wykhodz, also a tailor. On the other hand, Abraham saw little of his younger brother Salomon who also lived in Paris, but with whom he did not get along.

Herschel arrived in Paris in a state of exhaustion and depression. A court-ordered inquiry undertaken during the pre-trial investigation by Mlle de Loustal, a social worker, as well as the testimony by Abraham and others confirmed that Herschel had suffered greatly (and continued to suffer) from the stress and pressures to which he had been subjected. Even though welcomed into Abraham's household, Herschel's forced separation from his closely-knit family had been emotionally devastating. Everything seemed to be falling to pieces around him. He found himself alone and adrift. For a young, sensitive boy of fifteen, the departure from home under such conditions was terribly unsettling. When he arrived in Paris, he complained of acute gastric pains and was subject to frequent vomiting which could have stemmed from either neuropathological causes or from an ulcer. Given the sensitive youngster's experiences during the preceding months, either cause would hardly have been surprising.

Abraham arranged for medical attention, which helped to ameliorate Herschel's attacks and generally improved his health. When he kept rigorously to his diet, he had fewer difficulties. Not surprisingly, his pains reappeared later during detention.

Though his health improved after his arrival in Paris, it still left much to be desired. Herschel came from a family of small stature. He weighed only about 100 pounds and measured five feet, one inch. His eyes were brown with heavy black lashes, his skin dark, and his hair brown. He gave the impression of being more a child than an adolescent. In fact, his aunt and uncle still considered him a child at seventeen and always referred to him as such. (His lawyers would later also refer to him in the same terms, but their motive is perhaps slightly more suspect.) His physical development was somewhat below average. As a youngster in Hanover, he had undergone surgery for appendicitis. During childhood he had contracted what the Germans called the "English" sickness, a form of infantile rickets. He had a scar on his right thigh, probably from an accident he had had at age thirteen.

Herschel Grynszpan was a devout Orthodox Jew and regularly attended religious services. He suffered from the trials and tribulations to which "his people," as he always referred to them, were subjected. As he said to the medical experts: "I have always followed religious services regularly for, to me, religion is a serious matter." He confirmed during the investigation: "I am, like my parents, a strict observer of religious precepts, as opposed to those who rarely practice or are free thinkers."

Everywhere he saw the Jewish people insulted, hated, and abused. He had great pride and these affronts caused him to suffer for himself and for others like him.

Herschel always was something of a loner, yet his life in Paris was not that of a recluse. He went out occasionally, had a few friends, but spent most of his time with his aunt and uncle, helping in the apartment and the shop, and going shopping for the family. His recreational activities were innocent and included outings into the country, walks along the boulevard, and long strolls through the city. He occasionally participated in events of the Sportsclub l'Aurore, located at 110 rue Vieille du Temple near the Cirque d'Hiver. Its members were mainly young Jews from Eastern Europe with moderate socialist tendencies.

Herschel liked the movies (he preferred films such as *Ben Hur, Michel Strogoff*, and *Dark Eyes*), the theater, cafés, swimming, and dances at the Eldorado dance hall on boulevard Strasbourg.[5] When Herschel was not with his uncle and aunt (they went to the movies together once a week and occasionally had supper with the Wykhodz family), he would usually be out with acquaintances, often with friend and neighbor Nathan Kaufmann. They would meet at the Café "Tout Va Bien" at 15 boulevard St. Denis. After the crime, the Germans tried their best to label it a hangout for homosexuals and other disreputable elements, without, however, directly trying to tie Herschel to those activities. In any event, for reasons of economy, Herschel rarely entered the café, but met his friends in front of the entrance.

On Saturday, November 5, two days before the crime, Herschel went with Nathan to the nearby St. Martin movie theater and returned home at midnight. The following evening he went to a dance at the Sportsclub l'Aurore. Nothing in these amusements would presage the events to come.

Abraham regularly bought *La Journée Parisienne* and *Pariser Haint*, the Yiddish newspaper for emigrés. His nephew read the latter daily and was particularly interested in a series on the Dreyfus Affair. Through this paper he kept abreast of the anti-Semitic excesses in Germany, Austria, and the Sudetenland, the latter handed to Hitler at Munich in late September 1938, in a last desperate effort to appease Hitler's territorial appetite. The newspaper was not extremist in its coverage, but it did report in detail and editorialized on the suffering of the Jewish people.

Yet important as these things were to Herschel, almost everything was secondary to settling his status in France. From the moment of Herschel's arrival in Paris in September 1936, he and his uncle were preoccupied with efforts to obtain an identity card which would in effect be a residence permit. As a first step, Abraham registered his nephew at the local police precinct station, where he was fined 100 francs because Herschel's passport did not have an entry visa. He then requested the Central Committee for Aid to Immigrant Jews to assist him in the preparation and submission of the residence application. Either through negligence or design, the Committee did not transmit the request for a foreigner's identity card until January 25, 1937.

The request was received by the Ministry of the Interior on February 9, 1937, and was transmitted to the police prefect for action on February 20. While awaiting the outcome, Herschel was issued a receipt for the application for an identity card; this, for the time being, took the place of a residence permit.

During the long waiting period after the submission of his residency application, Herschel tried to straighten out his situation vis-à-vis the German and Polish authorities. His German reentry visa, issued prior to his departure to Belgium, expired April 1, 1937. It was extended to June 1, 1937, at the request of Sendel Grynszpan in Hanover. Herschel's Polish passport, a prerequisite for his return to Hanover, expired on June 3, 1937. Soon Herschel was going to find himself with neither a valid passport nor a visa.

On May 24, 1937, Herschel reported the loss of his passport to the Polish consulate in Paris. It is not known whether he had actually lost it or just hoped to obtain one valid for a longer period of time, but on August 7, 1937, he was issued Polish passport no. 75686, valid to January 7, 1938. This passport, however, lacked the reentry visa permitting his return to Germany (which in any event would have expired on June 1, 1937). On September 17, 1937, Herschel therefore wrote to the German consulate in Paris, requesting the renewal of his reentry visa. He explained the request by noting that his studies in Paris were taking longer than anticipated.

The letter was followed up by a visit to the consulate, also in September 1937, by Abraham. With the French residence permit still outstanding, and given his precarious health, which at least in part was probably attributable to the youngster's separation from his parents, it was felt that Herschel should retain the option to return to Hanover. But a check by the consulate with the Hanover police revealed that Herschel's original request for an exit visa had been based on his projected emigration to Palestine and not for study in Paris. Presumably pleased to have an excuse to react negatively, an oral refusal was issued. On January 4, 1938, Sendel Grynszpan reportedly wrote a letter to the German consul general in Paris, requesting the return of his son to Hanover, but that too received a negative response.

Finally, on July 8, 1938, the prefect of police rejected the residency request, and on August 11 issued a decree of expulsion, effective August 15, 1938. In other words, after almost nineteen months, and over a month after the final decision had been made by French authorities, the seventeen-year-old youth was given four days to leave France. He could no longer legally stay in France or return to his parents in the absence of a valid German return visa. The number of options available were limited indeed.

He could still go to Poland, even though he did not have a good command of Polish and hardly knew the members of his family who still resided there, provided that the Polish consulate would extend his passport beyond the January 7, 1938, expiration date. Still in Poland were his paternal grandmother, Gitta Grynszpan, who lived in Radomsk, and his maternal grandmother, who had remarried after the death of her husband. Also in Radomsk were an aunt and two uncles.

Another possibility was joining the Foreign Legion, which, however, seemed somewhat less appropriate in view of his youth and slight build. During his interrogation Herschel said that he had considered enlisting in the Foreign Legion, but finally had hesitated because his parents had already lost several children. Abraham later testified that "he refused to eat and wanted to enlist in the Foreign Legion. I even gave him 200 francs to take the necessary steps."[6] For whatever reason, he did not further pursue that possibility. There seemed to be one other possible "solution" to the young man's desperate situation. His relatives and his friend Nathan Kaufmann reported that he contemplated suicide. Who could blame him?[7]

Just when he first considered suicide was never clearly established. Was it during the early days of his stay in Paris because he missed his family, as reported by the medical experts who examined him, or when he learned of the refusal of his request for residence papers in Paris (as reported by Nathan Kaufmann in the course of his interrogation by the police on the day after the shooting), or after having received the news of his family's deportation?

Herschel's preoccupation with suicide recurs throughout his declarations. It was mentioned by Beimis Berenbaum, Chawa's brother, when asked about Herschel's quarrel with his uncle on Sunday, November 6. On November 25 and 30, 1938, he wrote about it to his parents. He also mentioned it on July 26, 1939, the last time he was questioned by the examining magistrate, when he tried to convince the judge that he went to the embassy, not to kill someone, but rather to commit suicide in a spectacular fashion.

There was indeed much talk of suicide but the medical experts felt that the intent to take his own life, if it truly existed, could not be taken too seriously.

Once Herschel's residency request had been rejected, Abraham had to worry about legal complications due to the youngster's presence in his home. After his arrest, both would claim that after the rejection of his application, Herschel had duped his uncle into believing that he had appealed to the Interior Ministry for a reversal of the decision and that the appeal had succeeded. Actually, in his youthful naïveté, about all that Herschel had done was to write to the president of the United States, asking for permission to immigrate on behalf of himself and his family.

In early October, 1938, Herschel's aunt and uncle moved once again, this time to 6 rue des Petites Écuries, not far from their previous home. Herschel remained in the old apartment house on the rue Martel, occupying a maid's attic room under the eaves on the sixth floor. This allowed his uncle to claim, in the event of a police check, that his nephew no longer lived with him. A search of the rue Martel apartment by the police did, in fact, take place during October. The police found the apartment empty and obtained Abraham's new address. Herschel was not found at the new address, the neighbors did not volunteer any information, and so the matter was not pursued further.

During the day, Herschel usually stayed in his room or at his uncle's place in order to avoid the police. In the evening, however, he continued to go out with friends, notably Nathan and Salomon (Sam) Schenkier. Though he was not completely isolated after receiving his expulsion order, there is little doubt that the enforced solitude during the day was distressing for this youth of seventeen.

Given the material at our disposal, what can one say about Herschel Grynszpan? The task of dissecting the character of an individual on the basis of secondhand information is in itself difficult and precarious. When the object is an adolescent in his formative years, and when these are years of great physical and psychological upheaval, one obviously must tread carefully. When in addition one is dealing with a highly emotional issue and some of the information available is contradictory, as might be expected since it comes from interested, and not necessarily impartial parties, the problems are magnified.

If there was one attribute which characterized Herschel, it was that of an emotional person who cared a great deal about the people close and dear to him. His eyes filled with tears when there was talk of his family or the misfortunes of Jews. He read a great deal, exhibiting an interest mainly in questions that concerned Jews, particularly their persecution.

Some might have considered him excessively emotional, but given the circumstances in which he grew up, who could blame him? He was loved by his parents and loved them equally in return. He couldn't explain clearly enough, he said, how much he loved them and how much he suffered knowing that they were so unhappy. Everywhere he saw the Jewish people insulted, hated and abused. He had great pride in his Jewish heritage and these affronts caused him to suffer for himself and for others.

Herschel's negative image, as conveyed by the Germans, is in direct contrast with the testimony of his immediate family and the tenants who lived in the same building in Paris that he was a gentle, self-effacing, obliging, affectionate and sensitive young man with occasional sudden mood changes, that is, a temper. His guards at the Fresnes prison would later describe him as a polite youth, although not very communicative.

Herschel appears to have been something of an idler, a kind of stroller of streets, a dreamer. He was a tinkerer; he loved things mechanical and wanted to become a plumber, electrician, or mechanic, but these hopes never materialized. He was chided for his lack of sense of urgency in looking for work or helping his parents, but the precarious atmosphere in which the family lived and the probability of imminent departure would have discouraged all but the most forceful and ambitious. Herschel was not such an individual. True, his brother and sister with difficulty had found temporary work at low salaries, but both were older.

He admitted to smoking about three packages of cigarettes a week, but never drank alcohol. This youngster, whom the Germans later sought to depict as a rake or libertine, was not only poor and temperate but also, by his own account, inexperienced sexually. In apparently separate discussions he confided to his lawyers de Moro-Giafferri and Weill-Goudchaux that he was a virgin.

And so it was that this emotional young man, torn from the family he loved, persecuted for his heritage of which he was proud, apparently decided to become an avenger for his people.

8

The Deportation of the Grynszpan Family

The wisdom of Herschel's departure from Germany became increasingly apparent as time went on. His brother and sister both lost their menial jobs shortly before Herschel left for Belgium and France. Sendel's tailoring business became dependent on a shrinking Jewish population as German clients became more and more hesitant to patronize a Jewish business and incur the wrath of the party watchdogs.

Government policies designed to exclude Jews from the economic life of the country moved on inexorably. The decree of April 26, 1938, required German and Austrian Jews to register their personal and real property, both in Germany and abroad, if in excess of 5,000 RM ($2,000). Foreign Jews were required to register their German possessions. With this information in hand, it would be easy for the Nazi authorities to tighten at will the economic screws on the Jewish population.

As if being Jewish in Nazi Germany were not enough, another major problem loomed on the horizon for Polish Jews. By now it had become abundantly clear that the Nazi government actively "encouraged" the departure of Jews, both German (and Austrian) nationals and foreigners. Foreign Jews were for the most part fortunate in that they were able to return home; their home countries readmitted them, albeit at times without enthusiasm. Poland, on the other hand, did everything possible to obstruct and impede the return of its nationals, many of whom, like the Grynszpans, had spent most of their lives outside the country.

During the mid- and late 1930s, opposition to the rightist Polish government was on the increase, stemming in part from Poles residing abroad. Presumably to counteract this threat and in order to prevent the mass deportation to Poland of Polish Jews, as Germany had occasionally threatened in the past, the Polish Sejm (legislature) in late March 1938 passed a decree authorizing the revocation of Polish citizenship of any citizen who

(a) was guilty of actions against the interests of Poland, while residing abroad;
(b) had resided abroad continuously for more than 5 years without maintaining any [official] contact with Poland; and
(c) did not return to Poland from abroad if requested to do so by the Polish authorities.[1]

According to Article 5 of the decree, "Persons who have been deprived of their Polish citizenship in this manner are not permitted to stay temporarily in Poland, even if they have acquired another nationality."[2]

At first, Germany, which needed Poland's acquiescence in connection with the planned liquidation of Czechoslovakia, could not afford a public squabble with its eastern neighbor over a mere 30,000 Polish Jews in Germany and another 20,000 in Austria. (Some Nazi statistics estimated that there were as many as 70,000 Polish Jews in the Third Reich.) For whatever reason, Polish authorities also initially delayed the strict application of the law.

But life for Polish Jews in Germany was clearly becoming precarious. Many, like Sendel and Rivka Grynszpan, had come to Germany already before World War I and had settled in major cities such as Hamburg, Bremen, and Hanover. They had severed their ties with their impoverished (and openly anti-Semitic) homeland—except for ties with family members still residing there—and had built up new lives in Germany over the years. Now it became increasingly apparent that they had no future in the Third Reich.

It was probably in order to meet with relatives and assess the possibilities of returning to Poland that Herschel's mother made two trips to Poland in 1938. Rivka Grynszpan first went in April to Radomsk where family members still lived, which gave her an opportunity to meet Salomon and his wife who had come from Paris on a visit. She went again in August and was forced to remain for several weeks, longer than she had anticipated, after coming down with the flu and a stomach disorder.

Rivka took advantage of her presence in Poland, and away from under Nazi censorship, to write Herschel a postcard on August 14. In it she told her son that they had arranged to send him 10 RM ($4) every month and asked him to save some of it for the day when they all would have to emigrate, "because it is clear that we cannot remain [in Hanover]." However, she cautioned her son not to write them in Hanover about receipt of the money, since this could cause them very great harm. (The unauthorized export of even such a small sum was a major offense in Nazi Germany.) Instead, she instructed her son to include the phrase "the food is good" when he wrote, thereby signaling them that the money had been received.

Rivka went on to ask what Herschel had found out about the possibility of emigrating to the United States. She also asked him to write in detail about his French papers, since they were worried, having heard about several people whose residence application had been rejected by the French.[3] They would get their answer within three months.

Soon their worst fears were to be realized. A German Police Order of August 22, 1938, decreed that

1. all residence permits for foreigners living in Germany and Austria would become invalid by March 31, 1939;
2. requests for new residence permits would have to be submitted not later than December 31, 1938; and
3. new residence permits would be given by the German government only to those "considered worthy of the hospitality accorded them because of their personality and reason for their stay."

Local jurisdictions were given authority to pass on the applications. It was obvious to the Polish Jews residing in Germany that they were in real danger of being forcibly deprived of a place to stay. Yet where were they to go? The traditional countries of refuge were closed to all but a lucky few. Should they return to an inhospitable Poland that actively sought to exclude them and was unlikely to provide even the limited economic opportunities which still remained in Germany? Here they were at least able to cater to the still substantial Jewish population and the few Germans willing to patronize them in the dead of night. The choice was certainly not an enviable one, and it is not surprising that while many actively sought to leave, many others hesitated.

It was at this point that Poland decided to act. An order of the Polish Ministry of the Interior dated October 6, 1938, was published on October 15 in the *Dziennik Ustaw* No. 80, Item 543. The order provided that within the next 15 days,

1. all Polish citizens living abroad must submit their passports for inspection to Polish offices (consulates);
2. after inspection, an endorsement will be placed in all passports submitted; unless
3. revocation of Polish citizenship is appropriate under provisions of the decree of March 31, 1938.

Those persons whose passports did not receive the required endorsement would automatically become stateless. Poland made it clear that it would in that case no longer feel obliged to accept its former citizens.

The decree became effective on October 29, two weeks after publication, thereby threatening to make stateless most of the estimated 50,000 Polish Jews living in Germany and Austria. In order to escape future responsibility for Polish Jews, Germany quickly initiated diplomatic efforts designed to persuade the Poles to permit the return of Jews living abroad even after the deadline. Specifically, the German government asked the Poles publicly to declare that in the event Polish Jews were in the future expelled from Germany, they would be admitted to Poland even without a visa.

The Polish government on two separate occasions refused to make such a declaration which would, of course, have been counter to the primary purposes of the laws. Under the circumstances, the Germans decided to act before the October 29 deadline. At the recommendation of the Foreign Ministry, beginning on October 26, the Gestapo sought to arrest and expel immediately all Polish Jews residing in Germany.

The Poles did not take kindly to these German actions and informed the government in Berlin that not only would the expelled Jews be refused admission to enter Poland and left in no-man's-land, but as a reprisal the German residents in Poland would also be expelled. Hitler, who liked presenting his adversaries with a "fait-accompli," was enraged by this attitude but was at the time unable to counter it. The Polish countermeasures effectively stymied the operation so that only

17,000 of the 50,000 Polish Jews were in fact forcibly expelled. However, within a year, the whole matter became largely moot with the German occupation of Poland.

The great human suffering caused by the expulsions cannot be laid solely at the door of the Nazi government. The actions and attitude of the Polish government seemed designed to cause the maximum hardship among its citizens living in Germany.

Herschel Grynszpan anxiously followed the events in the Jewish press, knowing of this dilemma faced by his family in Hanover. During the pretrial investigation he mentioned an article in a Jewish paper which foretold the consequences that Polish Jews living in Germany would suffer due to these decrees. There is no evidence, as the Germans later sought to maintain, that he read some of the more extremist newspapers. The situation of Polish Jews in Germany was becoming so desperate that even totally objective reporting was likely to sound alarmist.

On November 3, 1938, Herschel received from his sister the postcard, written on October 31, 1938, from Zbaszyn which he had in his wallet at the time of his arrest.[4] He must have answered almost immediately, for a second postcard, also from Zbaszyn and dated November 7, 1938, arrived in Paris after Herschel's arrest:

> We received your dear letter. Up until now nothing has changed our very unhappy situation. I'll continue with the description. We weren't allowed to leave the Rusthaus to return home. On Friday night at 9:30 P.M. we all left Hanover. There was crying and wailing so loud it could have awakened the dead. But it didn't help us. On Saturday morning we were ordered to get out somewhere in the deserted countryside. It was a nerve-wracking spectacle—the manner in which we were chased through fields and forests. After that we were forced to settle in barracks. Those who have money can lodge in private places. A committee from Warsaw has come here. These people do what they can for us. We are very poorly fed. We sleep on straw sacks. We have received blankets. But believe me, Hermann, we won't be able to stand this much longer. Since we left we have not yet been able to undress. Aunt Sura stayed behind. She is considered of "undetermined nationality." Aunt Ida is here. Uncle Schlojma is in the hospital. He has had an eye operation and he stayed there. Our hopes rest with him, if God grants his recovery. Everything depends on the Jewish community. We haven't yet received money from you. What do they say there about what will happen to us? We can't go any further. Berta.

> Dear Brother and Sister-in-law. We are in a very sad situation. We are poor and in misery. We don't get enough to eat. You, too, once were in need. I beg you, dear Brother, to think of us. We don't have the strength to endure this. You mustn't forget us in this situation.
> Sendel.[5]

Independent press reports published in France, the United Kingdom, the United States and elsewhere bear out to a large extent the stories of suffering. An article on November 3 by the correspondent of *The Times* of London described the events as follows under the headline "Polish Jews' Expulsion—Refugees Despoiled in Germany."

> The deportees include more than 2000 children. The first train at Chojnice was simply driven to the Polish frontier station and left there. The officials at the station were asleep, as no train was expected at that time of night. Among those who crossed at Zbonszyn is an 82-year-old whose oft-repeated request is that he may be allowed to die in his bed. This batch was expelled from the train on the German side of the frontier and compelled to make the last four miles on foot. They declare that they were driven by soldiers with a machine gun, which now and then fired a few rounds into the air to make the crowd hurry. Disease has broken out among them, especially among the children, but medical aid from Warsaw today is relieving the distress. Poles as well as Jews have joined in the relief work, especially at Katowice.

Some twenty-three years later, on April 25, 1961, in a calm atmosphere charged with emotion, Sendel Grynszpan recounted the details of his deportation in his testimony at the trial of Adolf Eichmann in Jerusalem:

> On [Thursday] October 27, 1938, in the evening, a policeman came to my home and asked us to go to the 11th precinct with our passports. He assured us that we would be returning directly and that it was unnecessary to take our belongings with us. When I arrived at the precinct with my family, we found many people there, seated and standing, and some of them in tears. A police inspector was shouting at them, "Sign this paper. You are expelled."
>
> The signing was required. We signed like everyone else. Only one man by the name of Gershon Silbery, or Gerschl Silber, refused. To punish him they stood him in a corner of the room for 24 hours. Afterwards, about 600 of us, from all quarters of the city, were crowded into the concert hall on the banks of the Leine [River].

On Friday night they put us in police vans, 20 to a van, and took us to the station. The street was full of people chanting, "The Jews to Palestine!" We were taken to Neu-Bentschen, the last German city before the Polish frontier, arriving at 6:00 A.M., Saturday the 29th.

Trains were arriving from all directions: from Leipzig, from Berlin, from Cologne, from Düsseldorf, Bielefeld, Essen and Bremen. All together, there were 12,000 persons.

At the border we were searched and our money taken from us. They left us with only 10 RM each. German law forbade the export of capital. They said to us, "When you arrived, you only had 10 RM; there's no reason for you to leave with more than that."[6]

During his testimony, Sendel Grynszpan spoke rapidly, words tumbling out, one after another. The president of the court, Moshe Landau, requested him to speak more slowly. Sendel was deeply disturbed by the remembrance of the events. He described the manner in which he was forced to cover on foot the two kilometers that separated the station from the Polish border:

The SS came with whips and struck us. Those who couldn't walk were beaten. There was blood on the road. Packages were snatched from their arms. The SS treated us in a cruel and barbarous manner. It was the first time in my life that I had suffered German brutality. We were made to run and they shouted at us, "Run, run!" I was struck and fell on the side of the road. My son helped me get up and pulling me by the hand he said, "Come, Papa, let's run, otherwise they will kill you."

There was a heavy rain, some people sank to the ground, some fainted, others had heart attacks. There were many old people among us. We hadn't eaten since Thursday night. We didn't want to eat the bread of the Germans and we were starving. When we arrived at the Polish frontier, the Poles fired shots at us, not knowing who we were. Then a Polish general and some officers, astonished to see such a tremendous crowd, looked at our passports and found that we were Polish citizens.

They decided then to let us enter. We were taken to a little village with a population of 6,000. There were 12,000 of us! Due to lack of space, they put us in the stable of the military post.

On Sunday, October 30, 1938, the Poles gave us the first meal we had had since Thursday. A truckload of bread from Poznan was distributed. Only those who could scramble for it managed to eat. The others got nothing. Then other trucks filled with bread arrived and everyone had some.

On that day, October 30, Sendel was able to send a card to Herschel in Paris, signaling that he should no longer send mail to Germany since the whole family was now in Zbaszyn, Poland.

Due to the many negative accounts of the deportations in the international press, the Germans went to great lengths in their efforts to justify and defend what had transpired. Various government reports prepared at the time claimed that there was at no time either brutality or crying and wailing. The deportees, they said, did not have to leave their trains in open country, but "apparently" were bused to the frontier, where they then crossed the German-Polish border on foot. The reports denied that the deportees were "chased across forests and fields." Later, they hoped that testimony by German doctors and Red Cross nurses would prove more effective than propaganda tracts.

The official German account of the expulsions in the Ministry of Propaganda's "Yellow Book" written by Wolfgang Diewerge (*Anschlag gegen den Frieden*), recounted the German version of the assassination of vom Rath and its aftermath. It blandly noted that "Those persons under Polish jurisdiction who had been residing in Germany were made available to Poland. The matter was handled in the most proper and humane fashion. . . .Thus Grynszpan's family arrived in their country, where they were reunited with their relatives and friends. They could leave for America as easily from Gdynia as they could from any city in Germany." The report did not dwell on how these unfortunate people were expected to arrange for emigration with virtually all their worldly goods and life savings forcibly left behind in the Reich.[7]

Yet when it came to providing details of the deportation of the 484 persons reportedly expelled from Hanover, even Diewerge's book makes it amply clear that it did *not* go smoothly.

> At the frontier those expelled were conducted to Polish territory partly by train, partly on foot and partly by bus.
>
> Difficulties arose whenever Polish officials at the frontier refused to allow the Polish Jews on Polish soil. The Polish government, nevertheless, finally recognized its responsibility to admit the persons in question, and orders were then given to do so. The orders in some cases, however, were delayed at certain frontier posts. This made it necessary at times for the expelled persons to await specific orders for a long time before the Polish authorities decided to allow them entry. The situation was not the same at all frontier posts. Where the Polish authorities im-

> mediately accepted their nationals and conducted them to the interior of the country, whence they were able to depart for their respective places of origin, there were no disagreeable incidents.

According to the report,

> the measure expelling the Polish Jews from Hanover was carried out without brutality and without incident. The police and the members of the SS made an effort to treat properly the Jews whom they were obliged to expel. They even helped as much as possible to carry their baggage which was considerable. No one complained and even the Jewish organizations of Hanover, who took part in the undertaking, did not hear of grumbling or lamentations of any sort.
>
> Three regular roads were used to reach the frontier on foot. There were no serious difficulties. Whenever the Polish frontier officials made things difficult they were finally persuaded to be reasonable and do what was necessary.
>
> It is not true that the parents, brother and sister of Grynszpan underwent particularly harsh treatment during their deportation from Germany. They were treated like all the others, that is to say, in a proper manner.

It does not require exceptional skill in reading between lines to recognize that, even leaving aside the barbarous nature of the entire process, serious problems were encountered during the expulsion proceedings and that the deportees were subjected to much suffering. Assessing blame for what transpired at the border is more difficult, although it would appear that there is more than enough to go around for both the Nazi and Polish regimes.

According to a report of April 12, 1939, by the German Railroad in Hanover, prepared at the request of the Propaganda Ministry, *Train Sp Han 4199, Hanover-Neubentschen (New Zbaszyn)* consisted of 14 cars averaging 55 seats each, with approximately 35-40 passengers per car. According to the same report, the train departed Hanover at 9:40 P.M. on October 28; that is more than twenty-four hours after the almost five hundred men, women, and children had been rounded up. During the intervening period they had been confined to two large rooms at the restaurant "Rusthaus."[8]

It is possible that there were, in fact, transports where the deportees were reasonably well treated, traveled in relative comfort, and crossed into Poland like human beings. But there were obviously others where the hapless cargo was simply dumped near the frontier and driven toward the border much like cattle, only to be pushed back by Polish police. It is certain in any case that on October 28 and 29, thousands of persons wandered in no-man's-land between cordons of German and Polish police. The latter refused at certain frontier points to admit the refugees once they realized that the first arrivals were part of a mass repatriation. It was only in the course of October 29 that the situation began to ease up, when, after German-Polish talks, the Polish authorities finally agreed to accept the refugees on condition that the Germans cease "leaving the refugees at the disposition of the Poles" (i.e., dumping them at the border).

The Germans would later go to great length to demonstrate their "correctness" in dealing with the Grynszpan family possessions. The 1939 Ministry of Propaganda pamphlet contains a photograph of the dining room at 36 Burgstrasse with the furniture intact, clothes hangers on the table, supposedly in the state in which it was left the day of the deportation. According to the caption under the photograph: "Today everything is still as it was." (Later events would prove that this was not so.) The disorder in the apartment is attributed to the precipitous departure of the family which failed to put back in their accustomed places those belongings they could not take with them.

Moreover, five members of the Consistory of the Hanover Synagogue were called upon to attest before a Hanover notary that they visited the Grynszpan flat on February 13, 1939, and found it in perfect condition. A photograph of their declaration was included in the propaganda booklet.[9]

Eventually, a German-Polish agreement was reached regarding the goods left behind by those who were expelled from Germany, allowing for a partial recovery of these goods. According to a German report, the Hanover civil court on November 25, 1939, after the occupation of Poland(!), appointed one Max Israel Sternheim as trustee of the Grynszpan property. Sternheim was charged with settling and liquidating all business matters and effects of Sendel Grynszpan. He obtained authorization to ship the furniture to Zbaszyn and wrote to Sendel Grynszpan's family living in what was formerly Poland, asking for instructions regarding where to send items such as linens, beds, dishes, clothing, a sewing machine, and other household goods. He received an answer from Sendel's mother, Mrs. Gika Grynszpan, saying that she could not get in touch with her son who was abroad. That was indeed true. Sendel had escaped to Russia. Sternheim finally sent the remainder of the household goods, at the request of the Zbaszyn Committee, to Sendel Grynszpan's address by way of the port of Hamburg.[10]

The Polish Red Cross and the Jewish community did their best to aid the refugees, but government assistance was meager and given reluctantly. Once in Poland, the refugees' lives were no longer in danger, but their living conditions were precarious and their general situation unenviable. Apart from the cruelty inherent in the deportation, the disagreeable welcome which awaited the Polish Jews on their return was an additional hardship. The Poland of Marshall Ridz-Smigly only very reluctantly accepted their return and did little to assist them.

The accommodations at Zbaszyn were hard but could not be described as a concentration camp. The refugees could enter and leave at will and were not forced to remain there once they found other lodgings. As soon as able, the Grynszpans left the camp to live in town at 5 Pilsudskiego Street. This was the address Herschel gave as that of his parents in a letter of July 27, 1939, to Dorothy Thompson.

The interrogation of Mordechai Grynszpan at the Eichmann trial provided some further details of the Grynszpan family odyssey. In August 1939, two weeks before the outbreak of the German-Polish war, the Grynszpans moved to Radomsk. The Germans kept well informed of the family's whereabouts. As soon as they arrived in Radomsk, during the war against the Poles, they searched for the Grynszpans. Fortunately the family had fled in time to Swislocz, a small town situated near Bialystock, north of Brest-Litovsk. (The area was Polish from 1919 to 1939, became Russian in 1939 after the division of Poland, and was returned to Poland by the USSR in 1945.)

In 1940, Sendel—who, it must be recalled, was born in the Russian part of Poland—and his family went to live in Astrakhan on the Caspian Sea. He lived in the USSR for six years while his son Mordechai enlisted in the Russian army for the duration of the war. The family emigrated in 1948-49 to Israel where they lived near Haifa.

The Grynszpan family received its last communication from their youngest son in March or April 1940. It was a preprinted Red Cross postcard with a list of general statements which could be crossed out if not applicable. There was only his signature. Shortly thereafter, France was occupied and all correspondence between Herschel Grynszpan and his family ceased.[11]

9

From Despair to Vengeance

By the fall of 1938, the world of Herschel Grynszpan was rapidly disintegrating; a cool head and steady nerves were required to cope with the stresses of the rapidly deteriorating situation. For this, he was poorly equipped. The events which directly affected his family and "his people" deeply distressed him. His own plight further drained his meager emotional resources. Herschel was overcome with anxiety.

His friends and his uncle tried their best to comfort and console him. They argued that his family now at least was out of immediate danger in Poland. Nathan tried to reassure and encourage him to view the future more optimistically. But the lack of news, after having received the initial postcard, and the vivid descriptions in the local press only exacerbated his depression.

On the afternoon of Sunday, November 6, Herschel and his uncle had a violent argument at the dinner table in the presence of the couple Wykhodz and Mina Berenbaum, the wife of Chawa's brother Beimis Berenbaum. The argument played at least a peripheral role in the events to come and became the object of considerable speculation, but due to the discreet silence of the participants in this family scene, the exact reasons for the quarrel were never fully divulged.

Herschel's father had apparently sent uncle Abraham 3000 francs ($85), a respectable sum in those days, to care for Herschel. The export of money from Germany was, of course, illegal, but they had arranged to have it smuggled out. Herschel now asked Abraham to return the money to his parents, but the uncle wanted to await future developments before doing so. Hence the argument apparently ensued.[1]

The one outsider present for at least part of the argument was Herschel's friend Nathan, who, in his interrogations following the shooting, reported that Herschel had accused Abraham at one point of not appreciating the misfortune which had befallen his parents. To this Abraham had retorted that he had always done just about everything he could for Herschel and that if the youngster was not satisfied, he was free to go. Herschel at that point started to put on his coat in anticipation of leaving, but Aunt Chawa had held fast to the coat and started to cry. Nathan also intervened and was able to calm Herschel somewhat. However, the dispute soon started all over again, whereupon Herschel departed with the words, "I am leaving, goodbye," but not before Uncle Abraham had given him 200 francs.[2] Nathan followed his friend after having calmed the uncle and aunt by assuring them that he would bring Herschel back.

While apparently never fully convinced that he knew the entire story, the examining magistrate and even the German indictment of late 1941 came to the conclusion, for lack of other evidence, that the dispute between the uncle and his nephew had indeed concerned money. Given the precarious position of Herschel's parents, and indeed Herschel himself, it must have been difficult for the youngster to keep emotions under control.

It is, of course, possible that the break between Herschel and his uncle may not have taken place solely on Herschel's initiative. It is possible that Abraham, who was usually calm and well balanced, in this instance lost his temper, and at the end of his patience showed the boy the door. Nathan, who arrived toward the end of the argument and was not fully aware of what had gone on before, confirmed that, far from hindering his nephew from leaving, he had the impression that Abraham actually showed him the door. Yet if there had truly been bad blood between Herschel and Abraham, it would be hard to understand the reasons for the 200 francs allowance.

Diewerge, who clearly had an ax to grind—the subtitle of his propaganda tract was, after all, *A Yellow Book about Grynszpan and His Helpers*—proposed in his book the hypothesis that the future assassin informed his family during the meal of his determination to take vengeance for the deportation of his family.[3] There is no evidence to support this argument. However, if it were so, it is most probable that

Abraham would have done everything possible to dissuade his nephew from carrying out his plan.

The rather vague and somewhat conflicting declarations of the Grynszpans and the Wykhodzes as to the reasons for the hasty departure of their nephew after Sunday dinner are suspect. But then, who would want to tell the world that the argument was precipitated by the unwillingness of an older relative to assist financially the parents of a youngster living with them. Even if the decision were entirely correct, it would be difficult to justify.

It must be remembered that all those present, except perhaps for Nathan, were in a precarious position. Even if unalterably opposed to Herschel's stated intentions, whatever they might have been, alerting the police would have made it necessary to reveal the illegal presence of the boy in their midst. Their position was extremely delicate.

Nathan certainly seems to have been unaware of the full range of subjects under discussion between the boy and his uncle. The family only encouraged him to help divert his friend and to keep an eye on him. Nathan caught up with Herschel and together they went to the "Club Sportive l'Aurore," as they had already planned earlier that day, to meet some friends. Herschel accompanied Nathan the rest of the afternoon but did not participate in the games and other amusements.

When evening came, Nathan tried to convince Herschel, who had by then calmed down but was still in a gloomy and somber mood, to return to his uncle's place. Herschel angrily refused, exclaiming, "I will not go back. I'd rather die like a dog from hunger, than go back on my decision."[4] The friends parted at 7 P.M. near the municipal building of the 10th arrondissement.

Herschel would later testify that it was while wandering aimlessly, alone and upset, he came across the shop window of "À la Fine Lame" with its revolvers in the window. Such a chance encounter may well have crystallized Herschel's perhaps still vague intentions to give vent to his thirst for vengeance.[5]

As the evening wore on and Herschel did not return home, his relatives became disturbed by the continued absence and Abraham Grynszpan and his brother-in-law, Jacques Wykhodz, decided to look for the youngster in his normal haunts. The reasons for their anxiety, which Nazi propagandists perceived as an ominous sign (after all, so went their reasoning, why should they have been anxious if Herschel had not told them that he would do something drastic like killing an embassy official) were fairly obvious. Herschel had often spoken of suicide, including in the course of that afternoon's arguments. At about 8:30 P.M., the two appeared at the home of Nathan Kaufmann, searching for their nephew. Nathan told them that Herschel had planned to spend the night at a hotel after eating at the Café "Tout Va Bien." After supper, Nathan went to search for his friend, but a visit to the café at about 9 P.M. was in vain. Nathan later met with Messrs. Grynszpan and Wykhodz and tried to reassure them.

Meanwhile, a little before 8:30 P.M., Herschel had gone to the Hotel de Suez at 17, boulevard Strasbourg and rented a room for the night. He paid 22.50 francs in advance and registered as Heinrich Halter, born in Hanover, eighteen years of age. He spoke French in a halting manner. The daughter of the owner, M. Adrien Laurent, speaking German, drew him out to say that he had come from Germany. When asked for his identification papers, he replied that he had none. He asked if it would be all right if he went out, which caused the porter of the hotel to suppose that he was going to fetch his baggage at the nearby Gare de l'Est (railroad station), since the hour of his arrival coincided with the arrival of the train from Germany. On his return near midnight, the bellhop took him to his room which he did not leave again. The night clerk noticed on the control board that the occupant kept his light on long into the night.[6]

Herschel slept badly. On November 30, 1938, during one of his interrogations, Grynszpan declared in the presence of his attorney, Maître de Moro-Giafferri:

> I had a very restless night. I dreamed a lot. In my dreams I saw my parents mistreated and beaten and the dream made me suffer. In my dreams I also saw Hitlerites who grabbed me by the throat to strangle me. I also saw boycott demonstrations such as those I had experienced in Hanover where, for example, I saw Germans mistreated and spit at when they went into a store owned by a Jew. Demonstrators screamed at them, "You are damned! You are selling the German people to the Jews!" I was obsessed by that question. Again and again I asked myself, "What have we done to deserve such a fate?" And I couldn't find any answer to the question.[7]

During the investigation by the medical authorities, he gave a somewhat different description of his dreams.

> I went to bed, but I did not sleep well because of the bad dreams I had. I

> saw myself going into the gun shop. I also had visions of my family's plight. I woke up three times during the night. Each time my heart was beating fast. To make it calm down, I put my hand on my chest.[8]

Herschel arose Monday morning at 7:30 A.M. Fifteen minutes later he rang for breakfast and had a cup of black coffee in his room. Before leaving his hotel at about 8 o'clock, he wrote to his parents the farewell postcard, addressed to his uncle, which was found in his wallet at the time of his arrest. Its message was clear.

The young man checked out of the hotel after paying 2.75 francs for the continental breakfast, and on this extraordinarily mild November day then walked directly to M. Carpe's small store at 61 rue du Faubourg St.-Martin. He arrived at 8:35, just as Mme Carpe was rolling up the store's iron shutters.

Herschel told Mme Carpe that he wanted to buy a gun; she in turn called her husband, who asked the young man the reason for the purchase. Herschel, calmly opening his wallet which contained a number of large bills, explained in his accented French that he often needed to carry large sums of money to the bank for his father and wanted to have a pistol for protection. (The sale and purchase of firearms was legal in France, provided the purchaser was of sound mind. The only requirements were for the merchant to keep a record of the sale and the buyer to register the purchase with the police.)

Young Grynszpan clearly was not knowledgeable when it came to guns. However, after looking at several models, he took M. Carpe's suggestion and purchased a 6.35 caliber revolver for 210 francs and a box of 25 bullets for 35 francs. The gunsmith asked the youth for his name, address and identity papers. Herschel showed his passport and gave his address on the rue Martel. M. Carpe demonstrated the use of the weapon, wrapped it and told Herschel to make the required declaration of ownership of a firearm at the neighboring police precinct. He also gave Herschel a properly filled-out declaration form. Herschel stuck the form into his pocket and left the store in the direction of the nearby precinct station, but shortly thereafter changed direction.

The youth then walked the three blocks to the Café "Tout Va Bien," arriving there at 8:55 A.M., loaded the gun in the restaurant's washroom and placed it in the inside left pocket of his suit jacket. Thus prepared, he walked to the Metro station Strasbourg St.-Denis and at 9:05 took the Line 8 train to the Madeleine, where he changed for the Line 12 train to Solférino. (Apparently, at this point Herschel still had not yet fully made up his mind what he would do when he arrived at his destination, for he tried to buy a roundtrip Metro ticket; however, they were on sale only until 9 A.M.) From there it was only a short walk to his final destination at 78 rue de Lille, the German embassy, arriving at 9:35 A.M. The lives of tens of thousands of people were about to be changed dramatically.

10

The Prosecution

The first police official to question the handcuffed Herschel Grynszpan on the morning of November 7, shortly after his arrest, was Commissioner J. Monneret. It was to be the first of many interrogations. The youth was subjected to further questioning at the beginning of the afternoon during the search of the hotel room and his room on the rue Martel. In the meantime, the police took the first depositions from members of the embassy staff, from Abraham Grynszpan, and from M. Carpe, who had sold the gun. Towards 11 P.M., after a full and exhausting day, Herschel was interrogated once again, this time by Commissioner Badin.

The following day, on November 8, Public Prosecutor M. Frette-Damicourt, taking account of Herschel's age, appointed Judge Jean Tesnière, a specialist in juvenile cases, as chief examining magistrate. This placed the case in the hands of an experienced magistrate with a good reputation.

At 3:30 P.M. on the day following the shooting, Herschel Grynszpan appeared in the public prosecutor's chambers where Judge Tesnière had his office. He was surrounded by three particularly burly police inspectors. Unless they were expected to protect Herschel, this display of force seemed a bit superfluous in view of the slight physique of the adolescent prisoner. Grynszpan was led at once into the examining magistrate's office. At his side were two attorneys, H. Szwarc and R. de Vésinne-Larue, while guards stood near the door.

After the usual formalities, Judge Tesnière asked the youth if he wished to explain his motives and the circumstances of the crime. Herschel responded with a deeply moving account of the suffering of his fellow Jews. He talked at length, searching for words, struggling to express himself in French. At frequent intervals, Judge Tesnière, who knew enough German to forego the aid of an interpreter, helped him find the right words. At times, Herschel was forced to stop, overcome by fatigue and depression. But he readily acknowledged his responsibility and without difficulty recounted the motives of his act. He said that above all he sought, through a spectacular act, to attract the attention of the world to the suffering and persecution of the Jewish people at the hands of the Nazis. The Paris newspaper *l'Oeuvre* of November 9, 1938, quoted him as follows:

> The Jewish people have a right to live, and I do not understand all the sufferings that the Germans are inflicting on them. I don't understand this long martyrdom. If you are a Jew, you can obtain nothing, attempt nothing, and hope for nothing. You are hunted like an animal. Why this martyrdom?

Le Temps of November 10, 1938, published a statement given by Grynszpan during his first full interrogation in which he sought to sum up his motives.

> It was not with hatred or for vengeance against any particular person that I acted, but because of love for my parents and for my people who were unjustly subjected to outrageous treatment. Nevertheless, this act was distasteful to me and I deeply regret it. However, I had no other means of demonstrating my feelings. It was the constantly gnawing idea of the suffering of my race which obsessed me. For 28 years my parents resided in Hanover. They had set up a modest business which was destroyed overnight. They were stripped of everything and expelled. It is not, after all, a crime to be Jewish. I am not a dog. I have the right to live. "My people" have a right to exist on this earth. And yet everywhere they are hunted down like animals.

After recounting how he had come to France and the reasons for remaining, he spoke of the murder itself. He described the events in detail, with some modifications from the previous night's account.

> I did not wish to kill. I could not consent to live like a dog in the German Reich. When I committed that act, I was obeying a superior and inexplicable force. What's more, vom Rath, the secretary at the embassy, called me a dirty Jew.

"Was that before or after the shooting?" asked the magistrate at once. "I couldn't tell you exactly—my mind was in a great emotional turmoil," replied the young prisoner.[1]

With those words, the inquiry terminated. It was by then 5:30 P.M. Herschel Grynszpan was taken to Fresnes prison which had a special "re-education center" area set aside for young offenders. By French standards a model prison, it provided its inmates with clean and airy accommodations and a certain amount of freedom.

As soon as vom Rath died, Herschel Grynszpan was indicted for murder, which automatically brought with it a longer and more detailed pretrial examination. The task of the examining magistrate was delicate since French public opinion was bound to be deeply split in its attitude toward the case. Both the plaintiff—here the German government nominally representing the family of vom Rath—and the defense were inexorably heading toward the sort of political trial that in the past had often divided the French. To be lenient in a case such as this, one would have to accept political murder—taking justice into one's own hands by killing an innocent person—as a justifiable right. To be severe would mean being insensitive to the rash actions of an adolescent who had been seriously traumatized by experiences well before he had committed this act.

Judge Tesnière consciously tried to limit the investigation to facts that *preceded* the shooting, an approach which was greatly appreciated by the Germans, who several times remarked on it favorably in the press. Tesnière's attitude was less warmly welcomed by the defense, which hoped to see such aspects as the events of *Kristallnacht* and Nazi barbarism addressed more expressly.

A full-scale trial undoubtedly would have brought this conflict of aims much more into the open than the pretrial investigation required under French law. It was apparent that with the possible exception of the defense (and Herschel himself, who did not consider himself an ordinary criminal), no one—least of all the French government—was in a great hurry to get on with the trial. The investigation was repeatedly delayed by German interventions, and France's Justice Ministry did nothing to speed up the process. "The trial," wrote defense attorney

Maître Weill-Goudchaux after the war, "could have been presented to the criminal court in July 1939. But Georges Bonnet, the Minister of Foreign Affairs whose efforts to accommodate the Germans were already evident, did not wish it, for he feared. . . acquittal."[2] He probably equally feared acquittal and conviction, for in both cases he would have had to deal with malcontents.

The Germans were, of course, not content to let French justice take its course without some "assistance." On November 8, by special order of the Fuehrer, Friedrich Grimm was charged with defending German interests in the case.[3] Shortly thereafter, Minister Counselor Diewerge was given responsibility for the coordination of the case on behalf of the Ministry of Propaganda. The two had worked together once before, on the Gustloff case, and they made a good team, determined that "Justice—German Style" would prevail.

Grimm agreed to this assignment with alacrity. He liked being in the limelight. In addition, he had made the acquaintance of Ernst vom Rath during a trip to Paris a month earlier and they had gotten on well together.

Dr. Grimm was born in Düsseldorf on June 17, 1888, the son of a railroad surveyor. After studying for the bar, he opened a law practice in Essen (Ruhr) shortly before World War I, which he spent as an (French language) interpreter. After the war, he established himself as a trial attorney, quickly taking up nationalist causes and becoming the spokesman for some of those seeking the demise of the Weimar Republic. Before long, Grimm appeared as defense attorney at many major trials of German rightists. In 1927, he became professor for international law at the University of Münster.

Given his record during these turbulent years of the Weimar Republic, it is not surprising that Grimm made the personal acquaintance of Adolf Hitler already in 1932. (In his memoirs published in 1953, Grimm recalled that he had met Hitler twice that year, the first time when the future Fuehrer, in the company of Walter Funk, had visited Grimm's home in Essen to discuss the concept of law as enunciated in the NSDAP party platform. Grimm says that he expressed some reservations with the formulation of the party platform, but Hitler assured him that there was no fundamental disagreement between them and that the wording was still in a state of flux and would be remedied. Grimm in 1953 would argue that everything would have been all right had Hitler's ideas prevailed, but eight years after Hitler's suicide, he apparently had come to the conclusion that such was regrettably not the case.)[4]

Already on the afternoon of November 11, while the body of vom Rath was still in Paris, a meeting took place in Berlin under the leadership of Propaganda's Diewerge to plan for the anticipated trial and ascertain as expeditiously as feasible the possibility of German participation.[5] In addition to Grimm, participants came from the Ministry of Propaganda, the Foreign Ministry (Dr. Kastner), and the Foreign Organization of the NSDAP (Dr. Luebbe).

According to the minutes of the meeting prepared by Diewerge, Grimm made several points:

1. The extradition of Grynszpan (to Germany) is out of the question under French law because the youth is not a German citizen and because French law precludes the extradition of anyone accused of political crimes.
2. The participation of the parents of vom Rath (as plaintiffs) in the anticipated trial is feasible.
3. The designation of a French attorney to represent the German interests is possible.
4. The admission of a German attorney to represent the parents is questionable, but in the absence of a legal rule is at least theoretically possible.

In view of later developments, Grimm's contention that the extradition of Grynszpan was out of the question is particularly significant.

Kastner of the Foreign Ministry reported that since Grynszpan was a juvenile under French law, it was highly unlikely that he would be condemned to death or, if given the maximum penalty, that it would actually be carried out. Those present agreed that Grimm should proceed to Paris at once to ascertain, in cooperation with the embassy, the NSDAP representative in Paris and the Ministry of Propaganda attaché there, how the accreditation of a German attorney might be accomplished as quickly as possible, to identify a French attorney who would be prepared to work with Grimm, and when the start of the trial might be anticipated.

Finally, Luebbe of the Foreign Organization of the NSDAP suggested that Grimm's *Politischer Mord und Heldenverehrung* (Political Assassination and Hero Worship) and Diewerge's *Ein Jude hat geschossen* (A Jew Has Fired), both booklets prepared in connection with the trial of David Frankfurter for the murder of Wilhelm Gustloff, be translated into French as expeditiously as possible. In a separate recommendation, Diewerge proposed to Goebbels that the funds made available to the Propaganda Ministry's attaché at the Paris embassy "for the purpose of supporting anti-Jewish propaganda in France be increased from 1,600 Marks to 5,000 Marks."

Lest it be left out in the cold, on November 15, the *Institut zum Studium der Judenfrage* (Institute for the Study of the Jewish Question) proposed to Diewerge a program for the propaganda utilization of the anticipated murder trial. The Institute estimated that it could mount a three-month campaign, complete with speakers and printed materials, for about 15,000 RM. While not averse to the suggestion, several communications from Diewerge to his superiors make it clear that, at this point, he needed additional office staff and typing assistance more than anything else.

A number of meetings were held in Düsseldorf, taking advantage of the presence of officials from both Paris and Berlin for the state funeral on November 17. One such meeting took place on November 16 at the Hotel Breitenbacher Hof. Among those present were Welczeck, Diewerge, Bohle, Grimm, other top officials of the Ministry of Propaganda and the vom Rath family. On that occasion the vom Rath family was urged to enter the case as plaintiffs and to accept the appointment of Grimm as their attorney. This would permit the Foreign and Propaganda Ministries to become indirectly involved in the trial, instead of merely following it solely as observers.[6]

Gustav vom Rath, in the presence of his wife and two sons, indicated that he would have preferred to bear his grief silently and in private. However, he realized that larger forces were here at play and he agreed to appoint Grimm in order that the trial could be conducted in the appropriate manner. As was to be expected, the designation was merely a formality and the vom Raths as plaintiffs played only a very minor part. It was, in fact, limited to one appearance by Herr vom Rath before Judge Tesnière on January 7, 1939.

Once vom Rath had agreed to this arrangement, Grimm received special powers from Ribbentrop, making him at the same time the representative of the Ministries of Propaganda and Foreign Affairs and of the family of the victim.

At another meeting during this period, Diewerge took up the question of the objectives of the trial against Grynszpan, that is, the objectives which the Nazi authorities hoped to achieve. "Exposure of World Jewry as the initiator of vom Rath's murder by which the Fuehrer's peace policy was to be frustrated" was to be the theme, one which was to be repeated time and again during the following years.[7] In his 1953 memoirs, Grimm still insisted that Grynszpan could not have acted on his own and that the murder of vom Rath was an effort by those behind the scene who sought to prevent any improvement in Franco-German relations.[8]

Immediately after the funeral services, Grimm returned to Paris to present his credentials to the president of the French bar, M. Charpentier. On the advice of Maurice Loncle, who was the lawyer he customarily used in Paris for civil affairs, Grimm requested Maurice Garçon, a distinguished criminal trial lawyer, to look after the interests of the plaintiff. Since French law did not permit foreign lawyers to plead or intervene directly in French courts, and as the embassy's staff attorney convinced Grimm that if he tried to be heard, he would be subjected to the "gravest vilifications and libelous accusations" by the defense, it was decided that Grimm would stay in the background as a "technical advisor."

Grimm had known Maurice Garçon since 1919, when they were opposing lawyers in a French court-martial in Landau (Palatinate), then occupied by French troops. Garçon was defending a French officer (Rouzier) accused of murder, while Grimm was representing two young Germans who, along with the murdered German soldier, were accused of having insulted and molested the officer. The court acquitted the officer, but the Germans were given prison terms. In spite of having won his case, Garçon was so disturbed by the injustice of the verdict that on his return to Paris, he made a personal appeal to the minister of justice and obtained an immediate pardon for the two Germans.[9] Grimm and Garçon had stayed in touch ever since, and when the Grynszpan case came along, Grimm was pleased with the idea of Garçon as the ostensible representative of the plaintiff.

Maurice Garçon agreed to take the case, provided that: (1) the affair be treated as a regular criminal case, without any resort to racist arguments, and (2) he be officially designated. Accompanied by one of his aides, Maître Garçon went to Berlin and met with the minister of justice. He also had a brief meeting with Ribbentrop who gave his accord to the conditions, which were then confirmed by letter.

Thanks to these arrangements, the German government was able to follow the pretrial examination very closely and exert considerable influence over the investigation. German officials were kept fully informed of everything that went on and thus were spared any surprises.

Grimm periodically sent reports to the embassy, the Foreign Ministry, and to the Foreign Section of the Ministry of Propaganda. Frequent meetings took place, usually in Berlin at the Foreign Ministry, with Minister Kruemmer and a representative of the Legal Section, Ministerial Counselors Diewerge and Faber of the Propaganda Ministry, Ambassador Welczeck from Paris, and other aides of lesser importance.

Grimm's task was twofold: first, to prevent the French inquiry from highlighting the evident causes of the crime, that is, a detailed examination of anti-Semitic excesses in Germany; and second, to eliminate to the extent possible any element which might reflect negatively on Germany and thus influence French attitude towards the Third Reich.

Other tasks were rapidly added to the assignments of the working group, such as the discovery of conspirators. Members of the group were asked to prepare papers on various aspects, including possible ways of avoiding inquiries into the expulsion of Polish Jews residing in Germany, reporting on the nature of the German-Polish conflict which was the reason for the expulsion, and, finally, a study of the entire history of the Grynszpan family. This latter task was assigned to the Hanover Police Department.

His manifold responsibilities made Grimm's work an extensive undertaking. To handle all these matters, he set up two offices, each with its own staff, one in Paris at the German embassy headed by Baron von Stempel, and another in Berlin at the Franco-German House under the direction of Dr. Schramm. With the aid of this organization, established under the guise of the plaintiff's representative, the French magistrate was carefully "guided," at least as far as it concerned the German side of the inquiry. As a result, the investigation discreetly skirted such burning issues as politics and anti-Semitism, and in particular that of *Kristallnacht*, an event which took place after the assassination and which therefore was judged not of immediate or direct interest to the pretrial investigation.

All the while, of course, the German government was hard at work trying to obtain information that might be of value to the prosecution or the public defamation of Herschel Grynszpan. Just having the name Grynszpan, or something akin to it, was enough to attract the attention of Nazi authorities. On November 21, 1938, the Czechs had deported to Poland, as an undesirable alien, the Pole Adolf Gruenspan. On December 23, he had illegally returned to Czechoslovakia, only to be rearrested and sentenced to one month in jail, after which he was to be once again deported to Poland. Ever on the lookout for suitable juicy items, Goebbels' *Völkischer Beobachter* reported gleefully on December 29, under the headline "A Grynszpan Family Pickpocket—Cousin of Murderer Grynszpan a Pickpocket," that Adolf Gruenspan, a well-known pickpocket, had been arrested in Czechoslovakia. Described as a cousin of Herschel Grynszpan, he had, according to the newspaper, admitted his relationship to the murderer in Paris.

The German authorities requested the extradition of this "German resident non-Aryan," a request with which the Czech authorities were only too happy to oblige. On January 26, 1939, the unlucky individual was unceremoniously turned over to the Gestapo near Schoenbrunn (Svinou) on the German-Czechoslovak border. Adolf Gruenspan was immediately brought to Berlin for interrogation, where he admitted having been convicted as a pickpocket in Vienna in 1933 and 1934. The Gestapo on February 20 dutifully provided the Ministry of Propaganda with two interrogation reports. These were followed on March 1 by an (presumably tongue-in-cheek) urgent request for information regarding the source of the newspaper story since extensive interrogations by the Gestapo had yielded "no evidence that he [Adolf Gruenspan] is in any way related to the family of the assassin Grynszpan."[10]

Actually, the reputation of the Grynszpan and Silberberg families must have caused the Nazi authorities a great deal of frustration. They sent an agent to Radomsk to check on the Grynszpan relatives in Poland. His report of June 30, 1938, as relayed by the German embassy in Warsaw, informed the Ministry of Propaganda that none of the family members was politically active, that there had been no criminal cases involving either family and that there was no record of any prior convictions of either the Grynszpans or the Silberbergs in Radomsk.[11]

Not that this inhibited the inventive Diewerge. In the pamphlet produced on behalf of the Ministry of Propaganda, he listed thirty-two foreigners, all with the name Grynszpan or variations thereof (Grünspan, Gruenspann, Grinszpan, Grinspun, Grünspahn) who had appeared before German courts. While the author ruefully admitted that it proved impossible to ascertain to what extent any of these individuals were in fact related to the murderer of vom Rath—presumably despite intense German efforts—it goes on to say that this list of "Grynszpan relatives" is indicative of the human and racial qualities possessed by the Jewish immigrants to Germany with the name Grynszpan.

Since no dates are given, it must be assumed that the list goes back to the beginning of record keeping. All in all, those sharing the name Grynszpan or its variations apparently were a pretty peaceful lot with a record of which most families could be proud. Most frequently listed offenses were passport violations, although there were the occasional thefts, document forgery, fraud, and embezzlement. But these offenses were outweighed in number by such dastardly criminal activities as disturbing the peace, traffic violations, peddling without a permit, belated registration of property, illegal export of currency, illegal border crossing, and so on.[12]

Diewerge demonstrated his ingenuity in other ways as well. In *Anschlag gegen den Frieden*, he recounted the story of Captain Alfred Dreyfus, the French Army officer convicted of treason by a French court-martial in 1894, stripped of his rank, and condemned to Devil's Island. When in time it became increasingly evident that Dreyfus, a Jew, had been the victim of a grave miscarriage of justice, a segment of the French establishment sought to prevent the reopening of the case, lest it embarrass France. In 1904, after considerable national turmoil, Dreyfus was completely vindicated and restored to his rank; in 1906, he was made a Knight of the Legion of Honor. Diewerge used the story to illustrate how Jews and their allies agitated so long in support of "their man," creating all sorts of problems for France, until he had been completely vindicated and knighted. What is fascinating in Diewerge's telling of the story is that he is able to recount it without ever mentioning on whose behalf the espionage took place (Germany) and that the real traitor (Major "Count" Esterhazy) had actually been identified.[13] In preparing the book, Diewerge and his colleagues apparently used their imagination in other ways as well. A retired government counselor, one of those charged with reviewing the manuscript, identified a number of significant errors. Contrary to the draft, neither Charles Guiteau, the assassin of President Garfield, nor the killers of Czar Alexander II, had been Jewish.[14]

11

The Defense Team

While the prosecution mobilized the extensive resources of not one, but two countries, the defense proved to be more difficult to organize. In the confused and hectic hours after the shooting, with his brother Abraham and nephew Herschel being held by the police, Salomon Grynszpan rushed to the local courthouse, looking for M. Frankel, an attorney, whom he sought to engage to represent Herschel. However, Frankel was not to be found, so a bystander suggested a M. Szwarc. In much the same haphazard manner Salomon also engaged the services of M. de Vésinne-Larue. The two attorneys had small, undistinguished local practices, but they were able to converse in Yiddish with their client, a not inconsiderable advantage in those early hours.

Within two days, the situation changed dramatically. The death of vom Rath transformed the shooting into a capital crime. More importantly, the events of *Kristallnacht* propelled the entire matter from the inside pages into the limelight and onto the front and editorial pages of the world's most important newspapers, destined to remain there for months to come. Abraham Grynszpan, whose steady hands were now urgently needed to provide support for Herschel, suddenly found himself fighting for his own freedom, as did Chawa. After Herschel's first formal interrogation on November 8, they had been arraigned and taken into custody on charges of having harbored an illegal alien and suspicion of being accessories before the fact. As a result, they were forced to relinquish their responsibilities as Herschel's legal guardians. That vacuum was initially filled by a family council of Salomon Grynszpan (Sendel's brother), Abraham Berenbaum (brother of Chawa Grynszpan), and Jacques Wykhodz (Chawa Grynszpan's brother-in-law). Later, Salomon took sole charge, but before long he, too, was replaced.

The family council quickly realized that the two attorneys representing young Grynszpan were probably unequal to the task. On the death of vom Rath, they became the focus of the sort of attention they had not before experienced and for which they were probably ill prepared. For that reason, the family council went to Fresnes prison, hat in hand, asking Herschel to accept another lawyer. Herschel on November 14 recorded this meeting in his journal in solemn, almost biblical terms:

> They greeted me in the name of my family and in the name of World Jewry for whom I had risked my life. Then they explained why they had come to see me. They told me that my trial would be an important one, and that because of it, I ought to have the best lawyer in France, de Moro-Giafferri. For reasons of my own, I did not want him. Then I made a proposal, and said, "If you can arrange to have my dear parents and my sister and brother come to Paris, then I will choose de Moro-Giafferri as my lawyer." They answered my proposal by swearing on the heads of their children that as soon as I had appointed that lawyer to defend me, my parents would come to Paris in less than two weeks with the assistance of the lawyer, and that my parents would then come visit me at once. So it was because of my love for my parents and sister and brother that I consented. They gave me money so I could procure the special food I wanted and they told me not to worry at all since the whole world was behind me.[1]

On November 10, one day following the death of vom Rath, Salomon Grynszpan had written to France's best-known criminal lawyer, Maître Vincent de Moro-Giafferri:

> I have the honor to request that you assume the defense of my nephew Herschel Grynszpan.
>
> I have decided to dispense with the services of the two attorneys, MM. Szwarc and Vésinne-Larue, whom I had engaged initially. At the same time I request that MM. Frankel and Erlich, who speak Yiddish, work with you.[2]

This letter was followed the next day by one from Herschel to de Moro-Giafferri:

> Please excuse that I write in German. The reason is that I am not able to write in French. I would like to request that you assume the defense at my trial. I close the letter with the hope that you will accept my entreaty.[3]

Who was this individual to whom the family now turned? It was almost predestined that Maître Vincent de Moro-Giafferri would become involved in the case. Just as there were few trials of German far-right sympathizers that did not involve Grimm, so there were few sensational murder trials in post–World War I France that did not bear the imprint of France's great criminal lawyer. De Moro-Giafferri was born in Paris on June 16, 1878. His father was Corsican, his mother came from the Auvergne. At age twenty-four, he was admitted to the Paris bar and became its youngest member. In 1919 he was elected "Deputy" for Corsica, and in 1924 he was under secretary of state for Education in the cabinet of Premier Herriot. Already before World War I (during which he was wounded at Verdun and then was promoted to lieutenant), he had established a reputation as a defense attorney. But he fully came into his own in the postwar era, participating with great success in most sensational criminal trials. As he told this author proudly in 1947, during his entire career he had lost only one client to the guillotine—Henri Landru, a.k.a. Bluebeard—who had been executed twenty-five years earlier, in 1922, after being found guilty of eleven murders.

De Moro-Giafferri enjoyed a solid reputation as an antifascist, having thrown his considerable popularity, oratorical skills, and reputation behind a number of celebrated causes in Europe between the two wars. On September 11, 1933, in a mock trial of the actual perpetrators of the German Reichstag fire, he had argued convincingly that Hitler and Goering were the real culprits. In 1936, at an international conference in Paris on the Nazi judicial system, de Moro-Giafferri called for joint resistance against the Nazi brand of justice.[4]

The German authorities did not take kindly to de Moro-Giafferri's designation as Herschel's defense lawyer,[5] and so it was not surprising that the Berlin newspaper *Der Angriff* of November 19 referred to de Moro-Giafferri as a "Jewish lawyer." Four days later, Diewerge asked the Foreign Ministry to immediately send an enciphered cable to the embassy in Paris, requesting detailed information regarding those responsible for the defense of the assassin, "especially concerning the ancestry of Moro-Giafferri." The embassy on November 28 replied that the requested materials had been sent but indicated that the attorney's Jewish background regrettably was "questionable but probable." (This was later corrected to read "questionable but *not* probable.") The Paris embassy followed up on December 6 by forwarding to the Ministry of Propaganda a biography of de Moro-Giafferri, describing him as "Corsican, Catholic." However, presumably to save at least some face, the embassy went on to quote unidentified French legal circles as saying that for some unknown reason, the attorney "was totally in Jewish hands."[6] As for de Moro-Giafferri himself, he was clearly spoiling for a fight on his home turf with his longtime nemesis.

Dorothy Thompson wrote a colleague about having received a personal message from Moro.

> Moro has received innumerable threatening letters since he promised to take the case. He is a Corsican, and has officially warned the German Embassy that, unfortunately, his people, not being as civilized as the Jews, believe in the blood feud, and that if anything happens to him he fears there will not be one person dead in the German Embassy but they will be lucky if there is one alive.[7]

By virtue of his reputation and personal prestige, de Moro-Giafferri was well suited for the task. But before he could assume his new functions, certain changes were necessary. He obviously was not about to share either his responsibilities, or the limelight, with MM. Szwarc and Vésinne-Larue, but they were not ready to give up their prize without a fight.

On November 12, they addressed a letter to their "esteemed colleague" to inform him that they had been engaged to defend Herschel Grynszpan by the accused and his two uncles. According to the letter, their client now was under constant pressure to dispense with their services in favor of de Moro-Giafferri. "In order to prevent a formal complaint, which could only end up before the chairman of the Bar Association, it would be appreciated if you would declare yourself opposed to all machinations which are designed to exclude us from the case with which we have been entrusted in a regular manner."[8]

The entire matter would continue to simmer for a while, with charges and countercharges hurled back and forth. The two attorneys "went public" with their complaint in an article in the Parisian weekly *l'Intransigeant*. This, in turn, on November 21, provoked a letter by Salomon Grynszpan, Abraham Berenbaum, and Jacques Wykhodz addressed to de Moro-Giafferri, assuring him that he was the family's unanimous choice to defend Herschel and that he had complete freedom to proceed as he deemed appropriate.[9]

In the meantime, Edgar Ansel Mowrer and French journalist André Geraud, acting on behalf of Dorothy Thompson's Journalists Defense Fund, sought to identify a suitable attorney and not surprisingly they also focused quickly on de Moro-Giafferri. The attorney, who normally commanded fees in keeping with his fame, agreed in writing that he would be pleased to accept whatever remuneration the Fund would care to provide.

The French Bar Association had strict procedures governing the replacement of attorneys, and so it was necessary, in order to enable de Moro-Giafferri to enter the case, to settle with the replaced attorneys. Utilizing funds made available through the Thompson committee, MM. Szwarc and Vésinne-Larue were paid 22,000 francs ($550) each as compensation for their work on behalf of Abraham and Chawa Grynszpan and the preparations for Herschel's forthcoming trial.[10] Aside from these payments, minor amounts were made available by the Journalists' Fund to defray certain payments on behalf of Abraham Grynszpan which he was unable to meet during his imprisonment, some pocket money for Herschel, and an attempt to bring Herschel Grynszpan's parents to France.

Herschel badly wanted his parents to come to Paris. Writing them on March 3 from Fresnes prison, he thanked them for refusing to give information about him to journalists. He went on to say, "Concerning your coming here, the situation is as follows: as soon as I am certain that they do not want you to come here, I will be obliged to go on a hunger strike. I hope that this will aid me in my plans."[11] Before long his desire for privacy and his wish to see his parents would conflict.

In keeping with the promise to Herschel, it was decided to make an effort to bring the parents to Paris with the aid of A. R. Pirie, a British journalist. Pirie wanted the exclusive rights to Grynszpan's diary for his paper. (All young prisoners at the Fresnes prison kept a diary in which they were expected to recount their life story and express their hopes and aspirations. These were then used either by the psychiatric experts or by the pretrial judge. Grynszpan filled two notebooks with his diary.) Pirie proposed that, in exchange, he would go to Poland to find Grynszpan's parents and bring them to France at his expense. He did, in fact, go to Poland in the spring of 1939, at the expense of Thompson's Fund, but failed to return with the family.

One possible reason for the failure is discernable from Herschel's letters of March 3 and March 20 to his parents in Zbaszyn. While Herschel wanted his family in Paris, he was strongly opposed to letting the press gain access to his family or his own innermost thoughts as recorded in his journal, but he realized that efforts might be made to circumvent him.

> In regard to your trip, journalists who have taken the question of your trip in hand have been creating difficulties for me. They require me to grant them my "journal" in exchange. I do not wish to give it since I am against its publication. For this reason, I request of you that, in case you are asked to sign anything whereby you might promise to give them my "journal," you refuse. . . . I hope you will do as I ask.[12]

Herschel wished his family in Paris, but on his own terms. As a result, an idea presumably approved by his legal guardian and being financed at least in part through his defense fund failed to materialize. Herschel's parents, who must have been anxious to go to Paris, apparently did as their son requested. At about the same time, the ever busy Grimm asked the German embassy in Warsaw to persuade the Poles that it was not in their interest for the Grynszpan family to testify in France, and it is therefore of course possible that other factors contributed to the family being prevented from traveling to Paris.

Maître de Moro-Giafferri also encountered problems, having incurred the displeasure of his colleagues who felt that he had treated them in a high-handed manner. Although he did not himself handle the funds from the Thompson committee (the regulations of the French Bar expressly prohibited him from doing so), Miss Thompson clearly held him responsible for the payments which had been made from Fund resources. On August 4, 1939, she wrote him a strongly worded letter, criticizing the manner in which funds had been dispensed to lawyers who did not appear to be involved in the case, that is, Szwarc and Vésinne-Larue. There obviously was a communication breakdown between the Fund and those responsible for the disbursement of the money; for some reason, Thompson and her associates were not kept fully informed regarding what was going on in France.[13]

All the while, there also existed a certain amount of friction within the Grynszpan family, fueled largely by the absence of a single dominant individual and diverging ideas within the group. Grimm, who later had at his disposal the files and correspondence confiscated from various private and public offices by German troops entering Paris, sought to profit from this unique opportunity and devoted to it considerable space in his later publications. In actual fact, Grimm discovered very little of substance except that the two attorneys first engaged apparently were not willing to give up the case to their more prominent colleague without a fight or compensation and evidence of some intrafamily bickering which proved unsettling for the young defendant.

During the incarceration of Herschel's uncle and aunt, the family felt that in order effectively to aid Herschel's defense, a single person had to speak on their behalf. While Sendel's other brother living in Paris, Salomon, initially exercised that function on an informal basis, it was decided that a formal transfer of guardianship rights or parental powers was necessary. With this aim in mind, Abraham Berenbaum traveled to Zbaszyn on November 27, 1938. He returned with Sendel's signature and a letter of November 27 to his son.

> M. Berenbaum is here today. He has fully informed us about your situation. You mustn't torture yourself. With God's help everything will turn out right once again. You must confer with M. Berenbaum about everything and you must do what he tells you. He will do everything to alleviate your situation. You must remain strong now and not destroy yourself with self-reproach. You must not allow yourself, dear Hermann, to have gloomy thoughts in regard to us. Things are not so bad. We have enough to eat and drink and otherwise we lack for practically nothing. We are, thank the good Lord, all in good health. M. Berenbaum will be able to give you all the details. . . . So, dear Hermann, I close this letter with hopes that we will soon all be happily together once more. Again many good wishes and kisses to you, dear Hermann. We won't forget you.

Brother Mordechai and sister Esther added a postscript:

> M. Berenbaum has received full power to represent Father in all your interests. You must have entire and complete confidence in him. Whatever he tells you, you must follow his wishes as if he were Papa. Stay in good health and be happy. . . . Don't worry. With God's help, all will be well. Eat and drink and obey M. Berenbaum and everything will be easier.[14]

That letter and Sendel's power of attorney did not resolve the situation, for Herschel wrote to de Moro-Giafferri on January 27, 1939:

> As perhaps you already know, discord reigns in my family once again. If it weren't for the fact that I am involved, I wouldn't be concerned about it, but I am so tormented that, to speak frankly, I think I'll go mad if it continues. Because of this, I beg of you Maître, to be good enough to put an end to this situation. I ask you to convene a family council to resolve the following questions: Should M. Berenbaum come to visit me? Should Maître Frankel be my defense lawyer? And thereafter would you please see to it that no one bothers me with family affairs. I will withdraw the permission of anyone who ignores your instructions. I beg you to excuse me for inconveniencing you in this regard but I cannot do otherwise, or it will finally drive me mad.
>
> I request, therefore, that you arrange this matter as rapidly as possible, so that my family no longer causes me trouble.[15]

The matter was resolved shortly thereafter when Abraham Grynszpan was released from jail and, supported by Jacques Wykhodz, resumed his responsibilities as Herschel's adoptive father. Abraham Berenbaum and Salomon Grynszpan were once again relegated to secondary roles, a source of keen disappointment for both men.

The change of lawyers proved equally disconcerting for Herschel in spite of having himself requested the assistance of de Moro-Giafferri. Being caught in the middle of the dispute between Moro, his family, and the old attorneys (who sought to enlist Herschel to their cause) was unsettling. Neither Moro nor his client had the sunniest of dispositions and both lacked flexibility—Moro was not used to sharing decision making with various family members and Herschel increasingly saw himself as the heroic and glorious avenger. Also, instead of long visits and constant personal support which Herschel enjoyed from his first attorneys, who spoke Yiddish and had a lot in common with him both socially and culturally, de Moro-Giafferri—whose background could not have been more different from his own—was much less accessible to his client. Recognizing that his young client needed some handholding, de Moro-Giafferri did arrange for a Jewish associate, Maître Serge Weill-Goudchaux, to serve as his proxy and frequent visitor of "the little one," as they referred to Herschel. On the fringes there was also Maître Frankel, whom Salomon had originally sought to engage, and who now worked with Moro.

But the friction was not only due to personalities; there were also disagreements regarding the defense strategy. De Moro-Giafferri and the Journalists' Defense Fund wanted to save Herschel at all costs from the guillotine and expose the Nazis for what they were, without, however, endangering the safety of Jews still living in Germany; they were really hostages, threatened by the unleashing of yet further anti-Semitic outrages which the Grynszpan crime had exacerbated. One possible approach considered by de Moro-Giafferri was to depoliticize the crime, if necessary at the expense of disgracing the accused. Herschel, on the other hand, was anxious to dramatize his act and the persecution of Jews, seemingly unaware or unconcerned that this might be yet another excuse to whip up Nazi anti-Semitic fury against the 400,000 living under German domination.

The defense strategy considered by de Moro-Giafferri was far from conventional. He proposed that Herschel declare that his had been a crime of passion without any political significance. In so doing, the acquittal of Herschel could have been virtually assured, given his age. He would have been considered more victim than culprit. In addition, a German diplomat would have been disgraced—yet another plus.

This approach had certain advantages, such as Herschel's freedom, but obviously there were disadvantages as well. It would have completely diminished Grynszpan's stature, which ran counter to the youth's desire to play the hero. It might not have worked, yet if Herschel could sow doubt in the minds of the jury, it seemed worth the attempt. In addition, there was a sort of poetic justice in using this type of weapon against an adversary who had long ago perfected the art of falsehood.

However, Grynszpan refused to go along with the proposed strategy. As a result, the trial was sure to be fought in the political arena, where French juries were known to be fickle and unpredictable. It was therefore essential that de Moro-Giafferri have at his disposal evidence of the reasons which caused Herschel's despair. In order to make Herschel's crime comprehensible, Moro had to be prepared to present witnesses and documentation revealing the true nature of the anti-Semitic war of Hitler's Germany.

Accordingly, the World Jewish Congress (WJC) established a Documentation Commission. At its first meeting in Paris on December 1, 1938, Weill-Goudchaux, de Moro-Giafferri's associate and Herschel's second attorney, was instructed to gather documentary evidence of Nazi anti-Semitic activities. (The group also decided to translate

Diewerge's book into French.)[16] Weill-Goudchaux was assisted in his work through contributions from Jewish groups in France and abroad. Grimm would later call this, as de Moro-Giafferri had predicted, a Jewish conspiracy, when it was actually prudent defense strategy.

Herschel's pretrial testimony regarding his specific intentions varied considerably, although he remained completely consistent when it came to describing his motives. Initially, Herschel admitted premeditation, his intention to kill, and his desire for vengeance. Presumably it was his lawyers who, seeing the gravity of his situation more clearly than he, counseled Grynszpan to abandon the vengeful tone of his declarations, to express his regrets, and to maintain that he did not intend to kill vom Rath. Later he formally sought to retract his initial testimony. "I did not act in hate nor in vengeance but because of love for my father and for my people who are undergoing unheard of suffering. I profoundly regret having wounded a man." In the course of his interrogations, Herschel at various times claimed to have acted in a sort of dreamlike trance, that he wanted to shoot at the picture of Hitler or commit suicide in the embassy. However, presumably due to Herschel's volatile nature and view of himself, he apparently did not develop a consistent set of responses until long after his arrest.[17]

In the end, all these efforts seemed to have been in vain since the case never came to trial in France. And yet, in their own mysterious ways, they eventually had a profound effect well beyond anything that might have been anticipated.

Altogether, Dorothy Thompson's Journalists Defense Fund raised approximately $40,200. When the Fund was originally created, contributions were received with the understanding that any funds not needed for the case itself would be distributed to creditable organizations looking after the interests of victims of Nazi Germany. In May 1941, Miss Thompson announced that the final $3,000 had been presented to the Foster Parents Plan for War Children in London for the rehabilitation of children injured during air raids. Other organizations who had received donations included the Catholic Committee for Refugees from Germany, the American Friends Service Committee, the Intercollegiate Committee to Aid Student Refugees, the German Jewish Children's Aid, and the Loyal Americans of German Descent. The purpose of the latter organization was described in the press release as "protecting the rights of American citizens who are loyal anti-Nazis and for ferreting out saboteurs among German-Americans whose activities are throwing the entire German-American population into danger."[18]

A total of $3,000, in relatively small individual amounts, were given directly to various distinguished German writers and artists—such as Berthold Brecht—living in the United States, unoccupied France, or neutral European countries.

Fund expenses amounted to $2,846.08 for [clerical] salaries, printing, postage, and publicity.

A total of $2,500 was used in connection with the defense of Herschel Grynszpan. (Although initially $5,000 had been transferred to Paris, $2,500 was subsequently returned.) The money was used to compensate Herschel's first attorneys, Pirie's trip to Poland, the collection of background information in Poland, and some miscellaneous expenditures, such as Herschel's pocket money. Apparently neither de Moro-Giafferri nor any of his associates ever received any money from the Defense Fund.

Writing later about the case, Grimm had much to say about the attempts of some of those involved on Herschel's behalf to enrich themselves at the expense of the Journalists' Defense Fund. It is therefore interesting to compare the above expenses with those of Dr. Grimm, who between November 29, 1938, and June 10, 1939, had received 38,583 RM ($15,400) from the Ministry of Propaganda and between December 14, 1938, and March 17, 1939, 37,800 French francs ($1,050) from the embassy in Paris.[19]

Ernst Eduard vom Rath, June 3, 1909–November 9, 1938. Courtesy of vom Rath family.

Herschel Grynszpan, shortly before assassination. Courtesy of the Holocaust Martyrs' and Heroes' Rememberance Authority, Israel.

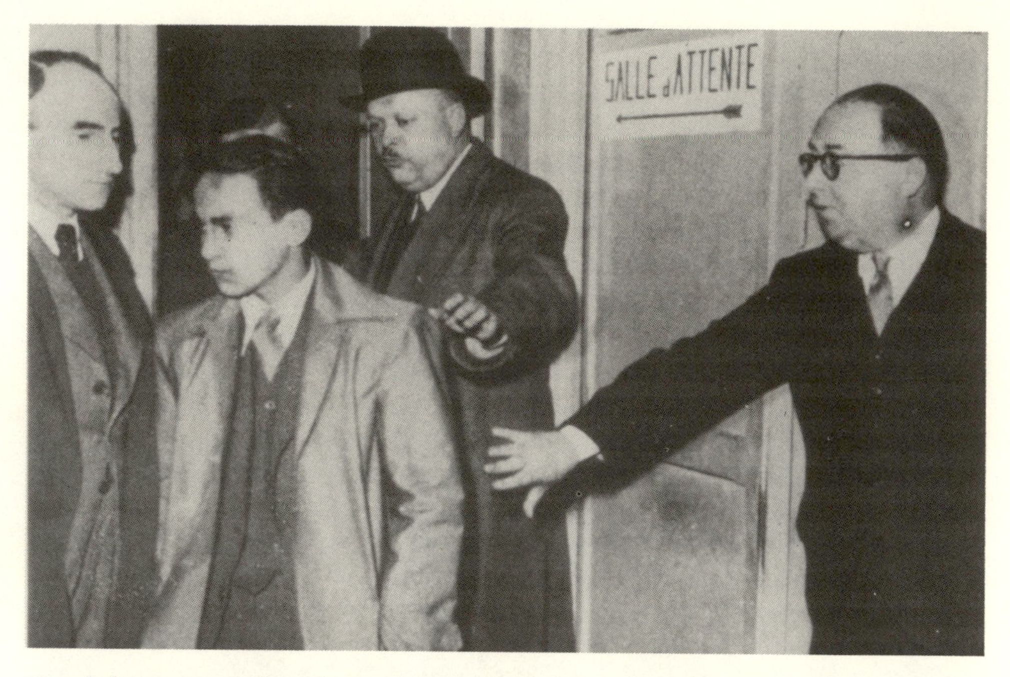

Herschel Grynszpan after his arrest surrounded by French detectives. Courtesy of Archives du Centre de Documentation Juive Contemporaine.

Repatriation of Polish Jews at Zbaszyn, October 29, 1938. Courtesy of U.S. Holocaust Memorial Museum: Main Crimes Commission Photo Collection, Warsaw, Poland.

On afternoon of shooting, Herschel Grynzpan being led from police prefecture.
Courtesy of the Holocaust Martyrs' and Heroes' Rememberance Authority, Israel.

Ernst vom Rath with members of his SA unit. Courtesy of Archives du Centre de Documentation Juive Contemporaine.

Funeral of Ernst vom Rath. In front row, father of the deceased and Foreign Minister von Ribbentrop. Courtesy of Archives du Centre de Documentation Juive Contemporaine.

Funeral ceremony for Ernst vom Rath. Hitler in front row, on right, next to Mrs. vom Rath. Courtesy of Archives du Centre de Documentation Juive Contemporaine.

SA standard honoring the dead vom Rath. Courtesy of Archives du Centre de Documentation Juive Contemporaine.

Abraham and Chawa Grynszpan on trial for harboring their nephew, Herschel Grynszpan. Courtesy of Archives du Centre de Documentation Juive Contemporaine.

Vincent de Moro-Giafferri during anti-Nazi manifestation, Paris. Courtesy of Archives du Centre de Documentation Juive Contemporaine.

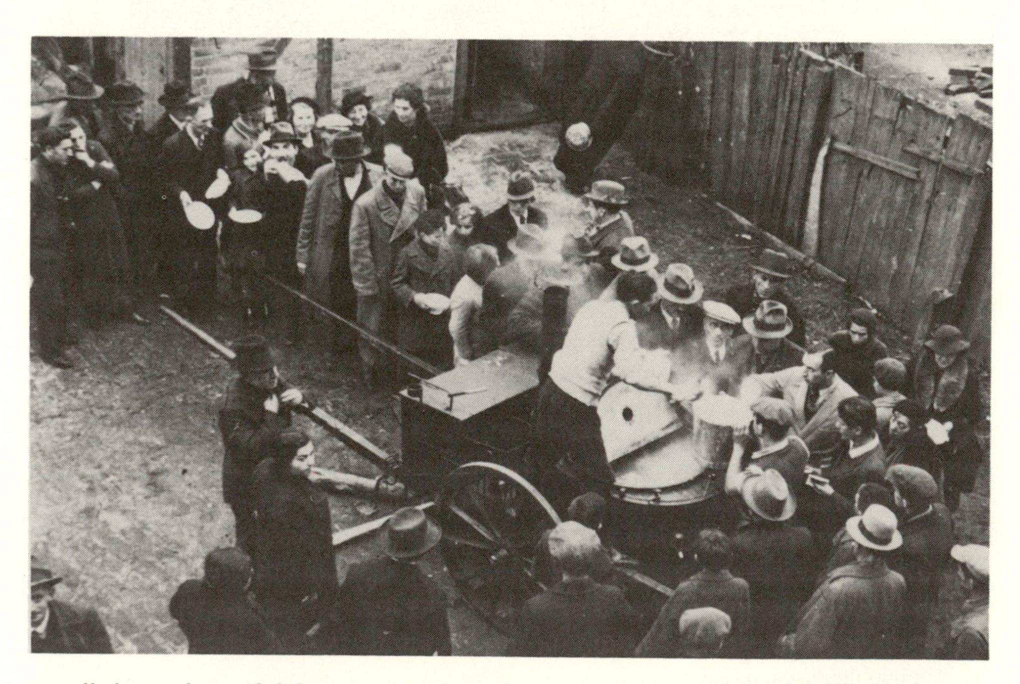

Expelled Jews being fed from soup kitchen, Zbaszyn, Poland, November 1938. Courtesy of the Holocaust Martyrs' and Heroes' Rememberance Authority, Israel. Copyright © All rights reserved, Yad Vashem.

Humiliation of the Jews of Baden-Baden: Jewish males marched through the street and led into the synagogue. Courtesy of the Holocaust Martyrs' and Heroes' Rememberance Authority, Israel.

Baden-Baden synagogue burning on *Kristallnacht.* Courtesy of the Holocaust Martyrs' and Heroes' Rememberance Authority, Israel.

Destroyed store, Germany, *Kristallnacht.* Courtesy of the Holocaust Martyrs' and Heroes' Rememberance Authority, Israel. Copyright © All rights reserved, Yad Vashem.

The deportees after their arrival in Zbasyn, Poland, October 29, 1938. Courtesy of the U.S. Holocaust Memorial Museum: Main Crimes Commission Photo Collection, Warsaw, Poland.

Prisoners in the Concentration Camp Dachau, 1938. Courtesy of the Holocaust Martyrs' and Heroes' Rememberance Authority, Israel.

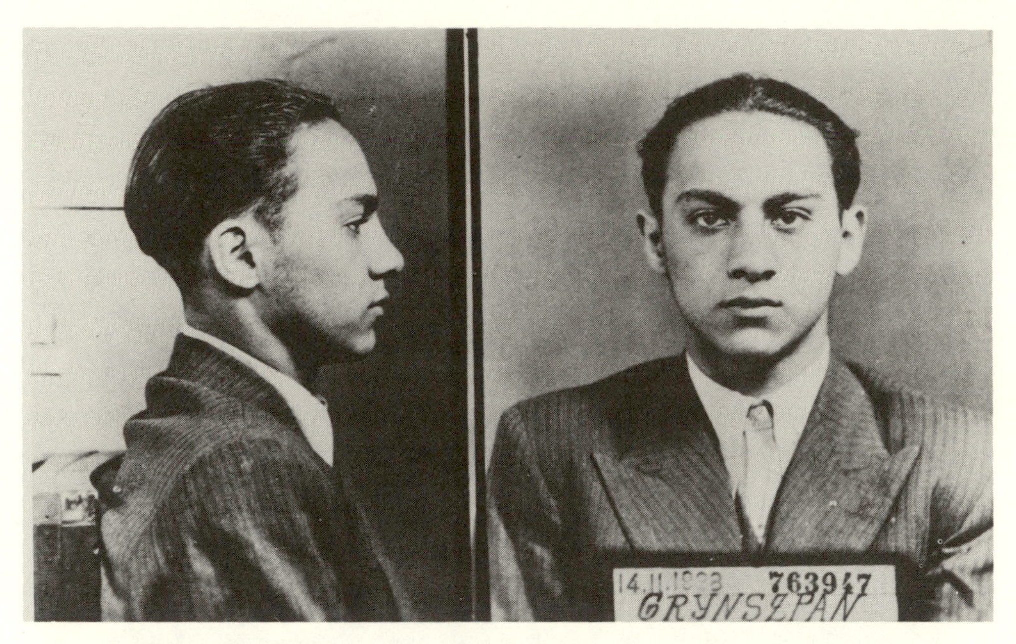

Herschel Grynszpan, police photo. Courtesy of the Holocaust Martyrs' and Heroes' Rememberance Authority, Israel. Copyright © All rights reserved, Yad Vashem.

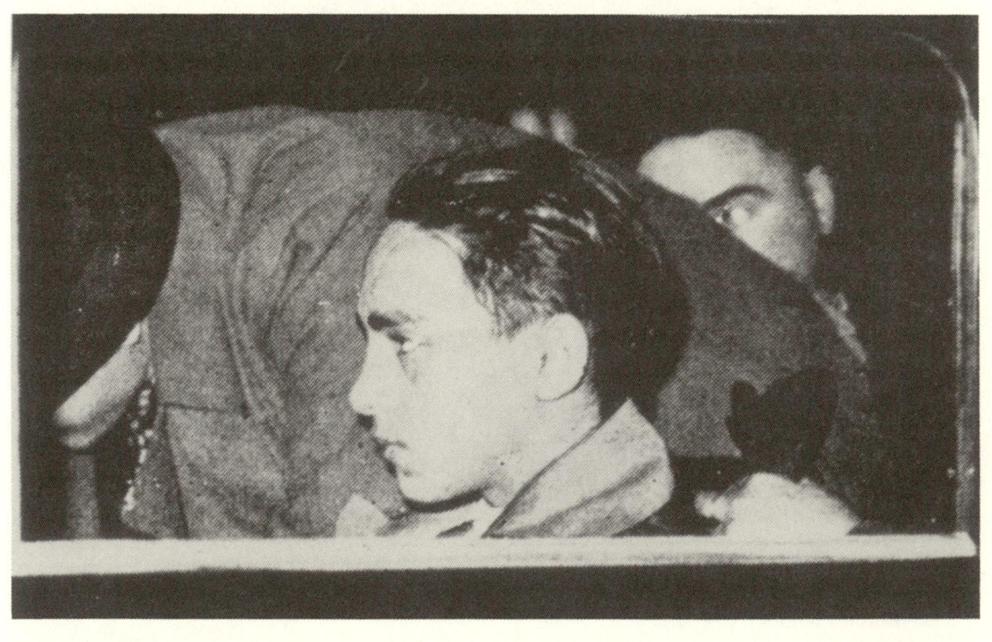

Herschel Grynszpan in police car after arrest. Courtesy of the Holocaust Martyrs' and Heroes' Rememberance Authority, Israel. Copyright © All rights reserved, Yad Vashem.

A postcard to parents, written by Herschel Grynszpan, and found on him after arrest. Courtesy of the Holocaust Martyrs' and Heroes' Rememberance Authority, Israel.

The expelled Jews after their arrival in Zbaszyn, October 29, 1938. Courtesy of the U.S. Holocaust Memorial Museum: Main Crimes Commission Photo Collection, Warsaw, Poland.

12

The Trial of Abraham and Chawa Grynszpan

After Herschel's first interrogation on November 8, his uncle and aunt were formally arraigned. They were taken into custody, charged with having given asylum to a foreigner whose entry and residence permit were not in order. Herschel had tried to spare his uncle and aunt during his first interrogation by Commissioner Monneret by stating that he had left France for Belgium on August 15, in accordance with the exclusion order received on August 11, but to no avail.[1]

By allowing their nephew to remain in France, Abraham and Chawa had committed a misdemeanor under the terms of Article 4, of the "Décret sur la Police des Étrangèrs" of May 2, 1938, which provided that "Whosoever, directly or indirectly, assists or attempts to assist the illegal entry and residence of a foreigner will be subject to the punishment provided. . . ." The offense called for a fine of 100 to 1,000 francs and imprisonment for not less than one month and not more than one year. Mme Grynszpan was sent to La Petite Roquette prison, while her husband was sent to La Santé. Herschel wrote them a letter of thanks from his prison:

> Thank you very much for all you have done for me. I will never forget it. I know I have brought you great trouble and misfortune by what I have done. I know that you are actually in danger because of me. But I hope that everything will work out well for you. I could not do otherwise.

> May God pardon me for what I have done. I did it because I could no longer bear the suffering of our persecuted brothers in Germany. I beg of you to pardon me, for otherwise I cannot be at peace. I beg of you to let me know if you should have any news of my dear parents, brother and sister. May God forgive me for what I did.[2]

The aunt and uncle were quickly brought to trial. Even though the original arrest warrants had charged them with being accessories before the fact, the examining magistrate (Judge Tesnière) decided that they were neither Herschel's accomplices nor responsible for his actions. However, M. Frette-Damicourt, the public prosecutor, feared that in view of the prevailing tensions between Germany and France, trying the two solely on charges of harboring an illegal alien would be poorly received in Germany. Checking discreetly with Grimm, Tesnière determined that the prosecutor's fears were groundless. As a result, the trial on the lesser charge was allowed to proceed, although the more serious charge was not dropped for another month.

Abraham Grynszpan and his wife were tried on November 29, 1938, before the 17th Correctional Chamber of the Department of the Seine. The trial was scheduled without fanfare in a small courtroom, presumably to signal that this was to be treated as a routine case. Yet it was anything but routine, for they were defended by de Moro-Giafferri. The couple's lawyer had in the past infrequently assumed the role of defense attorney at trials where the maximum penalty was one year in prison. Playing down the importance of the trial succeeded to some extent; there were relatively few spectators. On the other hand, for the legal community, any appearance by de Moro-Giafferri was always a major event, and so there were in the courtroom more than twenty attorneys not involved in the case, eager to see the famed lawyer at work.

One of those present in the courtroom who followed the trial with great interest was an agent of the Ministry of Propaganda. Thanks to both his detailed report and a German-language copy of the stenographic transcript submitted by Diewerge to Goebbels on December 12, there exists a complete record of the proceedings.[3]

The prosecution's charge was short, recommending that the couple "not receive an excessively long sentence," but asking the imposition of more than the minimum sentence. Abraham Grynszpan admitted that, contrary to his previous statements, he was aware that Herschel had received his expulsion order and that he had nevertheless remained in France. The couple pleaded, "When Herschel came to our home, he was in such a state of depression that it was pitiful. He was ill and suffering greatly from stomach trouble. Could we have thrown him out? It would have been inhuman. Moreover, we had been given the legal and moral responsibility for the child."

Then it was de Moro-Giafferri's turn, and those present were not disappointed. He spoke for over an hour and judging from the reaction of the German agent, it was an impressive performance. "Moro started right out. His well-known tactic: To wear down the court, if need be, with his exceptional knowledge of the specific provisions of the law in order to unleash, at the appropriate moment—towards the end—his tremendous oratory. So it was now."

Moro apparently argued convincingly—he obviously impressed Propaganda's informant—that the Ministry of Justice could not apply the law in this case since it had failed to provide, as required, a safe haven for the child (throughout his argument he referred to Herschel only as "the child") if no other destination was available. And indeed Herschel had nowhere else to go—he no longer had a valid Polish passport (and might have found it difficult to obtain an extension after receipt of his expulsion order) and the Hanover authorities had refused him permission to return.

Moro based his arguments primarily on humanitarian and legal grounds. He argued that Chawa should be judged innocent since she actually had only two choices—to leave her home in order to punish her husband for his sense of family obligation in giving shelter to his nephew or to report her husband to the police. In Abraham's case, he led the court through the regulations to demonstrate that in the absence of a domicile for Herschel, it could not be applied to the person providing shelter.

Moro's arguments were largely non-political, either because he knew from experience that political arguments were unlikely to sway the court or, as the Ministry of Propaganda's man surmised, because there had been some sort of agreement to that effect between the court and the attorney. According to the informant, the few times that Moro ventured into political arguments, a discreet wink by the presiding judge usually was sufficient to cause him to change his approach. Moro did, however, remind the court in his thunderous voice that Abraham and Chawa were accused of shielding a youngster who sought to escape from a country which had erected monuments in honor of two (Nazi) assassins of Austrian Chancellor Dollfuss and for Leo Schlageter. After World War I, Schlageter had been condemned to death by a French court-martial for sabotaging French military trains. (A monument in his honor stood at the site of his execution until the end of World War II.)

Arguments by de Moro-Giafferri notwithstanding, the couple was sentenced to four months imprisonment and 100 francs fine each for having sheltered Herschel after issuance of his expulsion order. Later, they were also ordered expelled from France, a potentially far more serious and far-reaching penalty, although execution of the order was stayed until after the completion of Herschel's trial. The sentences were appealed, but the two defendants remained in jail, still under suspicion of having been accomplices in the assassination. It was not until December 25, 1938, when this charge was finally dropped, that they were released on bail.

On January 3, 1939, the Court of Appeals increased Abraham's sentence to six months and reduced Chawa's to three months. After less than a month, both were discreetly freed without any reaction by either the French or the German press.

With the defeat of France and the occupation of Paris, Abraham and his wife fled to the unoccupied zone. However, as most of their fellow Jews, they were both soon deported to a camp at Gurs in southwestern France. Chawa remained there during the whole war, working on a farm. Her husband was less fortunate; he was deported to Auschwitz, from which he did not return. Since this was the fate of many (especially non-French) Jewish males interned at Gurs, there is no reason to believe that he was singled out for deportation as a result of his connection with Herschel Grynszpan. Being Jewish was all that was required to be consigned to death.

After the war, Chawa remarried, returned to her lodgings on the rue des Petites Écuries, and the "Maison Albert" became the "Maison du Tailleur."

13

A Complex Character

On November 10, Judge Tesnière, as part of his pretrial investigation, appointed three doctors to prepare a psychiatric report on the accused. They were: Dr. Genil-Perrin, director of the Hospital H. Rousselle, Dr. Georges Heuyer, professor of the Faculty of Medicine and member of the Academy of Medicine, and Dr. André Ceillier of Saint Anne's Asylum.

The panel compiled a report of eighty-two typewritten pages.[1] It was submitted to Judge Tesnière in late February 1939. The dossier was the result of numerous conversations with Herschel, carried out in the absence of lawyers. As a result, the responses were more direct, more spontaneous, and at times different from those made during police and court interrogations.

The panel found that the accused was mentally fully responsible. Mental disturbance and irresistible or unconscious impulses were ruled out as possible causes. The defense argument that Grynszpan acted under a kind of hypnosis and that he secured the gun in a state when he was not himself was not shared by the psychiatrists. They also gave no credence to his declaration at one of the early hearings that he had planned to commit suicide at the embassy before Hitler's portrait or to shoot at the portrait in a futile, but spectacular protest. The doctors were of the opinion that the anxiety caused by receipt of the postcard from his parents, together with contemporary press reports, resulted in fear which gradually gave way to a desire for vengeance, vengeance which he then satisfied deliberately and consciously, making intelligent choices from among the means at his disposal.

The report examined in detail the question of insanity with regard to Article 64 of the French Penal Code.

> It appears impossible for us to assume that Grynszpan was in a state of insanity, within the meaning of Article 64 of the French Penal Code, at the time he committed his act. It is evident that, when he carried out the act, he showed no signs of mental confusion, he did not act under any form of delirium whatsoever. His act of murder is not an act which is symptomatic of beginnings of mental illness. He shows at present no symptoms of the onset of mental illness. In his childhood he had neither epileptic fits nor convulsions. His act, moreover, does not show evidences characteristic of impulsiveness, nor the unconsciousness of epileptic actions. He retained an exact recollection of the various circumstances and all the details of his acts, and the hypothesis of an epileptic impulse has to be entirely rejected.[2]

The panel summed up its findings as follows:

> The young Herschel Grynszpan, 17 years old, accused of murder, was at the moment of the act not mentally disturbed in the sense of Article 64 of the French Penal Code. He is responsible for the act of which he is accused.[3]

The doctors noted that, in the absence of pathological or psychiatric abnormalities which would tend to reduce responsibility, it would be up to the judge and jury to decide to what extent the youngster's extreme anxiety should be considered an extenuating circumstance.

The panel commented on Grynszpan's passionate idealism and the great influence of the very devout Jewish milieu in which he lived. His inflexibility in regard to principles, his emotional nature and hypersensitivity, and the precariousness of his situation had combined to lead Herschel inevitably towards ever-increasing emotional strain and solutions of a more extreme nature. Under a calm exterior, seemingly timid and self-effacing, Herschel was not only nervous but also quick-tempered, given to precipitous actions. Under most circumstances, he was either for or against, without reflection but rather by instinct. He acted first and reflected afterwards.

The fact that he was physically somewhat underdeveloped for his age did not, in the eyes of the panel, reflect intellectual immaturity. Herschel was of at least normal intelligence. (The German authorities, not surprisingly, judged him to be of above-average intelligence, since this fitted their argument that his was a cold-blooded assassination, carried out under orders, and not the impulsive act of an immature, impressionable youth.) He displayed a keen interest in the world around him, was at least moderately worldly-wise, discussed events of the day, was interested in politics and newspapers, and enjoyed the normal pursuits of a person his age.

Herschel was a complex, multidimensional character. He had hoped that his family could come to France, if need be under pretext of testifying at his trial. Yet in this connection he provided a glimpse of his determination, which went well beyond his years, and which was only hinted at occasionally at the time, but which was later to be amply demonstrated in a much more dramatic fashion. The letter he wrote to his parents in regard to Pirie's visit[4] made clear that while he dearly wanted them to come, he was not prepared in return to forfeit his privacy.

Not long after Herschel's arrest, when the initial shock had worn off, he changed, at least in his own mind, from the tearful victim who in the past had occasionally been given to empty bravado, to that of avenger. Having suddenly moved from the anonymity of a young refugee, vilified for being Jewish and forced to hide from the authorities, to the object of world attention, Herschel quickly took to his new status. Instead of hiding in the shadows, he now talked of "his people," of "his mission," of the sacrifice of his life, of his protest before the whole world. He clearly relished being the center of attention—the feeling that adults would talk about him rather than only to him. His handwriting remained typical of a teenager, but his signature became elaborate and pretentious.

And with his new status came a boastful self-confidence. "I will take sole responsibility for the act which I committed," he said with emphasis. Herschel had in the past expressed himself rather vehemently. On November 6, when his friend Nathan urged him to return to his uncle's house, Grynszpan had answered, "I will not return, and I would rather starve than go back on my decision." Now some of his letters and statements exhibited this same quality. They were filled with phrases such as "I promised myself once and for all . . . ," "I insist that . . . ," "I'll do something desperate if . . . ," "I will find myself forced . . . ," "I will take the necessary measures . . . ," "I am exasperated . . . ,"

"I will revoke the permission I gave to anyone who acts counter your instructions . . . ," and so on.

In a letter to the editor of *La Journée Parisienne* requesting back issues to aid in preparing his defense, he wrote, "May I request that you come to see me, without fail, for I must absolutely arrange certain important matters, in my own interest as well as in the interest of the entire Jewish people. I beg of you to come immediately, since the matter is important."[5]

He was the object of much attention, more than he had ever had in his life, and he relished it. Writing in his diary about a visit from Weill-Goudchaux, he noted that the lawyer had told him "that never in his life did he think there existed a young man of seventeen who would have the courage to carry out an act as I had. He told me that he would be very happy if I would write a few words for him. I promised him I would, after which he left."[6]

He was given to theatrical gestures. His farewell postcard was a case in point. But then, he *did* wish to commit a spectacular act. His people, the whole world, and the press are mentioned repeatedly in his declarations. In the first letter from Fresnes prison to his parents he remarked with a certain pride, "You have undoubtedly heard talk about me in the meantime."[7] He assumed an air of self-assurance. In their report, the medical experts related that when Herschel entered the room for an examination, he assumed an important air and freely shook hands with them. As later events were to demonstrate, that self-assurance was superficial and fragile.

It would be inappropriate to characterize Herschel as merely a young man full of braggadocio. He exhibited in many of his letters an unusually sensitive nature, optimism, and gentleness which somehow runs counter to some of the letters quoted above.

He wrote to his Uncle Isaac on December 12, 1938, in a letter which certainly was not destined for publication:

> Unfortunately the man I shot is dead. I did not wish to kill him but only to wound him. I only wished by doing so to protest. May God pardon me for having killed a man who was perhaps not guilty. I console myself with this: In war, it is the guiltless soldier who always falls but never the diplomat who is responsible for war. I hope that the world and French justice will not consider that I acted like an ordinary criminal, but as someone who wished to demonstrate in favor of his rights on behalf of his innocent brothers.[8]

To his family in Poland he wrote on December 13:

> I could not write you until now because I did not have your address. I want to make up for lost time now and write to you every week from now on. I would like you to know, my dear ones, that here in prison I am well and have everything I need. You do not have to be concerned for me. I am in very good hands here. What is not available here in prison, I buy outside. Uncle Schlome [Salomon] sends me a little money every week to buy food. Even unknown people from America send me money, which I do not wish to accept.
>
> How is your health? Have you enough to eat there? It is possible that perhaps you might come to Paris. I talked with the examining magistrate. He hasn't given me any definitive information as yet on the subject.
>
> I met Uncle and Aunt Albert [Abraham] this week in the examining magistrate's offices. It is possible that their lawyers will arrange it so that perhaps they will be freed next week on bail.
>
> I have the best lawyers in France. Apart from that, I am well. Do not worry about me. Outside of that, there's nothing new. Loving greetings and 10 million kisses and hugs from your son and brother.[9]

His incoming correspondence included love letters, letters of encouragement, and adoring praise. There were letters with money, such as one from Dr. George Herzog, a San Francisco physician, to whom Herschel replied, "Many, many thanks for the money which you sent, but I cannot take it as I have done nothing to deserve it. If you want to do something which I want very much, I ask you to take the money and give it to the 1,200 innocent Jews robbed, exiled and suffering on the Polish border."[10] (It goes without saying that this letter was not included in the German propaganda tracts.)

Many of Herschel's letters showed a kind of youthful naïveté and immaturity. Thus, with the aid of Maître Szwarc, his first lawyer, he addressed letters and declarations to the world's leaders. In his journal, he recounts that in the early days of his confinement he had written a letter to Hitler, asking for "a humanitarian act," the reestablishment of past conditions, the rebuilding of what had been destroyed, and the return of those things which had been taken.

According to a court-appointed social worker, Herschel tried to understand the reasons and aims of the inquiry and answered most questions readily. He understood French and spoke it fairly well. This assertion is of interest because various witnesses mentioned his "ignorance" of French. There is some evidence that Grynszpan, depending on circumstances, would alternately profess knowledge or ignorance of the language, perhaps in order to avoid answering questions precipitously. During court interrogations, Grynszpan gave the impression of constantly being on guard, and according to one observer, his countenance never lost the expression of a hunted animal. All in all, though, his defense was coherent. He seemed to suffer from occasional convenient lapses of memory, and aided by his lawyers, he understood what would aid his defense or would thwart his accusers.

His facial expression was intelligent and open. He had no tics, though according to the social worker, he bit his nails as nervous people often do. His words and gestures were normal though he lisped slightly. His sleep was sound. His physical health while in jail was good, although he asked several times to go to the infirmary to seek relief from his digestive troubles.

All in all, Herschel apparently made a very good impression on the social worker, who described the youth as not being timid, and answering politely after reflection and without using trite expressions.

14

Moves and Countermoves

As the glare of world attention diminished, burned-out synagogues became parking lots and boarded-up stores were repaired and reopened under their new Aryan owners. Jews in Germany and Austria desperately sought to flee their homes; visas to places such as Haiti, Kenya, Madagascar, South Africa, and Argentina were eagerly pursued by those not fortunate to have affluent or influential relatives in Great Britain, the United States, or other such desirable destinations. With the change of countries came other changes—rabbis became carpenters, matrons became sewing machine operators and cleaning women, businessmen took up farming, and teachers changed into factory hands.

Meanwhile in Paris, preparations proceeded for the trial of Herschel Grynszpan. Since the defendant was charged with a capital crime punishable by death, they were extensive. The unusually close cooperation which had developed between the court and Nazi authorities, masquerading as representatives of the family of the deceased, was largely determined by the prosecution's dependence on information available only from German sources and the unspoken aims of the two parties. The French government, still hoping to reach an accommodation with Germany, fervently hoped that the unfortunate events in Paris would not impede its efforts to improve relations with Germany, while the Nazi authorities sought to minimize the potentially negative impact of the forthcoming trial. Those who perceived Grynszpan's action as the direct result of Nazi excesses and saw in the trial an opportunity to expose them, predictably reacted strongly and with anger. Committees for the support of Grynszpan were formed, seeking a trial which would provide an opportunity to expose before all the world the evil that was Nazi Germany.

The Nazi authorities, especially Grimm, were also very active, trying to leave nothing to chance. On November 18, Grimm already made his second trip to Paris on behalf of his "clients," and at that time arranged for Maurice Garçon and Maurice Loncle to assume officially the roles as representatives of the vom Rath family, with specific arrangements for the trial to be determined at a later date.[1]

Grimm frequently returned to Paris in the coming months. On one such occasion, in December, he learned from someone close to Judge Tesnière that Abraham Berenbaum, Chawa Grynszpan's brother-in-law, had traveled to Poland to meet with Herschel's parents. Informed by Grimm, Diewerge warned on December 19 in a secret memorandum that there now existed the distinct possibility that the well-funded defense would bring Herschel's parents to Paris to testify regarding their expulsion from Germany and their experiences with the Gestapo. Obviously Diewerge did not relish that idea, for he asked whether there was a possibility that the Polish government could be persuaded to deny an exit visa to Herschel's parents. Two days later, the German Foreign Ministry reported that the information had been conveyed to the embassy in Warsaw; word came back in early January 1939 that the Polish Foreign Ministry was agreeable to the suggestion. However, the German Foreign Ministry message tempered its good news by warning that there was no assurance that the wishes of the Polish Foreign Ministry would in fact be respected by other Polish government departments.[2]

Even though "represented" by Grimm, the actual involvement of the vom Rath family was minimal. In fact, it was limited to a one-time appearance of Gustav vom Rath, the victim's father. Initially scheduled to testify before the examining magistrate on January 5, 1939, his appearance had to be delayed to January 7, due to illness. Grimm and Diewerge used the opportunity to arrange on January 5 a major briefing for the German press representatives in Paris.[3]

Gustav vom Rath and his son Guenter, accompanied by Maître Garçon (the official representative of the plaintiff) and one of Garçon's associates, met with Judge Tesnière in private. The interrogation was quite limited in scope and concerned primarily personal matters, such as the character of the deceased and his relationship with his parents. The meeting between the examining magistrate and the elder vom Rath had been arranged at the behest of Grimm and Diewerge. As far as they were concerned, its aim was not so much to provide information to the French jurist, but rather to evoke sympathy for the vom Rath family and counter efforts depicting Herschel Grynszpan and German Jews as the primary victims. Furthermore, as Diewerge reported to Goebbels in his report of January 16, those responsible for guiding the trial preparations hoped that vom Rath's statement made in connection with the meeting and publicized by the German press would neutralize the rumors of a rift between the family vom Rath, the party, and the Fuehrer. Both Grimm and Diewerge were delighted with the final results and Diewerge reported triumphantly that "the planned result was fully achieved."[4]

Fortuitous circumstances and a cooperative magistrate apparently contributed to these achievements. About forty-five minutes into the meeting Grimm was invited to participate in the proceedings. As Diewerge recounted the story, when it was discovered that the translator was Jewish, Judge Tesnière removed him by saying that in view of vom Rath's good French, there was no need for an interpreter. Maurice Garçon then told the judge that Grimm was in the anteroom and Tesnière invited the German lawyer to join them. "This . . . gave us the opportunity to bring Professor Grimm as translator into the non-public interrogation. The participation of Professor Grimm was not noted by the opposing forces," exulted Diewerge.[5] It was indeed a most unusual gesture since hearings by the examining magistrate usually are strictly confidential and Grimm had no official standing. Grimm could, of course, be depended on to make the optimum use of such an opportunity.

Judge Tesnière seems to have been helpful in other ways as well. On January 3, 1939, Diewerge forwarded to Goebbels, under cover of a memorandum marked "Secret," German translations of a substantial number of personal letters to and from Herschel Grynszpan, primarily correspondence with his immediate family. Grimm wrote Diewerge on April 19, 1939, that the letters had been provided by the "examining magistrate" but cautioned that only those that had become public knowledge through the press or by other means could be used during the trial or in propaganda pamphlets.[6]

It is little wonder then that Grimm considered Tesnière a "decent" French jurist, one who had made good use of the extensive materials provided him by the German authorities. Among these apparently were a series of confidential "exposés" about "secret wirepullers" to assist in the investigation of those behind the scenes responsible for the assassination. The exposés had been prepared by Grimm on the basis of the various international trials in which he had participated.

With the French authorities so well disposed, the Germans now were anxious to proceed with the trial. Reporting on his trip to Paris from January 25 to 29, Grimm expressed the fear that the "other side" was seeking to delay the trial but noted that he was determined that the proceedings commence in March.[7]

Grimm visited Paris again a month later, from February 15-20. Reporting to the Ministry of Propaganda on his return, he now thought it possible that the trial could begin by early May, although appeals by the defense could further delay the start by another two months. Grimm was under the impression that the "opposing side" now was anxious to delay the start of the trial since they were not "comfortable" with the present government. Wondering whether he should continue to press for an early trial, Grimm noted prophetically that the desirability of an early trial depended largely on general political developments.[8]

Less than a month later, on his return from a visit to Paris from March 12-18, Grimm reported to the Ministry of Propaganda that "it is in our interest *not* to expedite the trial."[9] This abrupt and total about-face is readily explained. While Grimm was in Paris, on March 15, German armies invaded Czechoslovakia, breaking Hitler's solemn pledge made in Munich a bare 6 months earlier. Reaction in France and elsewhere was swift. As Grimm wrote, "if the trial were held tomorow, the assassin would go free." Since they now expected de Moro-Giafferri to press for a quick trial, Grimm agreed with Garçon to seek a delay by various interdictions and requests for additional avenues of investigation.

The report indicated that in other respects things also were not going too well. Grimm and Garçon had learned that de Moro-Giafferri had collected a large number of photographs of Zbaszyn. Judge Tesnière, presumably the source of the information, was quoted as saying that he did not think the scenes were too bad, and that he "would have been happy if [he] had had such nice barracks during the [last] war and had been housed that well." Grimm and Garçon apparently did not fully share Tesnière's positive viewpoint.

Garçon also expressed serious reservations about the photographs of the Grynszpan's Hanover apartment, feeling that they might make a bad impression even though the rooms had the typical look of a place someone had to leave in a hurry. (While the report gives no reason for Garçon's objections to the photographs, he probably recognized that a jury would not be positively impressed by seeing pictures of a home which the long-time residents had been forced to vacate with a few minutes notice.) Grimm expressed the hope that it might be possible "in the presence of a representative of the Jewish community to clean up the rooms and photograph them again." Later they would learn to their chagrin that this would not be possible since the furnishings and personal effects of the Grynszpan family had in the meantime been disposed of.

Finally the report discussed the difficulties inherent in identifying for the trial suitable witnesses who might testify about the train which took the Grynszpan family from Hanover to Zbaszyn. It was agreed that it would be politically completely impractical to call Gestapo officials to testify and Jewish representatives from Hanover were not considered reliable. Under the circumstances, it was agreed to seek some suitable witnesses among the attending Red Cross nurses or restaurant staff.

Grimm's next trip to Paris took place March 12-18. The report he submitted on his return was by far the most pessimistic yet. The Grynszpan matter was given scant attention. Instead, he described the general situation as worse than ever. Germany's friends were described as bitter and on the defensive, with no one willing to speak in support of Germany or the (French) policy of Munich.[10]

Whenever Grimm visited Paris, he usually made two reports to the Ministry of Propaganda, one dealing with the Grynszpan case, the other addressing political aspects. On his return from a trip to Paris from April 20-27, he made only a political report. Apparently not enough had transpired in the Grynszpan case, at least not enough about which he wanted to report. From the German viewpoint, things rapidly were going from bad to worse. Grimm reported that Jewish influence on the government was growing by leaps and bounds, as evidenced by the new French decree prohibiting racist propaganda. Deprived of their primary tool, Grimm and Diewerge quietly folded their tents, left Paris and, at least for the time being, the trial of Herschel Grynszpan. Grimm made at least one more visit to Paris, June 6-13, but his 12-page report never mentioned Herschel Grynszpan or his trial.

It is unlikely that those at the Paris embassy shed many tears about this turn of events. On May 6, Diewerge sent Goebbels a propaganda status report on the case. He took that opportunity to complain that the embassy was "neutralizing" the Ministry of Propaganda staff assigned to Paris. For example, the embassy on the morning of April 28 had received an advance copy of a speech Hitler was scheduled to make that evening and had promptly sent it to the French government. Yet not only did the embassy not allow the ranking Ministry of Propaganda official to give excerpts of the speech to his agents, he didn't even get a copy of the speech for himself.[11]

Grimm and his colleagues did not completely abandon their trial preparations. Grimm traveled to Warsaw on May 1, 1939, to meet with representatives of the German embassy. The embassy had, "when the atmosphere was still friendly," pointed out to Polish Foreign Minister Beck that it was in Poland's interest that the forthcoming trial against Grynszpan not be used for propaganda against the country, and urged the Polish authorities to prevent the Grynszpan family from traveling to France. (Unfortunately for the Germans, by this time, everyone of course realized that with the annexation of Czechoslovakia, Poland was one step nearer to a German onslaught. On March 31, England and France promised full support to Poland in the event of a German attack.) The Poles responded that their country already had a worldwide reputation for being anti-Semitic and that a bit more or less propaganda in this respect was of little consequence.[12]

The strained relations between Germany and Poland notwithstanding, the embassy felt that the Polish government would be reasonably cooperative. Grimm, however, feared a "double-cross" whereby "World Jewry" (which Grimm felt was guiding Herschel's defense) might seek an accommodation with the Poles and conduct a defense that would spare Poland and focus solely on Nazi atrocities. To be ready for all eventualities, Grimm proposed to prepare for three possible strategies:

1. To demonstrate, jointly with Poland, that the reports on the expulsion of Polish Jews were based on atrocity propaganda and that those returned to Poland had been treated well by all concerned.
2. To claim that the Polish Jews were well treated by the German authorities but mistreated by the Poles.
3. To claim that the expulsion measures were due to the Polish decrees and that the Jews were treated decently by German authorities, with no comments to be made about the treatment accorded the victims by the Poles.[13]

To this end, the Nazi authorities went to great lengths to collect data and testimony from many of those involved in the organization of the transports, making elaborate lists of the medical personnel and social workers involved and the amount of food purchased by the deportees in the station restaurant or on the platform. (It is likely that the deportees would have spent a relatively large amount of money for the purchase of food. They knew, after all, that they would not be permitted to export more than 10 marks from Germany and therefore probably sought to spend some of the excess on food, or whatever else might have been available.)

One aspect received a great deal of attention from both German and French officials during this period—accomplices or coconspirators. The French police assigned the task to an expert in this field, Inspector Valentini, who came to the conclusion that Herschel had acted on his own and that there were no mysterious persons behind the scenes.

The German investigation, despite strenuous efforts, was also unable to establish any connection between Herschel and his family with any radical activists or even with anti-German organizations. Much as they tried, they were unable to persuade French authorities that the "Sportsclub l'Aurore," where Herschel occasionally went for dances and outings, was actually a cover for a secret political activist group and a hotbed of Jewish intrigue. The embassy initiated its own investigations into the political activities of the "Club l'Aurore" and of Abraham and Chawa Grynszpan through one of its trusted agents. As the embassy reported to the Ministry of Propaganda on June 23, 1939, these investigations proved difficult since they had to be conducted in such a way as not to alert the other side. In the end, no evidence of any political activities on the part of the club or the family was found and the only strategy left to the German propaganda machine was the claim that the *absence* of any evidence was the best proof that something was amiss.[14]

The German inquiry concentrated on two specific points. One was the subject of the quarrel between Herschel and his uncle just prior to storming out of the house on the afternoon before the shooting. The Germans theorized that it was the result of Herschel informing his relatives of his plans to assassinate the German ambassador, or some other Nazi official, and their efforts to dissuade him. The other concerned that mysterious sum of 3,000 francs, which both Herschel and Abraham had mentioned in the course of their first interrogations, but the existence of which they later denied. For the German investigators, here was proof positive, the smoking gun, that there had been some secret payoff, especially since Herschel obviously had had enough money to buy the gun and stay overnight at a hotel even though he was financially dependent on a man (Abraham) who supposedly was quite careful with money.

As previously indicated, the explanation for both are quite simple, persuasive, and interrelated. In a letter to Oswald Villard of December 5, 1938, Dorothy Thompson wrote about a personal message received from de Moro-Giafferri to the effect that Herschel's father had sent the uncle 3,000 marks[15] to care for Herschel. This was of course illegal, but they had arranged to have the money smuggled out of Germany. The boy, so Moro wrote, learning of his parents' plight, asked the uncle to return the money to his parents. Abraham apparently was willing to comply, but wanted to await future developments before doing so, bringing on the quarrel.[16] It is perfectly understandable that both Herschel and his uncle would deny the existence of any such fund, since they presumably did not want to hand Nazi authorities yet another weapon to use against the family. Furthermore, the persons who assisted in the transfer of the funds were perhaps still under Nazi control.

As Europe girded for what seemed an inevitable war, the pretrial investigation slowly neared completion. Judge Tesnière questioned Herschel Grynszpan for the last time on July 26, at which time Herschel sought to diffuse some of the more serious charges against him. He argued that contrary to the testimony until then, it was not he who had loaded the pistol but rather that this had been done by M. Carpe, the seller. Furthermore, Herschel argued that his testimony immediately after his arrest, which seemed to indicate premeditation, had been recorded wrongly as a result of the lateness of the hour and the absence of an interpreter. He also claimed for the first time that he had been mistreated by the gendarmes. Finally, he hinted that he had planned to commit suicide in the German embassy.

Judge Tesnière, in his final report to the Office of the Public Prosecutor, in mid-August found that Herschel Grynszpan's version of events, given immediately after his arrest, was correct and recommended that the defendant be tried for premeditated murder. However, Judge Tesnière, in what appears to have been something of an about-face, also indicated in his report that it would not be inappropriate to discuss, in the course of the trial, the events in Germany which resulted from the act and the reactions thereto in the rest of the world. However, this did not diminish Grimm's admiration for Tesnière and he attributed it to "political realities."

Under normal circumstances the trial would have commenced in early or mid-September. However, the French Ministry of Justice felt that the strong anti-German sentiments, caused by the occupation of Czechoslovakia in March, made it unlikely that the case could get an impartial trial. It therefore decided to postpone the trial until the following year.

Herschel's attorneys, aware that conditions were propitious, given the animosity vis-à-vis Nazi Germany, urged an early trial for the youth. As for Herschel himself, on August 28 he asked Maître Frankel to transmit a letter to the minister of justice: "I know that France is passing through a tragic period. I therefore request that you allow me to enlist in the French Army. I wish to redeem the act which I committed with my blood, and thus repair the troubles which I have caused the country which accorded me its hospitality."[17]

The request was denied. On September 1, 1939, World War II broke out and France had other things to worry about. Judge Tesnière became Army Captain Tesnière and M. Glorian replaced him as examining magistrate.

There followed the era of the "Phony War," and probably nothing better characterizes that unreal period than the strange developments of the Grynszpan case.

At the conclusion of the pretrial investigation, Grimm drew up a report, in both French and German, which represents the most detailed single original account published on the affair.[18] Within weeks of the outbreak of the war, he became consul general in Berne, Switzerland, but continued to function as the nominal representative of the plaintiff. No longer able to commute to Paris, Grimm was apprehensive that Herschel's defense team would now make the most of the new situation and demand an early start of the trial. On October 6, 1939, Grimm proposed to the Ministry of Propaganda from his office in Berne that efforts be made through a neutral country to either postpone the trial until after the war or to obtain representation at the trial through an attorney from a neutral country. Grimm argued that, in spite of his new responsibilities, he would be able to continue his own involvement in the case and proposed that Marcel Guinand, an attorney from Geneva, Switzerland, be designated the new representative of the plaintiff before the French court. The Ministry of Propaganda concurred.

M. Guinand traveled to Paris on October 19, 1939, and remained there almost a week. On October 26, after Guinand's return to Switzerland, Grimm submitted a detailed report to Goebbels' ministry, marked "Strictly Confidential," recounting Guinand's amazing experiences as an intermediary between two governments at war with each other. The primary purpose for Guinand's journey was to prevent the case from coming to trial, since it was likely that under existing circumstances, the defendant would be acquitted by a jury. Attorneys Garçon and Loncle confirmed that if the trial of Herschel Grynszpan were to take place at that time, less than two months after the invasion of Poland, the youth would be acquitted if for no other reason than that he was Polish. De Moro-Giafferri, the group was convinced, would bring the entire Polish matter into discussion. "It is," the group agreed, "therefore imperative to prevent the trial from taking place." The best way to achieve the desired result, they agreed, was to have the French Ministry of Justice postpone the case *sine die* as long as it was impossible for the plaintiff to be present.

The French attorneys arranged for their Swiss colleague to be received by M. M. Batestini, Director of the Section for Criminal Affairs of the French Ministry of Justice, to whom Guinand presented a *Memoire* authored by Grimm. Batestini, according to the report, agreed that if tried before a jury, Herschel would undoubtedly be freed and de Moro-Giafferri would utilize the opportunity for an anti-German smear campaign. The French official thought that under the prevailing wartime conditions, there would be one possible way to prevent such a "scandalous" result—by bringing the case before a military court which would be staffed by professional civilian and military judges but would have no lay jury. If tried before such a court, Batestini thought, one could probably count on conviction and prevent political excesses by the defense. However, the military justice system had the drawback of having no provisions for the participation of representatives of the plaintiff.

M. Batestini thought the matter important enough that Guinand should present the matter personally to the minister of justice, by then none other than the ubiquitous Georges Bonnet. A meeting was arranged. However, it had to be cancelled on short notice due to the accidental death of Charles Bonnet, the minister's brother. A meeting instead was arranged with Bonnet's *Chef du Cabinet* (deputy), Victor Dupuich. Dupuich apparently proved to be somewhat more suspicious than some of his colleagues. He is quoted as describing his impression that behind Guinand's efforts were both the vom Rath family and the

German government, and he wondered why this was so. Guinand sought to convince the French official that German government interest in the case was understandable since vom Rath had been an embassy official. According to Guinand's report, he also explained his own relationship with Grimm and expressed hope that, through Grimm, he perhaps could help mediate "special prisoner of war problems" between the two countries.

The French authorities, so wrote Guinand, received him most cordially and agreed to do whatever was necessary to prevent the case from being utilized for propaganda purposes! They were as good as their word. Herschel Grynszpan would not even be indicted for another eight months, and then only when a trial was almost certainly out of the question.[19]

However, as the war went on, the cordial relationships began to turn sour. Grimm heard in early January 1940 that an anti-German film being made in Paris claimed Gestapo involvement in vom Rath's assassination. To Grimm, this presaged the beginning of a propaganda campaign against Germany. A German intelligence listening post in Geneva reported a few days later that the French were planning a series of new radio propaganda programs involving prominent personalities. One of those scheduled to participate, among such as de Moro-Giafferri, was Maurice Garçon. According to a red penciled notation by Diewerge on the margin of the report, Grimm was told to break off relations with Garçon.[20]

On December 27, 1939, the *Nationalzeitung* of Basel, Switzerland, carried a story from the French press agency HAVAS. Examining magistrate Glorian had questioned Herschel Grynszpan in response to the latter's request for an early trial, which would enable him to join the French Army and fight Nazism. Assuming that this was part of an effort to obtain an early trial, Grimm once again sent Guinand to Paris in early January 1940. Guinand's twelve-page report to Grimm was almost entirely devoted to political, economic, and military intelligence aspects, such as armaments observed, troop movements and morale, and public opinion. Guinand did mention that he had received assurances from the French authorities that, in spite of the ongoing war, the French government was prepared to conduct the trial in a manner that would safeguard the interests of the "*parti civile.*" Guinand was convinced that for the time being no action would be taken in the matter. He was correct.[21]

Not that the defense didn't try. On January 11, 1940, Herschel wrote to the public prosecutor:

> I have written you several letters in which I have asked you when my trial would take place. Up to now, you have not answered. I ask once more when you plan to hold the trial. If I don't have an answer by March 1, I will be obliged to go on a hunger strike for 24 hours as a warning. And if the trial is not held by March 31, I will find it necessary to go on a hunger strike until my strength fails.[22]

On March 19, 1940, de Moro-Giafferri followed up with an impassioned letter to the public prosecutor:

> I have repeatedly had the opportunity to express to you the wish that the case of Grynszpan come to trial. . . . Today I can no longer wait to express to you my opinion. This case must come to trial. My client requests his judgment—or freedom. There is no valid reason which empowers you to reject the request which is in keeping with law and justice. I don't speak of Grynszpan's decision. He plans to start a hunger strike. I naturally don't agree with that; I have done everything to dissuade him from his plan. But he has such a strong character, this seemingly weak child, I have lost hope that I can persuade him to wait longer.
>
> Shall we stand aside and view this drama of a youth who, faced with the passivity of the responsible powers decides to die because of the postponement for many months of a trial whose preparations have long been completed?

Moro-Giafferri went on to ask "If not now, when?", noting that Herschel, a juvenile, had already spent seventeen months in jail.

> I am not prepared to abandon one rule of law which precedes all others: Everywhere, except under dictatorships, an accused must be judged as soon as the pretrial investigation has been completed. And in all the world, today more than ever, the public. . . demands to know the motives for an unexplained delay. . . .
>
> You know that in America there exists a committee made up of the most famous writers—purposely selected from among non-Jews—which has taken in hand the defense of Grynszpan. They have honored me by requesting my help. They write to me, they query me [about the delay]. . . . I am humiliated that I am unable to respond. I suffer for the prestige of our country. . . . I join with Grynszpan in requesting that a date for the trial be set. . . .

If he can be tried, he should be tried.
Is that impossible? Then he should be freed.[23]

On June 8, 1940, three days after the evacuation of Dunkirk, two days before the French government hastily evacuated Paris and less than two weeks before the surrender of France, Herschel Grynszpan was indicted for the murder of Ernst vom Rath.

By then, a German victim who was probably a tepid Nazi had become a Nazi hero, while the assassin, who originally had few defenders among the French, suddenly found himself fiercely supported.

15

Evacuation from Paris—Extradition to Germany

Almost immediately after the shooting of vom Rath, some German newspapers had raised the question whether Grynszpan might not be legally extradited to Germany to stand trial since the crime had taken place on "German property."

This question was also raised in German official circles, for already on November 10, 1938, the Legal Section of the Foreign Ministry prepared the following report:

> In regard to the question raised in the press concerning the extradition of Grynszpan to Germany, the following can be said:
>
> The shooting took place in the German embassy, which is, however, according to the basic principles of international law, not German but French territory. In view of Paragraph 4 of the [German] Criminal Code, Grynszpan could in fact not be tried in Germany at all, since he did not commit in a foreign country any of the crimes listed in Paragraph 4 for which a foreigner could be tried in this country. [This would be changed in Paragraph 383 of the draft of the new Criminal Code.] Since there is no way the crime could be tried according to German law, there can from the very outset be no question of a German request for extradition.
>
> If Grynszpan had committed the crime in Germany, he would have to be treated as a minor in accordance with the *Jugendgerichtsgesetz* [Juvenile

> Criminal Code] of February 16, 1923, . . . and could be punished only with a jail sentence of one to ten years.[1]

In the light of later developments it is interesting that it was Grimm who, in the course of a meeting on November 11, 1938, in the Ministry of Propaganda, had pointed out specifically that there existed no possibility for the legal extradition of Grynszpan from France to Germany for trial.

On the same subject, propagandist Wolfgang Diewerge wrote in early 1939:

> An extradition of the perpetrator would have been out of the question in any event. French law provides that the country requesting extradition be responsible for judging the crime according to its own laws. That was here impossible. The crime was, as seen from Germany, perpetrated in a foreign country. The criminal was not a German, and could therefore be prosecuted by German courts only if the crime had been a case of high treason against the German Reich. Finally, the case in question was a political delict in which extradition on general principle does not take place. An exception would have been appropriate only if the assassination had been directed against the head of state or a member of his family.[2]

All agreed that Herschel could not be extradited since there was no possibility of trying him before a German court. But such minor details could not be allowed to impede the course of Nazi justice, and despite the fact that there existed a legal French government, Herschel was soon to find himself in German hands.

With the entry of German troops into Paris on June 14, 1940, there also arrived a special Gestapo unit under the direction of the infamous Dr. Helmut Knochen, who later was to become one of the most feared Nazi officials in France in his role as the head of the *Sicherheitsdienst* (SD), the SS counterintelligence organization. A member of this unit, which for organizational purposes was attached to the army's *Geheime Feldpolizei* (Secret Field Police) was SS *Sturmbannführer* (Major) Karl Boemelburg. A career police official, Boemelburg in 1938 had been assigned to the embassy in Paris as liaison to the French prefect of police. Another early arrival in Paris was Grimm, who arrived only a day later, on June 15, on behalf of Foreign Minister Ribbentrop.

Boemelburg and Grimm had been given the assignment to apprehend Herschel Grynszpan and to locate and confiscate any and all materials pertaining to the assassination of vom Rath. As Grimm recounted to Ribbentrop in a memorandum on April 6, 1942, arrangements were made, with the assistance of the Secret Field Police, to confiscate from "Jewish organizations, agents and lawyers in Paris" all documents relating to the case. In pursuit of this task, Boemelburg's men, within twenty-four hours of the German occupation of Paris, had ransacked the offices of de Moro-Giafferri and other lawyers associated with the case, as well as every Jewish or anti-Nazi organization that had in one way or another become involved in the case.[3]

On June 19, Grimm informed the Foreign Ministry that Grynszpan had been illegally removed from the Fresnes prison shortly before the occupation of Paris. He added that a "special troop of the Secret Field Police is following his trail."[4] In fact, Grynszpan had embarked on a journey from his prison cell in Paris' Fresnes prison which did not end until he was handed over to the Nazi authorities on the French-German demarcation line about a month later. The details of this extraordinary journey, as recounted by various sources, differ in some minor respects, but they are surprisingly similar and by and large agree with each other.

The rapid deterioration of the French military situation caused the government in early June to move the judicial administration and prisoners from Paris. As part of this process, the Paris court was moved to Angers and prisoners were distributed to other prisons throughout the country. As a first step, Grynszpan was sent in a convoy from Fresnes Prison to Orléans, about 100 kilometers (sixty miles) to the south.

That, however, provided only a temporary respite. German troops marched into Paris on June 14 and continued their relentless drive southward. On June 15, in the face of approaching Nazi forces, Grynszpan was one of a group of ninety-six prisoners who set out from Orléans for Bourges, approximately ninety kilometers farther south. En route, this convoy came under German fire. (The German Foreign Ministry liaison with the Army reported on June 23 that the transport had come under German artillery fire and that some prisoners were killed while others escaped. Other reports mention an air attack.) In any event, according to this Ministry of Propaganda message, "Grynszpan was not among the remaining 6 prisoners who arrived in Bourges; they reported that they did not know Grynszpan."[5]

As a matter of fact, Grynszpan made his own way, arriving in Bourges on June 17. The chief warden of Bourges prison and the public prosecutor, fully aware of the Nazi interest in their new arrival, decided to send him off immediately to Châteauroux, about fifty-five kilometers to the southwest on the only road from Bourges which was still open. In order to frustrate German efforts to locate the youth, and presumably also to protect themselves, they decided not to record Grynszpan's name on the prison register.

The move from Bourges came none too soon. On June 19, the Wehrmacht entered the city and German officials promptly called at the prison and demanded that Grynszpan be turned over to them. The chief warden declared that he didn't know the prisoner and asserted that no one by that name had been interned there. The Germans obtained confirmation of Grynszpan's arrival in Bourges during the interrogation of the noncommissioned officer responsible for the prisoner transfer from Orléans. However, by then Herschel was long gone and the trail once again turned cold. (The public prosecutor in Bourges, Paul Ribeyre, was imprisoned by the Germans for several weeks as a result of this incident and was released only after the intervention of high French officials in both occupied and unoccupied France.)[6]

Châteauroux also did not provide the haven so desperately sought as the German army rolled on, and Grynszpan once again was sent on his way, this time on his own, told to report to the prison in Toulouse, more than 300 kilometers to the south. There he apparently arrived alone and dutifully presented himself to the prison warden, who accepted his surrender.

Confirmation of the broad outlines of this account, based largely on German files, comes from other less suspect sources.

The New York Times of September 8, 1940, reported Herschel's strange odyssey, based on information from the United Press. According to the article, Gestapo officials took Grynszpan from the Toulouse prison "where he had persuaded prison officials to hold him" after the French police had abandoned a convoy of prisoners from Paris. As the article describes it, "Grynszpan's trip across France, knocking on prison doors in search of officials to accept his surrender, will probably remain unique in prison annals. It throws a curious light on conditions in this country during the disaster."

A slightly different version was recounted by Varian Fry, one of the unsung heroes of the war against Nazi oppression. When it was learned that the Franco-German armistice of June 22, 1940, contained a clause providing for the "surrender on demand" of German refugees, a group of U.S. citizens, shocked by this violation of the right of asylum and cognizant of France's status as the primary haven for political refugees in Europe, formed the Emergency Rescue Committee. The purpose of the committee was to bring political and intellectual refugees out of France before the SD or Gestapo—or the secret police of Germany's allies—could make use of Article XIX.

Article XIX read as follows:

> All German war and civil prisoners in French custody, including those under arrest and convicted who were seized and sentenced because of acts in favor of the German Reich, shall be surrendered immediately to German troops.
>
> The French Government is obliged to surrender upon demand all Germans named by the German Government in France, as well as in French possessions, Colonies, Protectorate Territories and Mandates.
>
> The French Government binds itself to prevent removal of German war and civil prisoners from France into French possessions or into foreign countries. Regarding prisoners already taken outside France, as well as sick and wounded German prisoners who cannot be transported, exact lists with the places of residence are to be produced. The German High Command assumes care of sick and wounded German war prisoners.

According to Fry, the second paragraph applied to political refugees. "'German' originally meant all inhabitants of the Greater Reich, i.e., Germans, Austrians, Czechs and many Poles, but was later stretched to include everybody the German government wanted to get its hands on."[7]

The committee selected Varian Fry, a newspaperman, who set out from New York for Marseilles in August 1940 with a long list of men and women whom he was to rescue. The mission, expected to last a month, in fact lasted until Fry was expelled from unoccupied France thirteen months later. During this period Fry and his collaborators facilitated the departure of such prominent refugees as authors Franz Werfel (*Song of Bernadette*) and Konrad Heiden (*A History of National Socialism* and *Hitler: A Biography*), musician Wanda Landowska, painter Marc Chagall and sculptors Max Ernst and Jacques Lipchitz, as well as a number of prominent European politicians.

Varian Fry wrote about his experiences in 1945. According to Fry, so far as anyone knew, there had been only one extradition under Article XIX until September 1940, that of Herschel Grynszpan. As Fry recounted the story in 1945, Herschel had been sent first to Orléans, then to Limoges. On the way to Limoges his train was bombed by German planes. Grynszpan escaped, but on his own continued to Limoges on foot and presented himself to the public prosecutor, who in turn made out papers for him in another name and sent him to Toulouse, in the company of two gendarmes. According to Fry, the trio arrived in Toulouse on a Sunday and, finding no one at the prefecture, the gendarmes told Grynszpan to take a room for the night and come back the next morning. He came back, was arrested, and placed in prison. According to Fry, "Grynszpan's case is typical of the attitude of the French authorities; they would give a man a chance to escape before they arrested him, but if he didn't take it, they would arrest him and turn him over, in obedient fulfillment of the terms of the armistice."[8]

And so it was with Herschel Grynszpan. A month after his incarceration in Toulouse, the police prefecture was ordered to transfer him to Vichy. From there he was taken to Moulins. Herschel Grynszpan's odyssey had come to an end. On July 18, 1940, he was turned over to agents of the Gestapo's Boemelburg at the demarcation line between occupied and Vichy France. According to Boemelburg, the French government gave every indication that it would have preferred the prisoner to escape and that pressure was necessary to effect his transfer into Nazi hands.[9]

In mid-July, the German ambassador in Paris reported to the Foreign Ministry that the prison director of Bourges had illegally released Grynszpan as the German troops neared the city. The telegram went on to say:

> Investigations [by] agents Secret Field Police in unoccupied area at first fruitless, then through Minister Justice Vichy government report that Grynszpan turned himself in to Toulouse prison. Professor Grimm requested Minister Justice through French offices extradition Grynszpan. At the request of the Secret Field Police, Grynszpan was turned over at the demarcation line and brought to Berlin.[10]

On July 19, a memorandum to the files initialed by Ribbentrop noted proudly that "the transfer of Grynszpan to the German authorities did not, as reported in the telegram, take place at the request of the

Secret Field Police but at the request of the Foreign Ministry through the Armistice Commission." Ribbentrop wanted to make sure that he and his organization got the credit for this coup.[11] To make sure that everyone got the message, the Foreign Ministry sent a copy of the note to the Ministry of Propaganda on July 24.

Somehow it seemed fitting that Grimm, the eminent legal expert who on November 11, 1938, had informed all concerned that Herschel Grynszpan could not be extradited to Germany for trial, should be the one to request his extradition on behalf of the German government. Since making that finding, Article XIX of the Franco-German armistice had entered into force. Yet its application could not be justified in this case because until then, and also thereafter, everyone seemed to agree that Herschel Grynszpan was a Pole. It was the doubtful legality of the extradition to which Grynszpan would later turn for his defense and which would create some anxiety among his prosecutors.[12]

Today, the Grynszpan odyssey seems nothing short of bizarre. Here was a fugitive from the onrushing Nazis, aware that they were looking for him, voluntarily giving himself up to French authorities. It seems most implausible. One writer has strongly implied—in part on the basis of this event—that perhaps Herschel was a Nazi *agent provocateur* who felt that he would be safe in the hands of German authorities.[13]

On further examination, perhaps the actions of the young Grynszpan were not so strange. Grynszpan, who had no money and spoke French with a strong German accent, had made his way south amid panic-stricken refugees. The odds against survival seemed slim indeed. He was without advice in a country of which he knew little. He was nineteen years old, without anyone to whom he could turn. His face was well known and perhaps he felt that the average Frenchman might blame him for the present disastrous situation. During his incarceration he had not been embraced by the Jewish community and it is unlikely that he would have sought them out for assistance. At the same time, legally considered a juvenile, Grynszpan had been well treated and protected by the French judicial authorities, and it is not unreasonable that he perhaps felt safer in their hands than alone out on the street. Finally, Herschel's behavior revealed him to be the sensitive, vulnerable, and insecure youngster that he actually was.

With the benefit of hindsight, we know today that several possible avenues of escape were open to Herschel. As the German armies advanced on Paris, most Jews and those who were likely to be identified as opponents of the Nazis fled to the south. Abraham Grynszpan and his wife actually were in Toulouse along with Abraham Berenbaum and Maître Frankel. De Moro-Giafferri took refuge in nearby Aiguilon. Much of Herschel's family and his lawyers were nearby. Unfortunately, Herschel did not know.

16

A German Trial for Herschel Grynszpan—A Proposal

After his extradition, Grynszpan was flown to Berlin for interrogation and incarcerated in the notorious Gestapo prison of the *Reichssicherheitshauptamt* (Reich Main Security Bureau) at Prinz-Albrecht-Strasse 8. Six months later, on January 18, 1941, he was transferred to the Sachsenhausen concentration camp and given the number 35181. He was housed in a special section—the "bunker"—reserved for prominent prisoners such as the deposed Austrian Chancellor Schuschnigg, former Reichstag Deputy Wulle, and others.

Apparently, Herschel received much better treatment than regular camp inmates. He was reasonably well dressed and not obliged to wear prison garb or his prison number, his head was not shaved, and during the day he was able to move about relatively freely within the building complex. He was assigned various tasks normally reserved for trusties. According to witnesses, not only was Herschel not mistreated by the SS guards, but they actually tended to treat prisoners better in his presence. Inmates who occasionally caught a glimpse of Herschel had the impression that he received considerably better treatment than most others in the camp.[1]

(Harry Naujoks, trusty and longtime political prisoner in the Sachsenhausen concentration camp and a source of the above information, reported that the prisoners in the "bunker" were strictly isolated from the rest of the inmates. Helpers such as barbers and janitors were selected from among prisoners due to be executed or willing tools ready to participate in any crime. As a result, the only possibility to obtain reliable information about the prisoners held there was through first aid personnel who occasionally visited the cell block. Within the cell block, the prisoners were also strictly isolated. However, since the individual cells had no toilets or running water, the prisoners had to go to the bunker toilet in order to empty their slop pails. This provided an opportunity to exchange a few words with fellow prisoners occasionally, as did trips to the washroom and showers, in spite of the vigilance of the SS guards.)

In March 1941, Herschel was moved to the Flossenburg concentration camp, where he was held until October, when he was transported back to Berlin, to the Moabit prison.

All the while, a number of people were promoting the idea of a German trial for Herschel Grynszpan. Grimm, Diewerge (by now *SS Oberscharführer* Diewerge), and their associates sifted through literally truckloads of files removed from the Paris offices of de Moro-Giafferri, the LICA (*Ligue internationale contre l'antisémitisme*), and others, ever on the lookout for those elusive coconspirators. Grimm wrote the Ministry of Propaganda in July 1940, a month following Herschel's extradition, that the trial against Herschel Grynszpan could now be conducted in Germany. Diewerge noted a month later that regardless of whether it was decided "to punish the offense by a show trial, a public execution or some other means," it was of the utmost importance that the entire juridical and criminal materials be readied expeditiously so that they could be used whenever necessary.[2]

In September, Grimm was able to report that former examining magistrate Tesnière was now in a German prisoner-of-war camp. He had, so reported Grimm, offered his cooperation in the hope of perhaps gaining his release from prison.

In mid-1941, the Ministry of Justice transferred to the Office of the Public Prosecutor of the People's Court two volumes of files with instructions to prepare an indictment of Herschel Grynszpan before the People's Court. Ernst Lautz, the court's chief prosecutor in 1941, recalled in 1955 that at the time questions were raised concerning the court's jurisdiction in this case. As had been determined by legal experts already in 1938, a German court would be competent to try someone for murder committed abroad only if it were directed at the head of state. High treason, on the other hand, could be tried before a German court regardless of where committed. On October 16, 1941, the chief prosecutor handed down the indictment.[3]

The document is a fascinating study of Nazi jurisprudence, intent on preserving the impression of strict adherence to the letter of the law. A notation at the top of the cover page indicates that the accused is a foreigner and was a juvenile at the time of the offense. Both "impediments" would be addressed in the indictment.[4]

Herschel Grynszpan was indicted not for murder but for *high treason*. The defendant, according to the indictment, meant "to prevent, through force or threats, the Fuehrer and Reichs Chancellor as well as members of the government from the conduct of their constitutional functions. . . . " The document further charges that vom Rath was killed to alert world opinion to the alleged mistreatment of Jews in Germany and "in order to bring pressure on the German government to cease its activities designed to eliminate Jewish influence."

As for the youthfulness of the accused, the indictment charges that "the accused, at the time of the offense, had the mental and moral capacity of a person over eighteen years of age, and the reprehensible attitude demonstrated by the criminal act and the well-being of the nation require that he be punished as an adult."

The indictment thus sought to address the problem of the court's jurisdiction to try Herschel Grynszpan as an adult for a murder he had committed as a juvenile and outside Germany. In so doing, it of course highlighted the questionable legality of the defendant's extradition to Germany and called attention to his youth. As events were to show, the indictment highlighted some other problems as well.

Those not familiar with wartime administration in Nazi Germany may be under the impression that, thanks to the country's centralized organization, there was ready coordination between government agencies. Propaganda's Diewerge found out, if he did not know it previously, that this impression was illusory when, as one of the early key players in the Grynszpan case, he learned of the indictment only by accident. Much to his chagrin, it had been drawn up without any "guidance" from either the Ministry of Propaganda or the Foreign Ministry's Grimm. Diewerge later self-righteously informed Goebbels that without the intervention of the Propaganda Ministry, the trial would have gone forward without adequate propagandistic preparation and that even the imposition of the death sentence would not have been assured.

To bring matters back on track, Diewerge quickly convened a meeting on October 29, attended by People's Court Vice President Karl

Engert and Chief Prosecutor Lautz, the Gestapo's Eichmann and Grimm. In a summary report of April 2, 1942, to Goebbels, Diewerge reported that the group had at that time agreed on the following "guidelines" for the trial:

1. The person of the assassin is basically of little interest. . . . World Jewry is in the dock.
2. The murder was World Jewry's signal for the start of the war against National Socialist Germany.
3. World Jewry drove the French people into this war against their own interests.
4. The blood guilt of World Jewry is evident from numerous parallel cases, proof of which is available.
5. Germany's battle against Jewry before the war, both inside and outside its borders, was a battle for peace. *The destruction of Jewry is a prerequisite for the coming European new order* [italics added].
6. The background of the murder demonstrates the overall responsibility of Jewry, including the intellectual complicity of the Jews remaining in Germany after the [National Socialist] accession to power.[5]

World Jewry, the bogeyman of the Nazi era, was finally to be "brought to trial" for its complicity in the murder of vom Rath. Diewerge had earlier, in his *Anschlag gegen den Frieden*, sought to imply some sort of connection between the murderer and international Jewish organizations, although he did not go beyond making inferences and mysterious, unsubstantiated charges. He had used similar arguments on two earlier occasions.[6] Grimm, there also representing the "*parti civile*," had broadly hinted at the same point in his speech before the Swiss court trying David Frankfurter for the assassination of Wilhelm Gustloff.[7]

That much was not really new. What was new—and emphasized by the presence of Eichmann—was that the "guidelines" called for the trial of Herschel Grynszpan to fix blame on "World Jewry" for the outbreak of the war, and to call for the destruction of Jews as a prerequisite for the coming new order. The trial, in other words, was to justify the "Final Solution," the total elimination of Jews, which at that point was in its early stages. Had the trial taken place as scheduled, it would have coincided with the Wannsee Conference (January 20, 1942) called to discuss the logistics of killing some 11 million human beings.

In addition to justifying the monstrous plan, the trial was expected to counteract sympathy for Jews among the European population, which was witnessing the forcible deportation of the Jews.

It was sometime during early November that Hitler, probably at the behest of Goebbels, authorized the trial of the assassin of Ernst vom Rath.[8]

On November 13, 1941, Diewerge assured State Secretary Gutterer, his immediate superior, that the ministry's propaganda preparations had been completed and that the trial probably would take place in mid-January. "The death sentence will be pronounced for treason," he predicted confidently.[9] He also wrote Grimm that the cooperation which had existed between the various ministries in regard to the Grynszpan case in 1939 was to be reestablished for this purpose.

It was late November or early December of 1941 when the Ministry of Propaganda, probably under the direction of Diewerge, prepared the following report for Hitler's information:

Reich Ministry for Public Enlightenment and Propaganda—Fuehrer Information

Reference: Propagandistic Possibilities of the Murder Trial of Grynszpan

Mid-January 1942 is scheduled as the date for the conviction [*sic*] of the murderer Grynszpan as ordered by the Fuehrer. The murder trial will take place before the People's Court in Berlin. The indictment will charge high treason together with murder. The circumstances of the act and the responsibility of the murderer are undisputed. The death sentence is legally possible.[10]

The murderer has always considered and described himself as a tool of World Jewry. After the murder, he was glorified by leading Jewish organizations throughout the entire world as a fighter in the front ranks against National Socialism. His act has been described by World Jewry as a conscious call to arms.

The trial, therefore, offers the possibility of proving before the entire world the decisive contribution of World Jewry to the outbreak of the present war. Through careful, minute work, all arguments have been collected; they prove World Jewry's spiritual responsibility for the shooting and its solidarity with the murderer after the act. Even the French witnesses of the murder are to a great part still available and prepared to make important statements; so, for instance, the French examining magistrate who can report mainly on the international intrigues during the pretrial examination. The well-known German hater, de Moro-Giafferri, who also played an important role in the Jewish trials in

Cairo, Chur, Basel and Berne, was retained as the main defense attorney for Grynszpan in Paris.

The entire material of judicial interest has been incorporated in the memorandum by Professor Grimm, [while] the propagandistic material has been compiled in the booklet *Anschlag gegen den Weltfrieden*.[11]

World Jewry will therefore sit in the defendant's dock, next to Grynszpan. It will be possible to give the testimony of witnesses a special political-propagandistic twist. A judgment which merely concerns itself with the person of the assassin would allow questions to be raised among the German people as to the meaning of such a trial against a Jewish murderer.

The head of the Foreign Organization of the NSDAP, *Gauleiter* Bohle, will speak about the persecution of Germans abroad by World Jewry. There are hundreds of indisputable cases and their publication would strangle any feeling of pity among the German population for those Jews currently being deported from Germany.

Furthermore, the (former) French Foreign Minister Bonnet has prepared affidavits concerning the extent to which pressure was exerted by World Jewry on the French government in 1939 to enter the war. He is prepared to testify regarding these matters before the People's Court. A connection between the Grynszpan trial and French foreign policy is above all proven by Jewish attempts to undertake demonstrations during the visit [to Paris] of the Reich Foreign Minister.[12]

The propaganda preparations are being made by the Ministry of Propaganda in close cooperation with the Ministry of Justice, the Foreign Ministry, the People's Court and the chief public prosecutor. The material collected by the Ministry for Public Enlightenment and Propaganda will be included in the indictment.

Does the Fuehrer agree to an interrogation of *Gauleiter* Bohle and former French Foreign Minister Bonnet?

Hitler agreed to the questions posed and the great show trial was soon to be under way. The pogrom of November 1938 represented the beginning of the Holocaust, and the trial of Herschel Feibel Grynszpan was destined to become its justification.

17

A House Divided—Nazi Trial Preparations

Once the decision had been made to hold the trial, the necessary preparations were rapidly initiated. Grimm and Diewerge could be counted on to do everything possible to expedite its realization. The Gestapo's pretrial investigation was completed by early December, and the case was assigned to the People's Court in Berlin. An exploratory planning session was called on December 10 by People's Court Vice President Engert and Chief Prosecutor Jorns, to which representatives of interested agencies were invited.[1]

The group tentatively agreed to begin the trial in February, since the January starting date, proposed by the Ministry of Propaganda in its report to the Fuehrer, was deemed unrealistic in light of the extensive preparations necessary. Engert proposed that every effort be made to prevent this from being turned into another "Reichstag Fire" trial, to instead "conduct it in a solemn and effective manner."

The specter of the Nazis' previous attempt to stage a major show trial some eight years earlier was clearly on everyone's mind. On February 27, 1933, the German *Reichstag* (Parliament) building was destroyed in a fire almost certainly set by a group of Nazi storm troopers acting under the direction of the president of the Reichstag, Hermann Goering. On the following day, Chancellor Hitler convinced the aging President Hindenburg that this had been part of a Communist uprising and prevailed on him to sign a decree "for the Protection of the People and the State," suspending several key sections of the Constitution guaranteeing individual and civil liberties. Hitler used the decree to usurp total power in Germany. Five "conspirators" were arrested and tried before the Supreme Court at Leipzig—Marinus van der Lubbe, a dim-witted Dutch Communist arsonist who had been found in the vicinity of the Reichstag (if he was involved, he could not have been the sole arsonist); Ernst Torgler, Communist parliamentary leader; Georgi Dimitrov, a Bulgarian Communist who later became prime minister of Bulgaria, and two other Bulgarian Communists. The trial was a total fiasco, especially for Goering, when Dimitrov, acting as his own lawyer, provoked him into making a fool of himself during cross-examination. Marinus van der Lubbe was convicted and executed; the others were acquitted, though Torgler was immediately taken into "protective custody," where he remained until his death during the war.

With the earlier experience in mind, and in order to complete the trial within one week, one of the first decisions was to limit the number of witnesses to be called. Among those prominently mentioned as potentially important witnesses were embassy officials, French police involved in the arrest and preliminary interrogation, and M. Carpe, the seller of the murder weapon. Also mentioned was the owner of the Hotel de Suez where Herschel had spent the night preceding the shooting. The group also decided to call several character witnesses for the victim, such as his father and Bohle. The latter was to discuss "vom Rath's relationship to the Fuehrer and the party," apparently an attempt to counteract some of the rumors alleging that the victim, and indeed his father, had been less than totally devoted adherents of the "movement." Mme Brun was to be called to testify about the effect of the shooting in France since she had "testified so splendidly on this point in the course of the preliminary investigation."

Yet according to Grimm, by far the most important testimony would come from former French Foreign Minister Georges Bonnet. Grimm reported that Bonnet was willing to testify being convinced that the assassination was not the act of a single fanatic, but a well-thought-out effort to sabotage Franco-German understanding and Ribbentrop's Paris visit of December 1938. While this and later reports concerning Bonnet's readiness to testify before the Nazi tribunal—which Bonnet would deny after the war—come from German sources which undoubtedly were influenced by some wishful thinking, there almost certainly was some justification for German hopes that he would appear as a star witness. Georges Bonnet was not above utilizing the anti-Semitism, which prevailed in France at the time of the shooting, to excuse his ministry's shortcoming.

Just what Ribbentrop hoped to achieve through the trial is revealed in an internal ministry communication.

> The Reich Foreign Minister has today decided that the Foreign Ministry should devote the greatest attention to this trial. . . .
>
> The assassination of Counselor of Legation vom Rath is clearly connected with the journey of the Reich Foreign Minister to the discussions in Paris on December 6, 1938, and was designed to sabotage the policy of Franco-German cooperation initiated in Munich. Over and above these immediate aims, the assassination reveals the basic plan of International Jewry to drive the world into a war with National Socialist Germany, and Counselor of Legation vom Rath therefore is to be regarded as the first casualty of this war.[2]

Ribbentrop not only claimed for his organization the "honor" of the war's first casualty, but also had no doubts about the importance of his own mission to France in December 1938. However, by 1942 it was obvious that German diplomacy, or more specifically Ribbentrop's efforts, had failed to prevent the outbreak of war, and the foreign minister was anxious to find a suitable scapegoat to blame.

It is clear that much of the Foreign Ministry's interest in the case depended on Bonnet's willingness to take the witness stand. Grimm had no doubts, and he reported to the Foreign Ministry's *Geheimrat* (Privy Councillor) Albrecht on December 22 that he "had discussed everything with Georges Bonnet in several long meetings and M. Bonnet completely agrees with me on all points and is basically prepared to appear as a witness."[3] All French witnesses would, of course, have to be invited officially, and French government approval would be required. However, Grimm felt that this would not be difficult to obtain, provided the negotiations emphasize the potentially beneficial result for Franco-German relations and the excellent effect in France.

Some others were not so sure. Minister Kruemmer raised the question with Diewerge, but was reassured in view of Grimm's favorable impressions. Not so easily convinced, however, was Ambassador (to France) Abetz who, in a telegram to his ministry, gave the definite impression that he did not expect much cooperation from the witness. He also questioned whether the French government would permit Bonnet to take the stand. As later events were to prove, the doubts were fully justified. Grimm's impressions turned out to be overly optimistic.

The first full-scale meeting to discuss the propaganda preparations of the forthcoming trial was called for January 5, 1942, by Ministerial Counselor Diewerge, who in the meantime had been charged by the Ministry of Propaganda with preparing "the propaganda aspects" of the projected trial.[4] The session, attended by representatives of the Ministries of Foreign Affairs, Justice and Propaganda, the Public Prosecutor's Office, the People's Court and the Foreign Organizations of the NSDAP, decided that the trial "should make clear to the German people and the world that International Jewry is primarily to blame for the outbreak of the war." The participants further agreed that "the actions of the Jewish Aid Committee for Grynszpan and its direct connection with the Roosevelt circles will also be revealed."[5]

To assure that these "revelations" would receive appropriate coverage, elaborate plans were prepared. On February 4, 1942, the anniversary of the assassination of Wilhelm Gustloff, the Ministry of Justice was to announce to the German people and the world that Herschel Grynszpan was in German custody and that his trial would commence in Berlin on February 18, 1942. A special "sensation" was to be created by the announcement that former French Foreign Minister Bonnet and *Gauleiter* Bohle would testify.

Grandiose plans were made for the press, both foreign and domestic. They were to be encouraged to place primary emphasis on the relationship between the assassination and warmongering. The foreign press was to receive special attention to assure broad and effective coverage; for instance, it was to be given the opportunity to interview the presiding judge, the prosecutor, and expert witnesses Grimm and Diewerge, as well as former Foreign Minister Bonnet. Foreign correspondents in Berlin would be allowed to "scoop" their German colleagues by being advised of the upcoming trial even before it was revealed in the German press. Aside from making maximum use of the foreign press in Berlin for covering the trial and disseminating its message, it was agreed that certain selected newspapers were also to receive "related" materials, not raised in the trial, proving the "Jews' . . . warmongering activities."

The primary theme of the foreign press briefings was to be the Fuehrer's announcement "that World Jewry had to disappear from Europe." Since emigration of Jews from Germany and Nazi-occupied territories had been stopped by mid-1941, the meaning of those chilling words must have been clear to all those present. Here was yet another bit of evidence that the primary purpose of the Grynszpan trial was to justify the forcible elimination of Jews from Europe.

On the domestic side, since the lack of newspaper space—most of which by necessity had to be devoted to reporting of Germany's war effort—would prevent adequate coverage of the trial, the Ministry of Propaganda proposed to prepare a cheap pamphlet for broad domestic dissemination. It was to hammer home the main propaganda themes of the trial. There was also to be a pamphlet with highlights of the testimony and the judgment of the court for distribution by German diplomatic missions abroad. By holding the trial in the 250-seat main courtroom of the People's Court, it was thought there would be enough room to provide access for interested parties while preserving the decorum of a courtroom, thus avoiding the circus atmosphere of the Reichstag trial.

As something of an afterthought, the Foreign Ministry on January 12 reminded the Ministry of Propaganda that the former's approval was required before any political discussions in regard to the trial could be conducted with foreigners. Diewerge replied that the Propaganda Ministry's Press Section had been informed and would comply.[6]

The next meeting to discuss the trial was called for January 22, 1942, by Roland Freisler, state secretary in the Ministry of Justice.[7] He called the meeting of representatives of the Ministries of Justice, Foreign Affairs and Propaganda, the People's Court, and the Gestapo to discuss two points which were to cast their lengthy shadows over the trial preparations from this time on. First, it was reported that Grynszpan had indicated during interrogation by the Gestapo that he might challenge the legality of his extradition and his trial before a German court. This, it was feared, would result in attacks on the Vichy government from sources outside Germany. The Foreign and Propaganda Ministries agreed to certify that they had no objections to the trial on these grounds.

The second problem, Freisler informed the startled group, was that Herschel Grynszpan would in all likelihood claim during the trial that he had homosexual relations with vom Rath and that this had been the immediate cause for the shooting. The minutes of the meeting do not record reactions to this news, but it is likely that for Propaganda's Diewerge and the representative from the Foreign Ministry (a colleague of the absent Grimm), this must have come like a bolt out of the blue. After all, at no time had there been any indication, either during the interrogations by Judge Tesnière or in the files of de Moro-

Giafferri—which had been examined in great detail—that there might have been a motive other than that claimed by the young assassin at the outset. At this point, Diewerge (and Grimm, when he heard about it) must have longed for the good old days when the assassination had been attributed to just ordinary Nazi atrocities.

This new revelation raised the question whether a trial was advisable at all in view of the negative propaganda repercussions to be expected from such testimony. After some discussion, it was agreed that Goebbels should be asked to raise the matter with the Fuehrer and obtain the latter's specific approval to go ahead with the trial in the face of this new development.

There was yet another complication. The Foreign Ministry representative reported that the French trial dealing with the question of war guilt and the causes of the French military disaster was scheduled to open in Riom on February 17, only one day before the proposed start of the Grynszpan proceedings. At Riom, Nazi Germany's allies in the new French government sought to "expose" the guilt of various French cabinet members and officers in starting World War II. Since the Grynszpan trial was designed to prove that World Jewry was responsible for the same thing, it somehow did not seem right that both trials take place concurrently. It was therefore the consensus of those attending that if the French trial started as scheduled, the date of the Grynszpan trial would need to be delayed to avoid a conflict. Shortly thereafter, Hitler concurred in the proposed delay.

Goebbels, confiding in his diary two days later, on January 24, reflected on the alleged unnatural relationship between the murderer and his victim.

> The murder trial of Grynszpan is again under debate. Grynszpan has invented the insolent argument that he had a homosexual relationship with the assassinated Counselor of Legation vom Rath. That is, of course, a shameless lie; however, it is thought out very cleverly and would, if brought out in the course of a public trial, certainly become the main argument of enemy propaganda. I therefore will arrange for only part of the trial to be open to the public, while the rest is to take place behind locked doors.

On reflection, Goebbels must have realized that a trial conducted under these circumstances would have only limited propaganda value.

Yet the fact that he was willing to consider such drastic measures is an indication of the importance he attached to the project.

With the decision taken to delay Grynszpan's trial until after completion of the Riom proceedings, from which the German propaganda machine expected so much, the preparatory work continued, although at a somewhat more leisurely pace. Diewerge went to Paris in early February and on his return reported to Goebbels that Bonnet in a conversation had confirmed his willingness to testify that he opposed the declaration of war against Germany but that the French government had been put under such heavy Jewish pressure that this step was virtually unavoidable. Goebbels confided to his diary on February 13, 1942: "This shows in what irresponsible fashion this war was started and how severely those must be punished who acted so irresponsibly."

The Riom trial began on February 17, and by late February it had become clear that German hopes were not about to be realized. The trial focused almost entirely on responsibility for the French military debacle, but not on the question of "war guilt." What might have been an ideal opening for the Grynszpan trial turned into a liability as a result of the vigorous defense put up by Léon Blum, Édouard Daladier and colleagues. Hitler characterized the turn of events in his Reichstag speech of March 15 as an "incomprehensible" attitude on the part of the Vichy government, and others echoed the Fuehrer's keen disappointment.

Goebbels' thoughts during this lull in the preparations for the Grynszpan trial turned to his old nemesis, the Ministry of Justice. Little love was lost between the propaganda chief and what he considered a group of stodgy paragraph-happy bureaucrats bent on frustrating his efforts on behalf of national socialism. They had foiled him repeatedly when he wanted the courts to pass "deterring" sentences, that is, sentences out of all proportion to the actual crimes in order to "deter" other offenders. Goebbels gave vent to his feelings in a diary entry of March 20, 1942:

> It is essential that the leadership of the Ministry of Justice, which has been completely orphaned since the death of Guertner, be placed in new hands. I will propose to the Fuehrer the President of the People's Court, Thierack,[8] who is a real National Socialist and who will undoubtedly not stumble over minor points. State Secretary Freisler has forfeited the right to be minister of justice in that he, who formerly was one of our most dreaded radicals, now has moved completely into the camp of the

> paragraph-true jurists. Schlegelberger[9] is out of the question for the leadership of German justice due to his bureaucratic attitude. The Fuehrer still does not know whom he is to place at the head of the People's Court instead of Thierack; because this post too must be filled in such a manner that at least the People's Court functions as the National Socialist judicial agency. . . . Justice cannot be the master of the life of the state, it must be the servant of state policies.

The Foreign Ministry, which continued to hope for an early trial, got things rolling again with an urgent and secret cable to Diewerge on March 21, passing on the news from Grimm that all French witnesses, without exception, would appear for the trial. Grimm had returned to Paris, where he was now consul general, to initiate negotiations regarding the appearance of French witnesses at Grynszpan's trial. The French government, according to this communication, had agreed without reservation to the interrogation of French witnesses and welcomed the trial which would permit the identification of the true enemy and the real initiator of the war. Not only that, but the French government also promised to provide propaganda support for the trial.[10] With the failure of the Riom trial, France's Nazi sympathizers were still on the lookout for *someone* to blame for the war.

Diewerge reacted by urging Goebbels to authorize the start of the trial by May 6, subject, of course, to Hitler's approval. By March 24, the Ministry of Propaganda had prepared a detailed "Fuehrer Information," entitled "Setting Target Date for Grynszpan Trial."[11] The "Information" called attention to Hitler's decision to delay Grynszpan's trial from mid-January to await the early results of the Riom trial and the need to obtain French approval for the testimony of French witnesses in general and former Foreign Minister Bonnet in particular. The document summarized the current status:

1. The Riom trial has not resulted in the hoped-for exposure and the severe punishment of the war guilty, but only in an examination of poor preparation for war. The enemy propaganda is already making use of that opportunity.
2. The French government has, after long negotiations, agreed to the testimony of French witnesses before the People's Court.
3. It has been agreed with Foreign Minister Bonnet that he will testify about the intrigues of Jewish warmongers during the decisive days of September

1939. "He will submit his testimony in writing prior to appearing before the court."

Finally, the Fuehrer was advised that the embassy in Paris considered the time ripe for the trial. The Ministry of Propaganda proposed, after consulting Justice and Foreign Affairs, the Public Prosecutor, and the People's Court, that the necessary preparations could be completed by early May. The trial, the Fuehrer was advised, would make it possible to:

- demonstrate to the European public, by way of the example of France, the general war guilt of World Jewry;
- demonstrate the interlocking relationship between Jewish circles in Paris and the warmongers in London and New York, including the "direct relationship of the murderer to those close to Roosevelt and Eden";
- counter the effects of Riom by raising the charges not brought up there and thereby to score some propaganda points in France; and
- neutralize foreign compassion for Jews by suitably related propaganda efforts.

Hitler was assured that steps had been taken not to repeat the errors of the Reichstag fire trial. Finally, Hitler's approval was once again requested for the trial to take place, beginning on May 11, 1942.

The "Fuehrer Information" is of interest not so much by what it reveals but by what it fails to discuss, that is, Freisler's startling news of January 22 regarding the alleged homosexual relationship and the possibility that Grynszpan might challenge the legality of his extradition to Germany. If solely dependent on the Ministry of Propaganda's "Information," Hitler would have been unaware of key developments before making his decision. (However, it has been established that Hitler *was* cognizant of Grynszpan's claim all along, having been advised of the results of the Gestapo interrogation already in the fall of 1941.)

Having gotten off the "Fuehrer Information," Diewerge convened a meeting on March 27 with representatives from the Foreign Ministry, the Office of the Chief Prosecutor, and the People's Court (but pointedly excluding the Ministry of Justice) to take up a number of specific problems. All present were anxious to start as soon as possible. The representative from the Office of the Chief Prosecutor announced that there was every indication Grynszpan would argue his extradition to Germany had been illegal and that his was not a political assassination but rather the result of a homosexual relationship with the victim. The Ministry of Propaganda was reminded in this connection that at the meeting of January 22, a promise had been made that Goebbels would obtain Hitler's personal approval to go ahead in spite of this possibility, but nothing had been received to date. Once again an early response was promised.[12]

Shortly after the March 27 meeting, Goebbels met with the Fuehrer, and on April 1, he had word from Hitler's Headquarters that there was no objection to the conduct of the trial as planned. On April 2 he confided to his diary that the Fuehrer had accepted his recommendation to begin the Grynszpan trial on May 10, but the entry does not reveal to what extent the probable defense was discussed.

Goebbels did, however, record with unrestrained glee that at his suggestion, Hitler had agreed to transfer the judicial supervision of the trial from the Ministry of Justice to President Thierack of the People's Court. The way Goebbels saw it, Hitler did not believe that the ministry, and especially State Secretary Freisler, had the necessary "political finesse" to deal with such difficult matters. Hitler, continued the same entry, also transferred responsibility for the "political supervision" of the trial from the Ministry of Justice to Goebbels personally.

Goebbels went on to comment that Hitler more and more frequently seemed to transfer responsibility to him whenever he did not completely trust the regularly responsible authorities. "That of course results in a tremendous increase of work for me, but on the other hand I then have the assurance that things will be dealt with and arranged psychologically correctly, and thereby achieve positive political effects. This is the deciding factor in this third year of the war, especially in the Grynszpan trial which of course is less a judicial than a political matter." To that end, Goebbels was determined that "the testimony of Bonnet, which will attribute the war guilt primarily to the Jews, is prepared correctly so that we can expect from it a great boost for our war effort."

While Goebbels' influence with Hitler was considerable, some of his diary entries must be treated with a certain skepticism. For example, while Freisler may have been judged as lacking in "finesse," Hitler later named him to replace Thierack as president of the People's Court, a position that Goebbels had described as being of great importance. There, Freisler quickly established himself as a ruthless and depraved individual. His "performance" as president of the People's Court trying the conspirators who attempted to kill Hitler on July 20, 1944—as preserved on film—is a chilling and horrifying spectacle. Freisler died in February 1945 in his courtroom during a bombing raid on Berlin.

In any event, Goebbels evidently lost no time in passing on the details of his "triumph" to the Ministry of Justice, for on April 3 he noted that they were extremely surprised and offended to learn that President Thierack, instead of State Secretary Freisler, was to be responsible for the judicial conduct of the trial. According to this diary entry, a protest directly to Hitler by Acting Minister of Justice Schlegelberger, was of no avail and Goebbels expressed his regret that neither Schlegelberger nor Freisler resigned in the face of this obvious slight. But still, it was gratifying to be now "in charge of the political side of the trial with Thierack responsible for the legal side."

On the morning of April 2, Thierack learned that the Fuehrer had designated him as the person responsible for the Grynszpan trial, not in writing from the Fuehrer's Headquarters, but verbally through the Propaganda Ministry. It was not exactly what the president of the People's Court had in mind. He wanted it in black and white.

Later that day, Thierack participated in the meeting at the Ministry of Propaganda called by Goebbels on receipt of Hitler's authorization to "guide" the trial.[13] Under the chairmanship of Propaganda's Gutterer, the group consisting of Vice President Engert of the People's Court, Grimm and Diewerge were designated a "steering committee" to which Goebbels would look for the "management" of the trial. Thierack agreed to undertake any measures necessary to safeguard the trial, subject, of course, to receipt of the Fuehrer's mandate. Without it, the president of the People's Court pointed out, he was unable to issue instructions to the Office of the Chief Prosecutor or the Justice authorities. Gutterer promised to obtain a decision later that day.

Thierack then brought up some subjects for discussion, including the question of the alleged homosexual relations between vom Rath and Grynszpan. The previous day, Grimm and Diewerge had learned to their chagrin that a reference to the alleged homosexual relations between vom Rath and Grynszpan had been incorporated in the indictment prepared by the Office of the Chief Prosecutor. A copy of the document having been delivered to the defendant, a change of the indictment was no longer possible. He would have no difficulty in bringing up the subject. (Reporting to Goebbels, Diewerge noted that "since there can be no suspicion of sabotage, given the responsible individuals involved, it can only be attributed to an absolute lack of sensibility.")

Diewerge launched into a detailed report on the subject, which included some well chosen words for the Ministry of Justice, and then argued that the problem could be handled in the courtroom in one of several ways. One could pass over it in silence or, if raised, describe it as a typical Jewish infamy. It was finally agreed to postpone a decision until a later date.

Also discussed was the potentially embarrassing problem of what to tell the public about Grynszpan's (illegal) extradition by the French authorities. The Foreign Ministry was asked to make that decision. The meeting closed with an agreement for the "steering committee" to reconvene for further discussions five days later, on April 7, in Thierack's office.

Gutterer passed on Thierack's concerns to Reich Minister and Chief of Hitler's Chancery Hans Lammers, requesting the written mandate for Thierack. Since it called for action by Hitler, it can be assumed that Goebbels was aware of the move.

Lammers wrote back to Thierack the following day that the Ministry of Propaganda had been in touch regarding the mandate. In the absence of orders from Hitler and since he (Lammers) was not physically located at Hitler's (Eastern Front) Headquarters, he told Thierack that he had passed on the request by wire with a suggested text of the authorizing statement. In response, word had been passed back from Hitler that he wanted to discuss the matter (with Lammers) within the next few days, before actually putting it to paper. According to Hitler, so Lammers reported, the matter was not so urgent that it had to be dealt with immediately.[14]

Thierack, anxious not to give Hitler the impression that he was pushing too hard, on April 4 thanked Lammers for his help, but pointed out that he had merely asked Gutterer for a copy of Hitler's "Notification" to the Ministry of Propaganda; it was needed in the event it should be necessary to give orders in regard to the trial. (If Thierack knew that there existed no such "Notification," he certainly did not let on.) He did not, he assured Lammers, mean to demand from the Fuehrer a special written authorization for himself. Thierack assured Lammers that while the Ministry of Propaganda was anxious to proceed with the meeting of the "steering committee" on April 7, he would await new instructions before taking any further actions and would request the same of the Ministry of Propaganda. He did, however, caution Lammers that under the circumstances it was doubtful that the trial could start on May 11 as planned.[15]

Diewerge, for his part, continued to move forward at full speed. In a memorandum to Gutterer, he listed some of the many administrative problems which needed to be addressed. They ranged from budget matters and the printing of the brochure which the Ministry had promised Hitler to probably the most vexing problem of all—the need to requisition a vehicle and obtain an increase in the gas allotment. Goebbels, considering himself empowered with Hitler's "authorization," lost no time in taking the initiative. As a start, he convened a group of individuals, including President Thierack of the People's Court, "in order to follow the trial in the background and to direct it correctly."[16]

18

The Trial

With trial preparations seemingly wrested from the Ministry of Justice, the "victors" in this internal power struggle intensified efforts to put their indelible imprint on the planned extravaganza. On April 7 Thierack convened a meeting of the "steering committee" to which he invited members of his own People's Court, the Ministry of Propaganda, and the Foreign Ministry, including Grimm and the cultural attaché of the embassy in Paris.[1]

It was a significant meeting on two accounts. Once again, no one from the Ministry of Justice participated, demonstrating graphically its complete exclusion. Furthermore, the group prepared a preliminary trial timetable, determining its course by deciding on the witnesses to be called, the time they were to spend on the stand, and the primary focus of their testimony.

Thierack began the session by asking the Foreign Ministry representatives to determine on what charge the French government had extradited Grynszpan, and especially whether it was solely for murder or with additional preparation of high treason. As Thierack explained, if the French extradited Herschel for murder, it would be impossible to enter into a discussion of high treason in the court's verdict—a potentially embarrassing situation when one considered that the German indictment was based on the charge of high treason. After all, it had earlier been agreed that high treason was the only crime for which

Herschel could legally be tried before a German court, but apparently the rules had been changed in the meantime. What was worse, if the extradition had been for murder, then it would be imperative to avoid in the verdict the connotation of a "political murder," since the French traditionally did not extradite persons charged with such crimes. And yet, all these motions were necessary in order to have a political trial for a political murderer. Treating it like just another criminal trial presumably would have made it impossible to include a detailed discussion about World Jewry and its "crimes" in the verdict although these issues could, of course, be addressed during the trial. But that would not provide the Ministry of Propaganda with a verdict to serve as the basis for a major propaganda campaign. It was all very frustrating.[2]

The schedule called for a seven-day trial, of which Diewerge said: "The external conduct of the trial has been reduced to the shortest possible period necessary for the presentation of the material in accordance with our wishes." The participants quickly agreed that Vice President Engert of the People's Court would preside over the trial, with Chief Prosecutor Lautz and *Reichsanwalt* (Public Prosecutor) Kuenne representing the State. (Engert certainly could be counted on to guide the trial in an acceptable manner. Personally acquainted with Hitler since 1920 and a party member since 1921, Engert had created a stir in 1924 when, as a local judge in Bavaria, he had collected over 700 signatures calling for Hitler's release from prison to which he had been sentenced as a result of the 1923 "putsch".)

DAY ONE

The first day was to be devoted to establishing the facts concerning the assassination. To that end, the trial was to begin with a general interrogation of the defendant. Thierack noted that Herschel Grynszpan had repeatedly declared he would refuse to testify. In that case, the group agreed, the interrogation of witnesses would begin immediately.

1. *Officer Autret.* The French policeman had been stationed in front of the embassy and had shown Grynszpan the entrance. After the shooting, Grynszpan had been turned over to him and had made to him his first comments about his motives.

2. *Embassy Clerk Nagorka.* He had taken Grynszpan to vom Rath's office and had turned him over to Autret after the shooting.

3. *Embassy Clerk Krueger,* who participated in the apprehension of

Grynszpan and who, more than a month later, reported that he had heard the youth say, "hopefully he is dead."

4. *Counselor of Legation Achenbach*, to whom the wounded vom Rath spoke about the shooting.

5. *M. and Mme Carpe*, who had sold the gun, were to testify concerning Grynszpan's demeanor while buying the murder weapon. However, the Carpes' appearance was uncertain, since it was not known whether they were Jewish and, for that matter, whether they were available to testify since they apparently had fled into unoccupied France. The Foreign Ministry's Kruemmer promised to make the necessary inquiries. In the event the Carpes were not available, their testimony would be replaced by reading the initial protocol of interrogation.

6. *Dr. med. SS-Sturmbannfuehrer Brandt* was to testify next. He was considered an important witness since, according to Diewerge, it had made a great impression abroad when Hitler had sent his personal physician to Paris. Furthermore, Brandt could, on the basis of the wounds, demonstrate that the victim had been shot in the back.

7. *Police Commissioners Dufailly* and *Badin* were then expected to testify about the constantly changing testimony of the defendant regarding his motive.

8. *Examining Magistrate Tesnière* was characterized by Grimm as one of the most important witnesses in view of his association with the case virtually from the start.

9. *A waiter or chambermaid* from the Hotel de Suez, where Grynszpan had stayed the night before the shooting, was expected to testify concerning the demeanor of the defendant.

10. *Dr. Genil-Perrin*, or another French member of the medical panel, was then to discuss the defendant's mental state. (According to Dr. Mueller-Hess, the German psychiatrist who was to testify on Day 4, his French colleagues had come to the conclusion that while Grynszpan "made a youthful impression, he was fully responsible for his actions.")

11. *Police Commissioner Valentini* was considered a potential witness, but Grimm cautioned that he might be "unreliable." (Valentini had been responsible for investigating whether the assassination had been part of a conspiracy and apparently had come to the conclusion that Herschel Grynszpan had acted on his own; testimony to that effect would, of course, undermine the aims of the show trial.) Instead, Grimm suggested the appearance of the French blood donor *Thomas*. It is not clear what kind of testimony Grimm expected him to give.

12. At this point, the schedule provided tentatively for the testimony by *Gestapo officials Jagusch and Boemelburg.* It was during interrogations by the Gestapo's Jagusch in Berlin that Herschel apparently claimed having had a homosexual relationship with vom Rath. Jagusch included the information in his final report which went to Hitler and also formed the basis of the subsequent indictment. Boemelburg would have been in a position to provide answers in the event the question of Herschel's extradition from France had been raised.

The final item on the agenda on this first day was to be a "reading of the defendant's correspondence with his family shortly *before* the act." [italics by Diewerge]. Grynszpan had received a second card from his sister, dated November 7, after his arrest. It described in graphic detail the harrowing experiences of the Grynszpan family during their expulsion to Poland, such as the fact that they had been taken to an open field and then "chased through woods and fields." It clearly was not in the interest of successful propaganda to give further publicity to this matter.

DAY TWO

The second day of the trial was to be devoted to an examination of "the motives of the murderer and the personality of vom Rath."

1. The Ministry of Propaganda promised to identify *two Red Cross nurses* who would testify about the "correct treatment" accorded the Polish Jews in general, and the Grynszpan family, during the deportation from Hanover during the night of October 28, 1938.

2. The next three witnesses were to be *Mlle Taulin*, vom Rath's language teacher, *Mme Simone Blanche*, and (French) prisoner of war *Andreas Malavoix*, all personal acquaintances of vom Rath who were expected to testify about his exemplary character.

3. They were to be followed by *Minister Schleier* who, in his capacity as *Landesgruppenleiter* (top Nazi party official in France), was described as being best qualified to discuss vom Rath's personality. (Presumably having a top party official discuss the victim was expected to counteract rumors of vom Rath's weakening ties with the party.)

4. *Gustav vom Rath*, the father of the victim, was expected to be the last character witness (to be followed by):

5. *Gauleiter Bohle*, head of the NSDAP's Foreign Organization, regarding "vicious Jewish rumors and persecutions to which Germans abroad were being subjected as a result of Jewish hate campaigns."

The text of Bohle's proposed testimony was submitted to the Ministry of Propaganda for its files. It is completely devoid of any facts having any bearing on the case on trial, and consists largely of a litany of horror stories describing the persecution of Germans around the globe (not necessarily by Jews), in countries such as the Netherlands, South Africa, Spain, and Switzerland.

Diewerge was not alone in recording the decisions of the meeting. The Foreign Ministry's Kruemmer also prepared a "schedule" for his files, and for the most part it was similar to that of his Propaganda Ministry colleague. However, at this point the first substantive differences appear. In addition to the witnesses listed by Diewerge, Kruemmer foresaw for the second day also testimony by a Foreign Ministry representative regarding German-Polish negotiations, designed to show "how the Polish government at that time actually treated the Jewish question." Perhaps more significantly, after the name of vom Rath's father, Minister Kruemmer had noted "If he is prepared [to testify]."

DAY THREE

On the third day, the trial was expected to examine the "political background of the act" with the aid of the testimony of "expert witnesses." It was to be the heart of this political trial, since the physical facts surrounding the shooting were largely uncontested.

1. The primary witness was to be *Professor Dr. Grimm*, charged with discussing his participation in Jewish trials, his experiences in the formulation of German-French relations, Jewish efforts to disrupt the Ribbentrop visit and the attitude of World Jewry at political trials. It was this testimony and that of Georges Bonnet the following day—"coordinated" by Grimm—which the Foreign Ministry hoped would prove that it was not Germany's policies and actions that had led to the outbreak of war.

After the war, Grimm would contend in his writings[3] and in letters to the author that his sole interest in the case was that of attorney for the plaintiff, that is, the vom Rath family. It is difficult to give any credence to this argument in view of Grimm's very active participation in the case, his projected testimony, and his preoccupation with having Georges Bonnet testify on the "Jewish conspiracy." Finally, of course, German judicial procedures make no provision for such a position. Grimm was fully aware of this when in April 1942 he asked Foreign Minister Ribbentrop that his "position in the German trial [be] clarified by means of an order from the Fuehrer, as in connection with the French trial."[4]

Whatever Grimm's position, thanks to meticulous planning, the projected testimony of this "expert" was preserved for posterity. At the request of Ribbentrop, Grimm in July 1942 submitted the "final draft," together with a request for an audience with the minister to discuss various aspects of the case.[5] This document provides a unique insight into the planned trial through the eyes of what was probably the most important and knowledgeable witness and one of its primary architects. Considering that Grimm at the time was working closely with both the Ministries of Foreign Affairs and Propaganda, and thus was undoubtedly familiar with their aims for the trial, the testimony sheds considerable light on its anticipated course and tone.

The testimony is divided into two parts. Part I entitled "The Assassination and the Proceedings in France" covers thirty-one typewritten double-spaced pages and twenty-seven specific subjects in the comprehensive index. Part II, "The Question of the Men Behind the Scene," covers the remaining 103 pages with fifty-one subjects.

Part I: The Assassination and the Proceedings in France

After a brief and essentially accurate description of the assassination, and despite the avowed purpose of this part of the testimony, the witness immediately planned to launch into the real purpose of the trial, the accomplishment of specific propaganda aims. The trial, it must be remembered, was to be conducted at a time when Germany sought to establish closer relations with the defeated France, while at the same time locked in a grim war with Great Britain and the United States. This probably explains why at the outset, the French were to be complimented on showing their moral character when revulsion swept France immediately after the murder, while "there was no lack of correspondence which glorified the act and the assassin. It, however, came almost exclusively from Anglo-Saxon nations, especially from America."[6]

The general tenor, if not the primary purpose, of the Grimm testimony was to become apparent within minutes after he took the stand. Arguing that both the defendant and his relatives had lied frequently during their interrogations, he volunteered the information that these lies were "extraordinary examples of the result of the Talmud teachings which allow Jews to lie to non-Jews and non-Jewish officials." Although the testimony specifically mentions only one such instance—in connection with Grynszpan's procurement of a French visa—the nature of these "lies" which so offended the witness can be discerned from the following: "These lies were not made solely for defense purposes, but also to carry on atrocity propaganda against Germany. After one enjoyed in Germany all the advantages of a humane treatment, Germany was slandered in this most shameless manner."

Early in his testimony, Grimm planned to utilize a device he was to use repeatedly, namely, the inclusion of many prominent names with little or no connection to the case. An example is a reference to Sir Stafford Cripps, a British Labor Party leader, which reads as follows *in its entirety*: "In the Grynszpan files of Soffer one has for instance found among the addressees with whom he was in touch the name Sir Stafford Cripps under the following notation: Sir Stafford Cripps, former Minister of Justice, Attorney General." No correspondence, no other reference to any connection with the case. Later mention of Paul Reynaud and Paul Boncour, both former French ministers who had refused to cooperate with the Nazis, are of an almost identical nature.

Part I of the testimony repeatedly strays from its avowed purpose in other ways as well. It concentrates chiefly on the defendant's personality and on his family and seeks to discredit both Grynszpan's French defense staff and those who sympathized with him. It was evidently designed to provide a backdrop for what was to follow.

Part II: The Question of the Men Behind the Scene

There is no clear organization of material throughout this longer and obviously more important section of the proposed testimony. Grimm's opening lines of Part II shed light on the trial's theatrical quality. "I have in the course of this trial frequently asked myself the question whether Grynszpan carried out the act on his own initiative, or if there are hidden individuals who have utilized him for their political purposes." Just a few pages after this thoughtful interlude, Grimm answers this question to his own complete satisfaction.

> I am . . . convinced that behind this assassination stand the higher powers of International Jewry and bolshevism and I base this belief on the experiences which I gathered in France as the attorney for the plaintiff, on the basis of the files confiscated in Paris, as well as on comparisons with

> other trials of a similar nature which were utilized by International Jewry as propaganda weapons against Germany and the National Socialist movement.

Thus convinced, Grimm set out to also convince his audience by expounding a line of reasoning which runs through the entire document and which for that reason must be presumed to have been contemplated as the primary trial argument. It is that the undefined and utterly mysterious factor called "World Jewry," or "International Jewry" stood behind Grynszpan when he first fired the lethal shots and that this "group" must be considered as guilty as the assassin himself for its part in the "plot" against Nazi Germany.

Grimm argued that World Jewry was violently opposed to the German regime and was prepared to resort to "atrocity propaganda" to further its goal, the destruction of the Third Reich. He accused the "Jewish press" and Jewish organizations—the chief target was the LICA, by virtue of having had among its honorary members such notables as Mayor LaGuardia, Eduard Benesh, Edouard Herriot, Pierre Cot, and Paul Boncour—of stirring up hatred against Germany, and charged that their glorification of any acts harmful to the Nazi government was bound to provoke further violent acts.

Had Grimm been content with this line of reasoning, his argument would not have been entirely unreasonable. The glorification of an act of violence might indeed provoke further acts of a similar nature, although certainly no newspaper or organization was needed to fan the flames of hatred against Germany among its victims, such as Herschel Grynszpan.

Yet for a successful propaganda trial, the mere assertion of guilt of some shapeless group was obviously inadequate. Specific "proof" was needed. It was Grimm's task to prove a direct relationship between the press and organizations on one hand and the murderer on the other. Since Grimm was to be the primary witness on this most important question of the "men behind Grynszpan," one must assume that he was in possession of all available evidence. Essentially, his arguments can be grouped into the following general categories:

- Reports of mysterious meetings with Russian agents, vague secret conspiracies against Germany, meetings and demonstrations by various groups protesting German actions, and so on. References to these had been found in various newspapers of the period prior to the shooting and in letters addressed to French authorities and found in the confiscated files. Although Grimm at no time either states that Herschel Grynszpan was involved or that he ever attended even one of these meetings, the implication is there.

- Attacking individuals and organizations, such as the LICA, which took Grynszpan's part *after* the assassination, and in some instances used the case for what the witness called "atrocity" propaganda against Germany. Especially sinister and suspicious in the eyes of Grimm was the interest by U.S. organizations such as the Journalists' Defense Fund, the World Jewish Congress, the Society of Friends (Quakers), Jehovah's Witnesses, and various individuals like the Mayor of New York. Grimm darkly hinted that this sort of sympathy could only be the result of advance planning and connivance on their part.
- Grynszpan must have been linked to one or another of the many anti-German organizations in France. Grimm was especially suspicious in this connection because a leading LICA official some time after the assassination had indicated that the youth had *not* been a member of the organization. The witness reasoned that there was no need for the organization to defend itself unless it had something to hide, and so "he who excuses himself, accuses himself." The fact that no tangible evidence of membership was found did not deter Grimm:

> One has . . . not found with LICA [or evidently any other organization] a trace of membership of Frankfurter or Grynszpan or of their families. It was [sic] easy for the LICA to remove such evidence, because, in violation of French laws, it did not maintain a permanent register but a collection of membership cards which could easily be removed.

- Grimm sought to cast doubts on Herschel Grynszpan's pretrial testimony, arguing that if the youth was lying, he must be covering up some other facts, namely those Grimm wanted to prove. There were indeed a number of discrepancies in Grynszpan's testimony before the examining magistrate. However, one example of a "lie" which Grimm claimed to base on the French medical report was that contrary to Grynszpan's arguments, the postcard from his sister could *not* have been the cause for the assassination. After all, so argued Grimm, "other Jews at that time received similar news under similar circumstances without resorting to such an act."
- Finally, Grimm invoked one other argument to prove his point:

> My conviction that Grynszpan's act is not that of a single individual finally is based on the recognition of the similarity of the Frankfurter and Grynszpan cases, both of which I have experienced, as you know. The similarity of the assassination and the conduct of the assassin after the act is so striking that it can only be explained if one supposes that one and the same "manager" is behind both and has instructed the culprit(s) in all details before the assassinations. One cannot at-

tribute this completely to the defense strategy, since the similarity of conduct exists during the assassination and in the first moments of the investigation, when the culprits were without any defense.

Little is accomplished by taking issue with Grimm's remarks, but since he indicated that the above argument provided "the best proof that both Frankfurter and Grynszpan had others behind them," it is necessary to examine it to determine the reliability of this key witness and his testimony.

The similarities listed by Grimm consist mainly of the facts that both killed their victims in their offices, readily turned themselves over to the police after the assassination, admitted without remorse that they killed their victims, wrote postcards to their relatives before committing the crime, and that both had relatives in Germany. In examining this reasoning somewhat more closely, it is fortunate to have on hand information about the Gustloff case which Grimm would consider reliable, that is, the text of his speech before the court at Chur trying David Frankfurter.[7]

When it comes to seeking the victim at the office, in Chur Grimm stated that "he [Frankfurter] assures himself that the victim is home" and "already on entering the apartment, he was composed enough." In actual fact, Frankfurter was shown by Mrs. Gustloff into her husband's office, which happened to be in his home. If Grynszpan had shot vom Rath in the latter's home, there would have been a similarity there as well.

Of greater consequence is Grimm's contention that both assassins readily turned themselves in to the police and thereby gave the signal for an extensive propaganda campaign against the Third Reich. In 1936, Grimm described the event as follows:

> The first thought of Frankfurter was to flee. He threatens all he meets with the pistol. . . . The path to the road appears too dangerous to Frankfurter. For that reason he runs to the rear into the park. Then he recognizes that escape is impossible in the snow-covered park. He says to himself: It is best to call the police whom he cannot escape anyhow and this at the same time affords protection against the enraged populace. With the same coldness which marked the act, he now thinks of his defense. Turning oneself in and admitting the act are extenuating circumstances.

In the course of the Grynszpan trial, Grimm planned to testify that "already in the course of the Frankfurter trial I had the impression that the young straying Jewish student could not have committed the crime on his own initiative, but that certain powers of International Jewry must be behind him." While Grimm vaguely implied that someone might have been behind Frankfurter, he specifically said at the time that "at the end of December around Christmas, when Christendom celebrates the festival of love and peace, he [Frankfurter] made the decision to kill and then let [the plan] slowly ripen to fruition."

It is probably not necessary to mention that Grimm's suspicions were especially aroused by both Frankfurter and Grynszpan having (or previously having had) relatives in Germany who were able to sample some of the German "humane treatment."

So much for Grimm's "best proof" that there existed a conspiracy. Yet while there is no evidence that the Gustloff assassination in any way influenced Herschel Grynszpan, he almost certainly knew about it, which might explain some of the superficial analogies between the two crimes.

Toward the end of his lengthy testimony designed to prove that sinister forces were lurking behind Grynszpan, Grimm planned to inform his audience that it was "of course not possible to prove any direct connection between the murderer and the Jewish organizations which later utilized the case so well." He expected to explain this strange fact in the following manner:

> When a man like Abraham Lecache or Zerapha or Jarblum [leading officials of anti-Nazi organizations and newspapers] actually orders a political murder, they take every precaution that no link is discovered between them and the murderer. Then matters are arranged so that either the murderer himself does not even know the men actually behind the matter, or there is every assurance that the murderer keeps quiet and the wire-pullers remain in the background.

And thus Grimm approached the end of his testimony. As far as he, and most probably the court were concerned, World Jewry (in the form of some prominent, though anonymous, Jewish leaders) had been exposed as the real culprits. All that remained for Grimm was to justify the trial by setting it in its "proper" perspective. This he did by closing as follows: "On November 7, 1938 . . . there fell in Paris in the modest office of Ernst vom Rath the first shot of the Jewish War."

As late as March 1950, Grimm would maintain in a letter to the author that the "shot of Paris" was to World War II what the "shot of Sarajevo" had been to World War I.

2. *Professor Kittel*, professor of theology at the University of Tübingen and a well-known anti-Semite, as the second "expert witness," was to follow Grimm and discuss the importance of the defendant's attendance of the "Talmud school" in Frankfurt and the goals of this teaching.

3. The day's final witness was to be *Professor Schoenemann*, a professor of English, on the influence of Jews in America and their attitude in favor of the defendant.

DAY FOUR

This was to be yet another day devoted to the examination of the "Political Background of the Shooting."

1. *Ministerial Counselor Diewerge* was to lead off the day's testimony, discussing the "systematic hate campaigns by World Jewry," the "lessons learned" in the course of trials of Jews, and materials found in Paris. It was Diewerge's contention that documents located during these searches "proved" that concerted efforts were planned to sabotage the visit of Foreign Minister Ribbentrop to Paris through demonstrations, press campaigns, personal attacks, and so on, and that Grynszpan was part of that effort. (As indicated previously, Grimm admitted that no such evidence was found.)

Diewerge planned to testify that when President Lecache of the Jewish League had to admit that the hate campaign would not lead to the desired results, he ordered the assassination, thinking that the "sensitive" Ribbentrop would in that case not come to Paris. The *sole* evidence Diewerge cited to support this scenario was that Lecache and Grynszpan had been neighbors.

The notes of Diewerge and Kruemmer regarding the former's testimony reflect some minor, though interesting, differences. While Diewerge planned to confine himself to generalities, the Foreign Ministry representative expected him to speak "about the preparations of World Jewry for a war against Germany, especially through Grynszpan's action." This was yet another example of the Foreign Ministry's preoccupation with using the trial as a means of fixing the war guilt on someone.

2. Next on the schedule was former French *Foreign Minister Georges Bonnet*, a witness of whom the experts from both Propaganda and For-

eign Affairs expected much. However, his testimony was viewed with some suspicion and reservation by representatives of the People's Court, who normally did not have to deal with witnesses over whom they had so little control.

According to Diewerge's memorandum, the main thrust of Bonnet's testimony was to deal with Jewish pressure on the French government to prevent an understanding with Germany. For Grimm, the theme of Bonnet's testimony was "the Jewish attack on the peace," with the witness expected to identify November 7, 1938, as the day World Jewry succeeded in destroying the policy of peace once and for all.

Grimm advised his colleagues that he and Bonnet planned to read their own testimony. Grimm specifically agreed to accept responsibility for Bonnet's testimony which was to be prepared in advance "to the nth degree." It was not for nothing, Grimm argued, that he had been charged with trial preparations by both the Ministries of Propaganda and Foreign Affairs. Diewerge supported Grimm's argument, confirming that Bonnet had agreed to limit his trial testimony to what had been agreed to in advance between himself and Grimm. Both Grimm and Diewerge obviously were anxious that their star witness be heard.

The arguments apparently convinced Thierack, at least partially, and he interposed no further objections to the appearance of Bonnet. However, still fearing that Bonnet might "deviate" in some way from his prepared statement, Thierack stressed the importance of selecting an interpreter who would be able not only to follow Bonnet, "but would also be capable of possibly circumventing on his own initiative difficult situations which might arise."[8]

3. *Professor Dr. Mueller-Hess*, director of the Institute for Criminal and Social Medicine of the University of Berlin, was then to comment on the accountability of the defendant.

In affidavits provided the author in 1947, Dr. Mueller-Hess and two associates stated that on October 15, 1941, he had been asked to examine Herschel Grynszpan and that he rendered a preliminary opinion on February 6, 1942. According to his recollection and that of his two assistants (the files had reportedly been destroyed through war actions), after extensive examinations he and his associate, Dr. Gerhard Rommeney, had come to the conclusion that Grynszpan,

> while not too well developed physically, was mentally very alert and gave no indication of a mental illness or mental deficiency. In fact one had to classify him as an individual with above-average intelligence in

> spite of his limited public school education. His judgment and ability for critical analysis, as well as his life experiences, were far above the average. As a result of these examination results, which coincided with those of the French doctors, I came to the conclusion that he was fully responsible for his actions.[9]

Dr. Mueller-Hess described this as a preliminary opinion since the youth had, during his German examination, attributed the murder of vom Rath to his homosexual relationship with the victim—an entirely different motive than that given his French examiners. As a result, Dr. Mueller-Hess wanted to await the testimony of French officials and doctors before rendering a final decision.

4. Although President Thierack had some reservations, it was agreed that the last witness of the day was to be a cell mate of the defendant. He was expected to testify concerning some of Herschel's statements in the course of his imprisonment regarding the motives behind the shooting. Grynszpan's remarks to his fellow prisoner, a police informer, were collected in the so-called *Grüne Hefte* (Green Pamphlets). In order to safeguard their secrecy, so that Grynszpan would not learn of their existence until the trial, they were kept under the personal control of President Thierack of the People's Court.[10]

DAY FIVE

This day too was to be devoted to "Further Political Background of the Shooting" with emphasis on "confiscated documents, articles and newspapers which prove the intellectual origin of the shooting in World Jewry." Grimm was designated to make a comprehensive statement about these documents. (The documents would later be made public in German as *Denkschrift* and published in French, under Grimm's pseudonym Pierre Dumoulin, as *L'Affaire Grynspan*.)

DAY SIX

"Final Arguments" were the order of this day.

Chief Prosecutor *Lautz* was expected to discuss political aspects of the indictment, while Prosecutor *Kuenne* was to take up the legal aspects.

Finally, the court-appointed defense attorney, *Dr. Weimann*, was to make his plea on behalf of the defendant. The minutes reveal agreement by the participants that Grynszpan's defense lawyer "will be instructed by Thierack in the appropriate manner regarding his duties in the course of the trial." Diewerge wanted to know what sort of individual would be designated to defend the young assassin. President Thierack noted that "the defense attorney also [like Bonnet's interpreter] would need to possess special qualifications, and above all should not be a young "gung ho" individual. . . ." Grimm volunteered to speak with the defense attorney "as a colleague."

They need not have worried. Weimann could be depended on not to disrupt a well-planned scenario. While he did not get to make an appearance on behalf of Herschel Grynszpan, two years later he was the court-appointed defense attorney for Carl Goerdeler, one of the leaders of the unsuccessful coup against Hitler on July 20, 1944. This is the sort of "defense" Grynszpan could have expected: "His official defense attorney [Weimann], whom [Goerdeler] met only once, on the evening before the trial for 45 minutes, left him completely in the lurch, and in fact accused him himself."[11]

DAY SEVEN

President *Engert* on this day was expected to pronounce the "Judgment and Explanation."

There are several points in the trial schedule that deserve closer attention. According to this timetable, if Grynszpan refused to be questioned at the very beginning of the trial, only a part of Day 6 would be taken up on his behalf by the court-appointed "defense" lawyer. Even if Grynszpan had been prepared to testify on Day 1, he probably would not have been expected or permitted to remain on the stand for long, since no fewer than fifteen other witnesses were expected to be called on the same day.

It is also interesting to speculate about potential witnesses who were *not* to be called. Thus, it was finally decided not to call the man who could have discussed most authoritatively the question of accomplices, Police Commissioner Valentini, who was responsible for the investigation of coconspirators. Instead those present would be treated to the more original arguments on the subject by Grimm.

Also not scheduled to testify was Mme Mathis, the wife of the concierge. This was certainly no oversight, for she was the only non-German to whom Grynszpan spoke after entering the embassy, telling her before the shooting whom he wanted to see. In order to buttress Grimm's argument that the shot of Paris was to World War II what the shot of Sarajevo had been to World War I (and thus to free the Third Reich from any responsibility for the war which had been unleashed), the Foreign Ministry hoped to argue—ostensibly on the basis of pre-trial depositions by Bonnet and Welczeck—that the youthful defendant, on entering the embassy, had requested to see the ambassador but was instead shown to the office of vom Rath.[12] A few years after the war, Grimm repeated the argument that Welczeck had in fact been the intended victim.[13]

According to a deposition in 1964 by Georges Bonnet, the French foreign minister in 1938 received an extremely agitated Ambassador Welczeck at his request a few hours after the shooting. The ambassador reported that on leaving the embassy he heard a young man at the door ask to speak to the ambassador, but seeing that the voice belonged to someone who could be taken care of by an assistant, he went on his way and on his return learned of what had transpired.

This version differs substantially from Welczeck's report of November 8 to the Foreign Ministry, wherein the ambassador had reported that on gaining entry to the embassy, Grynszpan had requested to see a "legation secretary." There is no mention of any kind of meeting between the assassin and the ambassador.[14]

Welczeck's story, as recounted by Bonnet, was almost certainly incorrect. Neither Mme Mathis, Officer Autret, nor the embassy staff whom Grynszpan encountered ever mentioned that the youth had asked for the ambassador. However, since neither contemporary reports of the shooting nor Welczeck's report to Berlin make any mention of the ambassador being present at the time of the shooting or being involved in assisting the wounded vom Rath, it is quite likely that the ambassador was not in the building at the time of the shooting. It is interesting to speculate why Welczeck did not wish the Foreign Ministry to know that he was not in the office at the time.

Had Welczeck been the intended victim, the assassination would, of course, have taken on considerably greater importance. Yet this version finds no support in the various contemporary reports. Diewerge in 1939 wrote in his *Anschlag gegen den Frieden* that Grynszpan entered the German embassy and asked to speak to "one of the higher officials," and even Grimm had written in 1940 that Grynszpan sought to give a document to one of the "embassy secretaries."[15] Furthermore, embassy clerk Nagorka, who actually showed Grynszpan the way within the embassy, in late 1946 confirmed to the author that the embassy's report was correct; Grynszpan had *not* asked for any specific individual. All efforts by Grimm and his colleagues now to claim that Grynszpan sought to kill the ambassador were bound to fail, for as the Foreign Ministry found out too late, even the indictment described the defendant as having asked to see a "higher official."

Other than Minister Schleier, the original schedule did not provide for either Ambassador Welczeck, or any of vom Rath's embassy colleagues who were present immediately after the shooting, to be called to the witness stand. Already in December 1939 Grimm had written Diewerge that there were some reservations on the part of embassy staff members Aechenbach and Auer about testifying on behalf of the victim at a future trial. However, Grimm indicated at the time that he had convinced Braeuer, the ambassador's deputy, that such testimony would be desirable to counteract foreign propaganda.[16]

In spite of Hitler's personal orders to proceed with the trial and elaborate preparations, such as the rebuilding of a courtroom to permit the accommodation of additional spectators, the setting up of a loudspeaker system, the erection of special telephone cells for the press, and the recruitment of appropriate interpreters, the matter did not progress as one might have expected.[17] The reason was the problems already raised during the meeting of January 22, that is, the possibility that Grynszpan might protest his illegal transfer to Germany and, more importantly, that he would testify that he killed vom Rath because the latter had made unnatural advances. The crime covered by Paragraph 175 of the German Criminal Code was to take on ever-increasing importance.

19

The Problem of Paragraph 175

Convinced, at least in his own mind, that he had finally excluded the Ministry of Justice from the forthcoming trial and that he and his like-minded allies were now in full control, Goebbels began to realize that perhaps a few problems still remained. He confided about one to his diary on April 5:

> I am having a great deal of work preparing the Grynszpan trial. The Ministry of Justice has deemed it proper to furnish the defendant, the Jew Grynszpan, the argument of Paragraph 175. Grynszpan has until now always claimed, and rightly so, that he had not even known the counselor of legation whom he shot. Now there is in evidence some sort of anonymous letter by a Jewish refugee which raises the possibility of homosexual relations between Grynszpan and vom Rath. It is an absurd, typically Jewish claim. The Ministry of Justice, however, did not hesitate to incorporate this claim in the indictment and to send the indictment to the defendant.
>
> This shows again how foolishly our legal experts have acted in this case, and how shortsighted it is to entrust any political matter whatsoever to the jurists.

Goebbels attributed the problem of Grynszpan's projected defense strategy solely to the phrasing of the indictment drawn up by Justice's inept officials. However, this was far from true. Grynszpan first revealed his intention to utilize this defense in mid-1941 during his interrogation by the Gestapo's Jagusch. Information to this effect was included in the RSHA's final report when the prisoner was turned over to the Ministry of Justice. It was on the basis of the RSHA pretrial report that Justice's Freisler informed his colleagues at the meeting of January 22 that there was a problem, whereupon the group agreed on the need to obtain Hitler's specific approval to proceed with the trial despite the possibility that Grynszpan might claim homosexual relations with his victim.

There is further evidence that Goebbels' version was motivated more by his thorough dislike of the Ministry of Justice than by facts. The inclusion of the homosexual angle was not due to some anonymous letter, as Goebbels had claimed. Dr. Mueller-Hess, the German psychiatrist due to be called as a witness in the trial, recalled in 1947 that he had been asked to examine Grynszpan on October 15, 1941, probably before a definite decision had been made to try the youth. In any event, the indictment was being drawn up at that time and could not have been available to the defendant. Dr. Mueller-Hess recalled that Grynszpan had told him:

> A man stopped [Grynszpan] on the street—either in front of a news stand or a public toilet—and had in the course of the conversation persuaded him to have homosexual relations. At the same time he gave his name and said that he was counselor of embassy [*sic*] at the German legation. Since the man promised to use his position to help [Grynszpan's] parents, he agreed and had relations with him on several occasions. How and in what manner this occurred I do not recall any more. Despite his pleas for positive action on behalf of his parents, Herr vom Rath repeatedly put him off. Infuriated by this, he committed the murder.[1]

Meanwhile it became known at Hitler's Headquarters that the Fuehrer had balked at formally transferring responsibility for the trial from the Ministry of Justice to the president of the People's Court. Probably in an effort to help things along, Grimm at this point asked Ribbentrop to arrange for an "audience" with Hitler to report on his work, as he had done in connection with the trial of David Frankfurter.[2] However, Grimm was out of his depth now and nothing came of this initiative.

Back in Berlin, everything seemed to proceed as planned, except for the mandate for Thierack. On April 11, Diewerge wrote to Goebbels that "in accordance with the Fuehrer's decision *as reported to me*, I have worked on the trial preparations, not with the Ministry of Justice, but with Dr. Thierack. The Foreign Ministry has followed suit" (emphasis added). He went on to say that if the dates for the trial ordered by the Fuehrer were to be met, Thierack's authorization would have to be announced quickly, since a number of steps could only be taken by the Ministry of Justice and the Office of the Chief Prosecutor. "I therefore urge that the Fuehrer Headquarters be advised of the urgency of the matter so that Minister Dr. Lammers can pass on the authorization to Dr. Thierack."[3]

Everyone involved in the trial preparations acted as if the transfer of power from the Ministry of Justice to the president of the People's Court were a "fait accompli"—everyone, that is, except Acting Minister of Justice Schlegelberger. He acted as if nothing had happened. On April 10 he wrote to Goebbels. It was a unique letter in many ways:

> Since the Fuehrer has ordered continuation of the criminal proceedings against Grynszpan and the trial is to begin on May 11, 1942, I would appreciate early confirmation that the Fuehrer, when he agreed to the trial before all the world, was aware that Grynszpan as part of his defense will allege homosexual relations with Counselor of Legation vom Rath.
>
> Permit me to refer in this connection to the meeting of 22 January 1942 with Dr. Freisler, attended by Ministerial Counsellor Diewerge, and the minutes thereof transmitted on 24 January.[4]

Knowing that the Ministry of Propaganda, in obtaining Hitler's agreement to hold the trial, had failed to make any formal reference to the homosexual aspect, Schlegelberger seemed to enjoy throwing down the gauntlet. It is unlikely that Schlegelberger on his own took up battle against the powerful Goebbels, but he must have had some strong allies in the highest echelons. In any event, the letter must have created more than a little consternation on the part of the Minister of Propaganda. (It is of course not beyond the realm of possibilities that the letter contributed to Schlegelberger's early retirement in August 1942, albeit with a sizable lump-sum payment. That, however, did not save him from being tried by the Nuremberg war crimes tribunal and sentenced to life imprisonment. He was pardoned in 1950.)

Diewerge advised Gutterer of Schlegelberger's letter on April 13, pointing out that in the recent past he had no longer worked with the Ministry of Justice but with Thierack, and requesting permission to disregard the acting minister's letter. Wiser heads prevailed and permission was refused. Instead, it was decided to try a new approach with a letter from Diewerge (on behalf of State Secretary Gutterer) to the liaison between the Ministry of Propaganda and the office of *Reichsleiter* Martin Bormann (chief of the Party Chancery and close confidant of the Fuehrer), seeking to enlist his help in obtaining Hitler's authorization to go ahead with the trial. In the letter Diewerge argued, in respect to Grynszpan's potentially damaging testimony, that internal press coverage of the trial would be well controlled and that the enemies of Germany would lie regardless of what was said in the courtroom. Under the circumstances, so reasoned the pragmatic Diewerge, Grynszpan's proposed testimony posed no problem.

All this must have started to affect Goebbels. He had expressed some doubts regarding the trial already in his diary entry of late January, when he considered holding part of the show behind closed doors. By April 14, he wrote:

> The Grynszpan trial is now supposed to start the middle of May. I still have to make some preparations for it. The preparations made on the part of [the Ministry of] Justice are in some respects psychologically not very clever. Thus, for instance, the problem of homosexuality, which is not under debate, has been drawn into the trial and the question of the evacuation of the Jews is also to be treated publicly. I consider this to be most clumsy. The enemy propaganda will immediately attach itself to these points and conceivably attempt to turn the trial against us. I will therefore see to it that these two aspects are not discussed in court. The remaining preparations are in accordance with my suggestions and will undoubtedly, if carried through, make the trial a complete success.

While Goebbels' rumination about the Ministry of Justice regarding the homosexual angle was old hat, all at once the "evacuation of Jews" was perceived as a problem. Up to that point, it had been planned to address this matter by calling various witnesses who could testify to the excellent treatment accorded the Polish Jews. However, by early 1942, the transports had taken on a much more sinister character (to the extermination camps) and Goebbels apparently decided that discussion of such transports would be counterproductive. Otherwise, however, everything was still on "go."

On the morning of April 16, the "steering committee" held another of its regular meetings under Thierack's chairmanship. One of the first items discussed concerned the foreign minister's request for certain changes in the trial schedule. Specifically, Kruemmer and Guenther had been instructed by Ribbentrop to insist that any testimony regarding vom Rath's personality had to come from a member of the Foreign Ministry. Furthermore, instead of having three days of the trial devoted to general descriptions of the political background of the shooting, they asked that one full day be devoted to a discussion of the opposition of World Jewry to Nazi party members abroad, and another to the immediate political background of the shooting "as conditioned by the political developments between Germany and France at that time."

In keeping with the ministry's aim to use the trial as a means of attributing the outbreak of the war to outside forces, they also suggested a number of specific changes of the subjects to be discussed by various witnesses. The most significant was the request that when discussing the immediate political reasons for the assassination, Grimm was to speak on "International Jewry as the saboteur of Franco-German understanding and the element primarily responsible for the outbreak of the war in September 1939."[5] Grimm was willing to go along with all changes, and indeed may have been instrumental in formulating them in the first place.

Thierack, in turn, pointed out to the assembled group, and specifically to the representatives of the Foreign Ministry, that the question concerning the crime for which Herschel Grynszpan had been extradited to Germany was taking on ever-increasing importance. In fact, it would not be possible to set a trial date as long as there was no official statement by the French government on the subject. Guenther and Kruemmer promised that they would give the matter their immediate attention and that it would be resolved in the very near future.

Once again, the group agreed on the need for some sort of formal statement from higher authority confirming that the trial preparations had been vested in the hands of President Thierack. The various ministries still only had Goebbels' word on the supposed transfer of responsibility, and in the absence of a formal edict, it was becoming increasingly difficult to answer correspondence from the Ministry of Justice, which continued to act as if nothing had happened.

Finally it was Diewerge's turn, and he surprised one and all with the announcement that for political-propagandistic reasons, Goebbels had decided that under no circumstances should there be any discussion at the trial of either the homosexual aspect or the transport of Polish Jews from Hanover. Furthermore, so announced Diewerge, the minister of propaganda planned to submit a new query to the Fuehrer whether to proceed with the trial in view of the danger that the defendant would testify about an alleged illicit relationship with vom Rath. This represented a complete turnabout by Goebbels within the past two days. Still anxious to proceed with the trial, those from the People's Court and the Foreign Ministry agreed.

Goebbels was briefed that afternoon on the results of the morning's meeting by Diewerge and the Foreign Ministry's Kruemmer. The minister of propaganda declared that he had the gravest doubts regarding the advisability of the trial. There was the danger, he confided to his callers, that the defendant would refuse to testify and limit himself to a short statement alleging homosexual relations with vom Rath. Such a statement would cause enormous reverberations throughout the world which would not be silenced by political, personal, and human arguments. Goebbels closed the session by announcing that he would ask Martin Bormann to convey these doubts to the Fuehrer.[6]

The formal, restrained memorandum by Minister Kruemmer, reporting on the meeting with Goebbels, does not reflect the utter chagrin which Kruemmer and Diewerge must have felt about this turn of events. Frustration is much more evident in Goebbels' diary entry of the following day, April 17. After restating his doubts about the proposed trial, the entry closed with: "That [Grynszpan's argument] is typically Jewish, a lie, dastardly and mean. . . . One can here once again recognize how perfidiously the Jews act if one goes after their neck."

The Foreign Ministry, in the meantime, pushed on with its preparations, anxious as ever to get on with the great show. By April 11, it had collected the current addresses of all German and French witnesses, initiated printing the French pamphlet about the case (the Dumoulin/Grimm book *L'Affaire Grynszpan*), and cancelled Grimm's projected lecture tour scheduled to begin May 11. The Paris embassy was advised that Grimm would come to Paris to meet with Bonnet between April 16 and 22 and to discuss propaganda aspects with the embassy from April 30 to May 2.

On April 14, the ministry informed the embassy that a number of well-known French journalists, authors, radio announcers and leading representatives of French public life would be invited to attend the Grynszpan trial. Primarily representatives of anti-Semitic organizations were expected, but hope was expressed that at least some others, including possibly a former French cabinet member and a leading jurist, could be induced to attend.[7] Within six days, the reply arrived, listing no fewer than thirty-two "suitable" candidates, including the former minister, Pierre Taittinger, and the author Céline.[8]

Then came the meeting of April 16 under Thierack's chairmanship. Knowing that the final decision to proceed with the trial would have to come from Hitler, and stirred to action by Goebbels' negative comments to Minister Kruemmer on the afternoon of April 16, the foreign minister on April 17 advised Bormann through his liaison at the Fuehrer Headquarters that he did not share the doubts expressed by Goebbels. The reply from Bormann was that "there is no question of dropping the Grynszpan case, but only of postponing it."

Despite Goebbels' pessimism towards a trial expressed on April 16, a last desperate effort to save the trial was made the following day. On April 17, a "Fuehrer Information" was submitted to Hitler, *Subject: Murder Trial Grynszpan: Information for the Fuehrer Concerning the Possibility that the Murderer will Allege Homosexual Relations with the Victim.*[9] The author of the document is not clear, although it probably was prepared within Hitler's Headquarters with the cooperation of those favoring a trial. The Ministry of Justice was not among them. The tone of the document was definitely slanted in favor of a trial, going so far as to identify possible negative propaganda results in the event the trial should be cancelled.

According to the document, the planned trial would "provide the opportunity not only to counter the effects of the trial at Riom, but beyond that to prove Jewish warmongering and war guilt." (The Riom trial had been suspended on April 4, 1942, never to be resurrected. It was, as far as the Germans were concerned, a great idea gone astray.) It further assured the Fuehrer that all precautions had been taken to counteract any negative testimony by Grynszpan and argued that the enemy, which must be aware of the forthcoming trial due to the involvement of the French witnesses, would undoubtedly capitalize on its cancellation.

The "Information" then posed the following questions:

1. Is the Fuehrer aware of the possibility of testimony [regarding homosexual relations] by the murderer?
2. Does the Fuehrer's decision of April 1, approving the initiation of the trial, stand?
3. Or should the trial materials remain unused in view of this Jewish lie?

Finally, the Fuehrer was reminded of the need to issue the necessary mandate for Thierack.

The document is unique for several reasons. First, it concerns itself exclusively with the alleged homosexual relationship and its effect on the trial, a subject which Goebbels tried to avoid putting to paper at all costs. Furthermore, it makes clear that Hitler made his initial decision to proceed with the trial of Herschel Grynszpan in the fall of 1941 after receipt of the RSHA/Gestapo report by Jagusch, which contained references to Grynszpan's allegations concerning his relationship with vom Rath. In other words, all those worries of the "steering group" had been for naught.

Within the ranks of the Ministry of Propaganda it was hoped that the Fuehrer Information would break the longstanding logjam. On April 18, one day after it was submitted, Diewerge informed his minister that the projected May 11 trial date was no longer feasible even though work had continued steadily in spite of doubts surrounding the proposed trial.

During this period of uncertainty, confusion continued to reign. The question of responsibility for the trial "direction" and supervision had still not been resolved. To compound the problem, Ambassador Abetz (evidently during a brief visit to Berlin) picked up the rumor that Grimm had been authorized to take over the "general guidance" of the case. He informed the Foreign Ministry and in turn was advised that:

> According to information which has to date not been confirmed in writing, the Fuehrer has made . . . Dr. Thierack responsible for the supervision of the Grynszpan trial. The Ministry of Justice, which normally would have this responsibility, to date obviously knows nothing of this change. President Thierack, Minister of Propaganda and we are of the opinion that the written authorization by the Fuehrer for President Thierack must be issued as soon as possible, since trial preparations cannot be continued until then. . . . Indicative in this connection is that the Ministry of Justice, namely State Secretary Freisler, in recent days has made written and verbal requests to the Foreign Ministry which are based on the assumption that the Ministry of Justice is the responsible authority.[10]

The communication went on to say that it had been possible to stall the Ministry of Justice temporarily with subterfuges, but that immediate action clearly was needed. For once taking cognizance of the doubts raised regarding the trial, the message cautioned that preparations should not progress so far that they become known publicly, which in case of cancellation would be extremely bad from a propaganda point of view.

Other difficulties were being encountered. Grimm brought back an unhappy report from his discussions in France. It seems that he encountered problems in regard to Bonnet's testimony, and it was difficult to get any statement out of him. The former French foreign minister had expressed grave doubts about the advisability of coming to Berlin, which, according to Grimm, was due to "the attitude of the United States and obviously the attempted intervention of the Chief Rabbi."[11]

Serious doubts about the advisability of a trial began to surface even within the Foreign Ministry, which had started to take a closer look at the indictment. According to Guenther, it "contained several points which from a propaganda viewpoint made their discussion in an open trial rather questionable." In other words, after all this time it had begun to dawn on Ministry officials that a discussion of alleged homosexual conduct between a diplomat and a Jewish refugee or the illegal extradition of the defendant might have negative effects. In a discussion with Prosecutor Kuenne, Guenther also pointed out that various points in the indictment were contrary to the testimony already submitted by witnesses. "This is especially detrimental to the argument that Grynszpan's action was an important cause for the outbreak of the Jewish war against Germany." The solution, according to Guenther, was to change the indictment (to fit the testimony). Guenther rejected Kuenne's reply that the indictment would not be read in court, fearing that someone in the course of the trial might bring up one or another of these points. The entire matter was left undecided, with Kuenne planning to check with his superior regarding the far-reaching request.[12]

The reply came from Chief Prosecutor Lautz the following day. He called Guenther at the Foreign Ministry to say that the request entailed numerous problems. After all, he explained, the initial indictment had already been delivered. Furthermore, it had been submitted to the minister of justice for prior approval, so that the Office of the Chief Prosecutor felt unable to make basic changes without his express consent. Guenther countered that the Ministry of Justice had been excluded from the case, to which Lautz replied that there was nothing official about the change. With the discussion getting nowhere, Guenther closed by saying that the Foreign Ministry reserved the right to return to this question "in a few days."

20

The End . . . ?

Time was beginning to run out on the trial to which the Ministries of Foreign Affairs and Propaganda had devoted great efforts and of which they promised themselves so much. Suddenly, there appeared two mysterious documents which were to prove even more disruptive than the Ministry of Justice.

As previously noted, the Office of the Chief Prosecutor, under the personal direction of Thierack, had been collecting Grynszpan's statements to his cellmate, a police informer, under the code name *Grüne Hefte*. By early May, after learning of their existence from Prosecutor Kuenne, Guenther first asked Engert, then Thierack, that the documents either be turned over to the Foreign Ministry for its perusal for two days, or that one of its representatives be permitted to inspect them. Thierack politely but firmly refused, saying that because of the need for absolute secrecy, the contents were known only to Engert, Prosecutor Lautz, and himself. (Thierack was in error, for the first word about these documents reached the Foreign Ministry through Prosecutor Kuenne, who gave every indication that he was familiar with their contents.) Thierack assured Guenther he did not doubt the Foreign Ministry's ability to maintain secrecy, but he did not wish to create even a theoretical possibility that Grynszpan would find out about their existence. The Ministry of Propaganda apparently was kept completely in the dark.

By this time, key officials of the People's Court and the Foreign Ministry were trying to cope with an even more explosive set of notes. The Foreign Ministry's Guenther first heard from Prosecutor Kuenne on April 29 that prison authorities had found concealed on Grynszpan's person a slip of paper written in Hebrew on which the youth admitted that his statements to the Gestapo regarding his relationship with vom Rath had been untrue. Even more startling was the prosecutor's report that Grynszpan, "chained and therefore unable to write himself" had, in addition, dictated several messages in cipher to a fellow prisoner.[1] (There is no indication what type of cipher Grynszpan utilized. However, it must have been one he was able to develop and keep in his head, such as a simple numerical code or one consisting of transposed letters, since his fellow prisoner obviously did not have the key.) Since the People's Court was not equipped to decode messages—presumably the reason why the Foreign Ministry was told of the coded notes—Guenther was given a copy for decoding. In view of these developments, the Foreign Ministry decided to refrain, for the time being, from further efforts to gain access to the *Grüne Hefte*.

On about May 8, the Foreign Ministry managed to decode the Grynszpan note and initiated some Byzantine maneuvering. It did not want it known by such "outsiders" as the prosecution, the court, or even their own man Grimm, that its code section was responsible for breaking the cipher, possibly in order to keep secret the existence of such a section in the ministry. It was therefore first suggested that the chief prosecutor be informed that the Army High Command (OKH) had succeeded in breaking the cipher at the request of the Foreign Ministry. However, the responsible officials decided instead to return the coded message to the chief prosecutor with the suggestion that he communicate directly with the OKH to have the message deciphered. In the meantime, the OKH would secretly be provided with the code and instructions how to handle this matter.[2]

It is not clear from available records just what subterfuge was eventually used, but when informing Ambassador Abetz of the contents of the Grynszpan message, Guenther advised him that to the outside, the Armed Forces High Command (OKW) was to be given credit for deciphering the following message, dictated over a period of six days.

4.24.42 I herewith declare that my second deposition which I gave to the Gestapo is untrue[.] the reasons for my false testimony are the following:

4.25.42 When France extradited me to Germany I thought that there would be no trial in that the Gestapo would murder me

4.26.42 This was naturally more to my liking than a grand propaganda trial whose results would be a death sentence and which undoubtedly would have resulted in bloody pogroms[.] time however proved the exact opposite[.] they did turn me over to the Gestapo as prisoner but they treated me exceptionally very well[.] as I heard there from other prisoners one is treated well by the Gestapo only if one has special plans for that person[.] in my case this could only be a propaganda trial[.] this I wanted to avoid in any event in order to prevent any possible pogroms which could result through my trial and so that I personally as a tool of German propaganda

4.27.42 would not be misused[.] in order to prevent this no means was good enough for me[.] I therefore utilized a touchy phase out of the life of Mr. vom Rath with which my attorney Godcheaux acquainted me and out of this made up false testimony to the Gestapo[.] I hoped that on the basis of this testimony they would murder me so that no outsider would get wind thereof (several days later I wrote a letter to the Gestapo in which I protested against my illegal extradition and therefore from now on will not testify during interrogations or the trial[.] I did this because I feared that I could contradict myself and would therefore nullify my statements which in any event are so implausible)

4.28.42 Shortly thereafter I received an order for protective custody and was sent to a concentration camp[.] here I was placed in a single cell and was treated quite well[.] almost every wish was fulfilled and I was very curious about this but did not believe that I would again leave the camp alive

4.29.42 Several months later there occurred what I did not expect[.] The Gestapo transferred me to the "UG" [interrogation prison] Moabich[.] one evidently wanted to make a trial with me anyway[.] in order to prevent this I turned to the last available means which remained for me to suicide [.] I did this twice but they were unsuccessful due to the vigilance of Guard Hollmurg[.] I have not given up the hope that I will still succeed[.] in case it should come otherwise I will not defend myself at my trial and refuse the judge all answers in order thereby to prevent perjury[.] I have entrusted this admission to three persons[.] in case they should someday wish to publish it so this is to serve as verification.[3]

By late April, even before the secret note had been deciphered, the end had clearly come and the "Grynszpan Trial" was destined to remain merely a title on voluminous secret files. The Ministry of Propaganda had bowed out the middle of April—the last item found in its files is the "Fuehrer Information" of April 17—and Thierack's People's Court and its prosecution staff lost their enthusiasm shortly thereafter. Only the Foreign Ministry valiantly continued its efforts to keep the patient alive, and as late as April 25, in a memorandum to the files, Kruemmer argued for an early trial. However, by the end of the month the handwriting on the wall could no longer be ignored, and the Foreign Ministry also ceased its ineffective rear guard action.

On May 13, Kruemmer recorded the death rattle of the trial in an internal memorandum to the files:

> On May 12 I was asked by Under State Secretary Luther to immediately get in touch with Minister Dr. Goebbels in regard to the following:
>
> The Fuehrer had asked Minister Lammers to query the foreign minister whether he thought that the time was right to undertake the Grynszpan trial. The foreign minister is of the opinion that the present time is not advantageous, firstly since the people would not understand why such a large trial was being planned because of a single murder while at the same time hundreds of Germans were dying on the front and secondly because after the beginning of the large battles in the East, world interest in the trial is not sufficiently great. Furthermore, the appearance at the trial of former French Minister Bonnet or even his indirect participation through the reading of his testimony would not be desirable from a foreign-political standpoint. For all these reasons, he considered a postponement to autumn advisable. He does not wish to inform the Fuehrer of this position without having discussed it with the minister of propaganda.
>
> I have transmitted the [foreign minister's] position to Minister Goebbels who responded immediately that he fully shared the opinion of the foreign minister. In addition, he welcomed a postponement in view of Grynspan's apparent plan to call attention to his illicit relationship with the victim.
>
> This response was immediately communicated to the foreign minister.[4]

The same day, May 13, Freisler wrote Chief Prosecutor Lautz that Hitler had ordered the trial of Herschel Grynszpan postponed and personally reserved the right to determine a suitable future date.[5] It is not difficult to imagine the pleasure this letter must have brought the Ministry of Justice, which had taken so much abuse in connection with the case and now found itself in the position of informing its adversaries of its final demise. On the following day, May 14, Goebbels wrote in his diary that after a discussion with Ribbentrop, it had been decided to postpone the trial "until autumn." He went on to say that it was now in the interest of German foreign policy neither to emphasize too strongly the role of former French Foreign Minister Bonnet nor to enter into such a "delicate" trial.

The Foreign Ministry's Guenther noted in his files that despite the "probable postponement" of the trial, it was necessary to keep certain points under constant review, so that no delays would be encountered if a new date were set. It would be necessary to collect the testimony of all German witnesses for submission to the foreign minister (!), decide on the utilization of the secret message and it was an "absolute necessity" to gain access to the "Green Pamphlets." Just so the case would not be forgotten entirely in the bureaucratic mill, Guenther directed one of the Ministry's lower officials to report to him every Monday about the status of the case, and he even went so far as to make provisions for alternates in the event he himself or the reporting officer were on leave.[6]

There is on record one other document of that period, the "Fuehrer Information" No. 60 of July 3, 1942, prepared by the acting minister of justice:[7]

> The Jew Grynszpan has admitted in an encrypted note that his claim of homosexual relations with vom Rath were untrue. However, he insinuates the suspicion that the murder victim had homosexual relations to others.
>
> In this connection it is of interest that a brother of the murdered vom Rath, First Lieutenant and chief of a cavalry squadron was sentenced to one year's imprisonment and loss of rank for sexual offenses with men by the Field Courtmartial of Division 428, Special Mission.[8]

There is no record of how frequently the case was reviewed, but on December 7, 1942, Ribbentrop ordered that the French pamphlet prepared by Grimm,[9] "showing the Jewish wire pulling behind the assassination aimed against the peace of Europe," be made available to the "broad masses" in a "suitable manner."

As for the then twenty-one-year-old Herschel Grynszpan, he was reportedly transferred from Moabit first to the Sachsenhausen concentration camp and then, on or about September 26, 1942, to the penitentiary at Magdeburg.

21

Summing Up

In looking back over this case, many questions remain. First and foremost, what was the reason for the assassination of Ernst vom Rath? Was there some sort of relationship between the two men, homosexual, financial, or otherwise, or was Herschel Grynszpan (as an East German author has implied) perhaps a knowing or innocent Nazi tool, playing a role similar to that of Marinus van der Lubbe at the infamous Reichstag fire? Was the coded "confession" a crude Nazi forgery or a singularly remarkable document? Why did the Nazi show trial never take place?

If vom Rath's murder indeed was the desperate gesture of an emotional young man, was it the work of a single individual or a conspiracy involving not only Herschel Grynszpan but also others? On balance, was the pogrom of November 1938 the sort of unmitigated disaster that it is historically perceived to be for German and Austrian Jews or can anything of a positive nature be attributed to it? And finally, how is history to judge Herschel Grynszpan—cowardly assassin, immature avenger, or hero?

Those who do not believe that Herschel Grynszpan killed vom Rath for the reasons he gave before the French court contend that there existed some sort of prior relationship between assassin and victim. For confirmation they rely on what they perceive to be a knowledgeable source—Herschel Grynszpan. The problem is, he is apparently responsible for different versions.

Harry Naujoks, the concentration camp inmate, wrote the author in 1951 about the indirect "conversations" with Herschel's fellow inmates, as described in Chapter 16. According to Naujoks, Grynszpan claimed that vom Rath had smuggled Jewish property to Paris on behalf of their owners and against large commissions. In the process, vom Rath is supposed to have embezzled large amounts and, so Naujoks says he seemed to recall, cheated the Grynszpan family, and others, out of their savings. This was the reason that Grynszpan reportedly gave for his shooting of vom Rath. Naujoks stressed in his letter that he was only relaying what he had heard through the "grapevine" and that he had no idea whether Grynszpan had spoken the truth, although he was quite certain that Herschel Grynszpan himself had given this description.

The story does not ring true. To date, no one has come forward with any sort of corroborative evidence which would support that scenario. Furthermore, vom Rath had only a short time earlier arrived in Paris and even if he had engaged in that sort of activity, it is highly unlikely that he would have dealt with a poor tailor when there were many more affluent people who needed this type of assistance.

Those arguing that there existed a homosexual relationship between assassin and victim naturally also rely to a considerable extent on the statements of Herschel Grynszpan. Occasionally also cited is a notarized sworn deposition of August 25, 1963, by Dr. Sarella Pomeranz, who stated that she was a doctor in the Institute of Radiology of Drs. Halberstaedter and Tugendreich in Berlin from 1929 until it closed in 1939. According to Dr. Pomeranz, Ernst vom Rath was treated at the Institute for rectal gonorrhea which, according to the referring physician, had been contracted as a result of homosexual relations. According to Dr. Pomeranz, she carried out the shortwave radiation therapy which, at the time, was considered the most effective treatment for the illness. Dr. Pomeranz stated that she remembers Ernst vom Rath because of who he was—not surprising when one considers that the Institute was operated by Jewish physicians, all of whom eventually emigrated. Grimm reported in his memorandum of April 23, 1942, that among the files confiscated in Paris was a letter from Tel Aviv dated August 27, 1939, from Dr. Schoroschowsky, a radiologist formerly from Berlin, who reported having heard essentially the same rumor. Dr. Schoroschowsky did not identify his source, but the information apparently was based on hearsay.

Questions have been raised about the veracity of Dr. Pomeranz's deposition. Actually, it is largely irrelevant. The question here is not what vom Rath's sexual preferences were, but rather whether there existed a homosexual relationship between vom Rath and Grynszpan. This writer contends that the question can be answered with an emphatic "no."

Too many facts speak against it. Grynszpan, when speaking to Mme Mathis or addressing the receptionist Nagorka, did *not* specifically request to see vom Rath. Even if familiar with the embassy routine, Grynszpan could not have known that on that particular morning he would be guided to his eventual victim instead of whoever normally received miscellaneous callers. Furthermore, if there really had existed a close personal relationship between the two, it is much more likely that the murderer would have killed his victim at vom Rath's home or wherever they met, thus giving himself a chance to escape. No one has argued to date that Grynszpan *wanted* to be arrested.

At no time during his incarceration in France did Grynszpan give any indication of a personal relationship with vom Rath, a fact confirmed by Judge Jean Tesnière and Maître Vincent de Moro-Giafferri after the war.

In fact, it was de Moro-Giafferri who in early 1947 provided the first hint of how Herschel Grynszpan probably came to use the ruse which eventually helped frustrate German efforts for a grandiose propaganda trial. The author had by that time located a number of relevant documents in German government files (but not the coded "confession") and in the course of a visit with Maître de Moro-Giafferri in Paris, told him of the youth's successful strategy. Herschel's erstwhile attorney was delighted with the story which he said was new to him, but for which he thought he had a ready explanation. According to de Moro-Giafferri, he had mentioned to Grynszpan that rumors were circulating concerning vom Rath's sexual preferences—although he stressed that he did not know whether vom Rath actually was a homosexual—and had brought up the possibility of basing the defense on this having been a "crime of passion." Such a defense, according to the wily attorney, would have been much more likely to be treated with compassion by a French court than a "political crime," and in view of the defendant's age might have resulted in a short, or even suspended, prison sentence.

It is, of course, likely that de Moro-Giafferri, who had a long record of opposing Nazi Germany and all it stood for, also saw in this defense a way of doing maximum harm to the Third Reich. It would have cast a shadow over Germany's official representatives, while at the same time probably not preventing the airing in court of the reasons for the shooting advanced by Grynszpan, that is, the Nazi treatment of his parents and his fellow Jews. In any event, de Moro-Giafferri recounted that the suggestion was immediately rejected by young Herschel. The attorney in 1947 conjectured that Grynszpan later recalled this conversation and resurrected the idea for his own use.

In his coded "testament," Grynszpan reports having heard of vom Rath's reputation from his attorney (Weill-)Goudchaux; however, a mistake in Grynszpan's recollection is certainly possible. It is also likely that Grynszpan's challenge of the legality of his extradition to Germany had its origin during his imprisonment in France. Presumably he was advised after his arrest why he could not be extradited to Germany and later used this information with excellent effect.

There exists an interesting letter, written in 1964, from an acquaintance of de Moro-Giafferri to Guenter vom Rath, brother of the victim, which was put in evidence during a trial in Augsburg, Germany. The writer, then living in Munich, identified himself in the letter as a former Communist activist who was born in East Prussia and had been editor of a Communist newspaper in Berlin until 1933; he then had fled to Moscow and Prague and in 1938 had moved to Paris.

> Thus it was that I was in Paris when your brother was assassinated by the young Grunspahn [sic] who wanted in this manner to alert world opinion to the frightening lot of his family who were agonizing in the no-man's land between the 3rd Reich and Poland. In assassinating your brother, he thought he had killed the German ambassador.
>
> What is important is to know how the calumnious legend concerning the homosexual relations between your brother and Grunspahn originated. I knew the lawyer de Moro-Giafferri who had been introduced to me by mutual political friends. One day, and unless I was mistaken it was in the spring of 1939, I met de Moro-Giafferri on boulevard St. Michel and I asked him for news of Grunspahn for whom he was the defense lawyer. He had just come from visiting him in his cell and was still revolted by the attitude of his client.
>
> "That young man is a fool, infatuated with himself," he said. "He refuses to give a non-political character to his act by saying for example that he assassinated vom Rath because he had had money quarrels with him following homosexual relations. Yet, such an attitude in regard to the murder of vom Rath is necessary in order to save the Jews of the Third Reich, whose lives are becoming more and more precarious in regard to their property, their health, their future etc."

De Moro-Giafferri appealed to the conscience of Grunspahn, implying he was responsible for the persecution of the Jews by his act which made Jewish blood flow. "If only," he added, "he would deny the political motives of his crime and assert that he only had personal vengeance in mind, vengeance as a victim of homosexuality, the Nazis would lose their best pretext for exercising their reprisals against the German Jews who are victims of his fit of madness and now, of his obstinacy."

I asked him then if Grunspahn really had relations with vom Rath. He replied, "Absolutely not!" I said to him then, "But as defender of Grunspahn shouldn't you protect not only the interests of your client, but his honor as well?"

It was at that moment that de Moro-Giafferri exclaimed, "Honor! honor! What is the honor of that absurd little Jew in the face of the criminal action of Hitler? What does the honor of Grunspahn weigh in the face of the destiny of hundreds of thousands of Jews?"

As to your brother, de Moro-Giafferri added, "Whether vom Rath might be a homosexual or not I don't know and besides it doesn't interest me. . . . "

De Moro-Giafferri acted in accordance with the desire of the Grunspahn committee, formed and directed by Dorothy Thompson, in insisting to Grunspahn that he agree to no longer maintain that his act had political and anti-Nazi significance, but solely a cause "Passionelle." In that event it would have been a matter of seduction of a minor [on the part of vom Rath] and according to de Moro-Giafferri and his collaborators, the court would have inflicted [on Herschel Grynszpan] a minimum penalty, perhaps even with a suspended sentence. [In France a remission of sentence is possible in cases of sentences of up to five years' imprisonment.] Even that argument, de Moro-Giafferri deplored, had no effect on Grunspahn.[1]

The writer specifically authorized the addressee to use the letter as he saw fit and indicated that he would be prepared to affirm its contents under oath.

There is of course also Grynszpan's coded note, admitting that his argument was merely a ruse. It is likely that many will doubt the genuineness of this remarkable document and will not be satisfied until either Grynszpan himself or one directly involved in its preparation can definitely testify to its authenticity. In view of past Nazi trickery, such skepticism is fully justified. However, there are a number of points which seem to argue very strongly against this contention, and they have in fact convinced this author that this is a "bona fide" statement.

Above all, as implied in the Ministry of Justice's "Fuehrer Information" of July 3, 1942, the confession is hardly suitable for introduction in court. It brings up the homosexual angle, and although it denies any connection with the case at hand, it does imply that vom Rath may have had a somewhat questionable reputation, certainly not a welcome admission in the Third Reich. The document also brings into the open the question of the illegal extradition, characterizes the trial as a propaganda vehicle pure and simple, and paints the Gestapo and its methods in a less than flattering light.

It might be argued by those who consider it a forgery that the confession would have been introduced in court only if Grynszpan had raised the question of Paragraph 175, that is, the homosexual relationship. However, in that event the introduction of the document would have automatically brought into the trial the extradition issue, confirmed rumors about Gestapo methods and would have failed to clear vom Rath's name. All in all, a forged document in all probability would have been unlikely to be of such dubious value.

Another telling argument against the contention that the coded confession is a forgery is the manner of its introduction into the system. Had it been a forgery, it probably would have been carried out by or on behalf of the People's Court or its prosecution staff, and it is questionable that it would have had to go through the very convoluted decoding process. As a matter of fact, for purposes of secrecy, it is highly doubtful that a copy of the document would have made its way into the files of the Foreign Ministry. It apparently was never made available to the Ministry of Propaganda.

And finally of course, there was the Ministry of Justice's "Fuehrer Information" of July 3 which confirms the existence of a coded message. To argue that the Fuehrer was provided false information as part of the deception process strains credulity.

Given the Nazi proclivity for dirty tricks designed to further their aims, it is not surprising that some suspect Nazi complicity in the shooting of vom Rath. After all, they had probably arranged for van der Lubbe's participation in the firing of the Reichstag in 1933, thereby giving Hitler an excuse to muzzle all opposition. After the war, the world was to get confirmation of a number of other, similar activities. Thus, Hitler is reported to have considered the assassination of the German military attaché in Prague as an excuse for a German invasion, but with the collapse of Czechoslovakia (at Munich), this subterfuge became unnecessary. Not much later, in late August 1939, an attack on the German radio station in Gleiwitz on the Polish border, ostensibly by Poles but actually by Germans in Polish uniforms, was used by Hitler as justification for the attack on Poland a few days later.

The assassination of vom Rath seemed to fit the same mold. It permitted the Nazis to escalate their persecution of the Jews, it greatly speeded up Jewish emigration, and allowed Nazi authorities to acquire Jewish property (through the billion-mark "fine," forced sales at outrageously low prices to party stalwarts, the outright confiscation of "abandoned" property, etc.) needed to shore up German war preparations. Proponents of this theory can cite a number of suspicious factors to support their thesis, such as that German concentration camps were ready to receive some 30,000 Jewish males on almost a moment's notice; the survival of several members of the Grynszpan family; and Herschel's seemingly strange behavior of turning himself in voluntarily to French authorities after his evacuation to the south of France. And finally, there is the rumored survival of Herschel Grynszpan, discussed below.

There is no doubt that Nazi concentration camps *were* ready to accept the sudden influx of a large number of Jewish males in early November 1938, not only through stockpiling of clothing but also through the rush construction of barracks during the summer of 1938. Furthermore, the secret telex to all stations from Gestapo chief Mueller at 11:55 P.M. on November 9, 1938 seemed to indicate that Nazi authorities had planned this action well in advance. On the other hand, the fact that Mueller's message made no reference to vom Rath or his demise suggests that the preparations were in place for implementation if and when a proper opportunity presented itself. In other words, the Nazis were ready to make use of any "suitable" opportunity, and Herschel Grynszpan provided it.

The survival of the Grynszpan family appears to have been the result of fortuitous circumstances, that is, their residence in the part of Poland occupied by the Soviet Union on the partition of Poland and their subsequent ability to stay ahead of the Nazi forces.

As for Herschel's turning himself in to French authorities after his escape on the way south, to understand the action one only has to place oneself in the position of this youth of eighteen, totally alone in a strange country whose language he did not speak well. Despite his ordeals, Herschel had until then lived a relatively sheltered life, always in the care of someone. Despite extensive Nazi research into his past, there are no indications that he was particularly streetwise. Unable to cope, fearful of capture by the Germans, having been well provided for by French authorities after his arrest and presumably assured that there was no legal way by which he could be extradited to Germany, it is really not surprising that he would have felt safer in prison. Little did he realize, of course, that the France he had known no longer existed, not even in the limited area outside direct Nazi control.

Finally, the apparent reluctance of the RSHA (Gestapo and SD) to press for the prosecution of Herschel Grynszpan (by, among other things, giving credence to his claim of homosexual relations with the young diplomat), evoked the suspicion of Friedrich Karl Kaul, the East German author of *Der Fall des Herschel Grynszpan*. It is not clear whether Kaul meant to imply that a sense of obligation or loyalty toward Grynszpan was at the heart of their attitude or whether there was fear that a trial might expose their duplicity. Neither scenario sounds reasonable.

Insofar as any coconspirators are concerned, the Nazis tried very hard to prove some sort of complicity by outside groups. However, despite great efforts, they were unable to find any evidence of a conspiracy, or even undue influence by outside parties. Neither the French investigators, the representatives of the plaintiff nor later searching Gestapo inquiries revealed any trace of a formal or informal conspiracy.

This did not stop the Germans from asserting right from the beginning that complicity existed between the murderer and Communist or Jewish groups. Diewerge, in 1939, was given the unenviable task of documenting the existence of "a Jewish conspiracy" and "Jewish atrocities" which he sought to discharge by preparing *Anschlag gegen den Frieden*, aimed at countering revelations by German refugees about the Nazis' anti-Semitic activities.

Grimm, having in the meantime gained access to the files of French police, Grynszpan's defense staff and various Jewish organizations in France, would try to do better during the 1942 German show trial, but to no avail. In spite of it all, the best the Nazis were able to do was to assert that the very absence of evidence of a conspiracy represented conclusive evidence that such a conspiracy existed—the sort of argument that would do honor to *Alice in Wonderland*.

Looking at the events of November 1938 with the benefit of hindsight, one might well come to the conclusion—some may call it cynical—that in the final analysis, Herschel Grynszpan performed a very valuable service for European Jews. In spite of the hundreds of dead which resulted from his deed, it saved many more than perished at the time. The pogrom represented the opening stages of the Holocaust.

Many Jews who until that point had lived in the hope that Nazism would wither away or become more tolerant, suddenly found themselves face to face with another reality. They arrived at the realization that this evil was here to stay and that the conditions of Jews under Nazi domination could only get worse. The result was a panic-like exodus. Children's transports were organized by various countries and people sought visas for safe havens they found difficult to locate on a map.

In 1933, when the Nazis came to power, an estimated 600,000 Jews lived in Germany and Austria. That year, approximately 37,000 emigrated from Germany. The number of emigrants decreased in subsequent years to about 25,000 in 1936, 23,000 in 1937 and 40,000 in 1938. (The increase in 1938 is attributable less to an increase of emigration by German Jews, but rather to Austria's "*Anschluss*" to Germany and the enthusiasm with which Austrians adopted and applied the German anti-Jewish measures; as someone observed, the level of repression of Jews reached by the Germans after five years was reached by the Austrians in five weeks.) All in all, during the period 1933–1938, about 200,000 Jews left, but about 400,000 still remained in Germany and Austria! Yet from November 1938 to the outbreak of the war in September 1939, the number of emigrés increased to 80,000. Had the emigration rate remained at the pre-*Kristallnacht* level, many of these people would have been added to the long list of Holocaust victims.

If one accepts the premise that the argument alleging homosexual relations is a pure invention on the part of Grynszpan, there remains the question why the trial never took place. The most obvious answer is fear of negative repercussions to such a propaganda show, yet perhaps that answer is too simple.

It can be argued, on the basis of past prominent trials in the Soviet Union, that had there been a real desire to bring Grynszpan to court without any embarrassing testimony, he could certainly have been "conditioned" sufficiently to assure a smooth and uneventful trial. Yet for some reason, the same regime which thought little of murdering millions of innocent people, usually endeavored to maintain an aura of pseudo-legality. In few cases tried before Nazi courts did the defendants, in the manner of Stalin's Soviet courts, compete with the prosecution in reciting their many crimes. In fact, the world witnessed Dimitrov's vigorous and successful defense during the Reichstag fire trial. And in the fall of 1944, Fieldmarshall von Witzleben and Carl Goerdeler, accused of participating in the conspiracy to overthrow

Hitler on July 20, defended the righteousness of their actions before a most hostile People's Court, though obviously without success.

Ambassador Abetz's memorandum of April 18 to von Rintelen informed Ribbentrop's aide that Bormann had indicated that the trial was being postponed "for. . . decisive reasons other than those mentioned by Minister Kruemmer." The reasons mentioned by Kruemmer had been the old standbys—illegal extradition and the threat of the homosexuality charge. Goebbels' last known diary entry on the case has the Minister of Propaganda noting that it was not then in the interest of German foreign policy to emphasize too strongly the role of former French Foreign Minister Bonnet.

One is tempted to describe these comments as efforts at rationalization by individuals unwilling to admit that their grandiose plans had been frustrated by a slight youth of twenty-one. That view is contested by Helmut Heiber, the German historian, who has argued that it was not Grynszpan's defense strategy but foreign political considerations which were responsible for the cancellation of the trial.[2] Heiber pointed out that the Riom trial, which began in mid-February, had been the scene of repeated demonstrations against the Nazi regime and that the tone and attitude of the defendants had caused the German government to support a halt in the proceedings by mid-March. As a result of that and other events of the period,[3] so reasoned Heiber, Hitler had come to the conclusion that in actual fact Vichy did not desire closer relations with Germany, and that the sympathies of the French leaders were still with the enemies of the Reich. Under the circumstances, according to Heiber, Hitler was in no mood to permit a trial which would have served to ease the accusations previously heaped on the French.

Heiber's argument is not convincing. The events mentioned by him took place in March and April, but the first real doubts about the advisability of trying Herschel Grynszpan surfaced on January 22 and never were completely dispelled. Furthermore, the Foreign Ministry—which presumably would have been most sensitive to these considerations—persisted longer than anyone else in its effort to bring the case to trial.

Under the circumstances, this writer chooses to stick to the more romantic interpretation that, assisted by opportune outside forces of a political nature, the twenty-one-year-old Herschel Grynszpan met, challenged, and defeated an awesome bureaucratic machine bent on using him as a justification for the Holocaust. Yet it is ironic that this apparent "victory" was largely meaningless, for it failed to impede the extermination of European Jews, while at the same time, what was initially perceived as Grynszpan's great blunder of unleashing the events of *Kristallnacht*, resulted in saving thousands of lives.

Epilogue

It has been over fifty years since the assassination of Ernst vom Rath and the pogrom of November 1938, and only about four years less since Herschel Grynszpan was known to have been alive, yet the fate of the youth continues to be shrouded in mystery. Initially, it was assumed that Herschel Grynszpan had died in Nazi hands, and since that fate had been shared by so many millions, few thought to question that assumption.

Discussion of vom Rath's shooting and Grynszpan's fate was revived and stimulated by two articles published in the 1950s. It all started in April 1952, when the German illustrated magazine *Wochenend*, published in Nuremberg, carried a long article by Count Michael Alexander Soltikow entitled *Geheime Reichssache* (Secret Reich Matter or Top Secret). The author, a former minor Gestapo official, counterintelligence officer, and author of anti-Semitic books, who after the war professed having all along been an active anti-Nazi, alleged that vom Rath's shooting was not a political assassination but rather was attributable to a homosexual relationship between the assassin and his victim.

What might have been a one-day sensation became a fixture in the German press—and to a lesser extent in other European newspapers—when Ernst's brother Guenter vom Rath, an attorney, sued Soltikow and the magazine for slander of a deceased person. The pretrial investigation of the case dragged on for years, until it finally came to trial in

1960, eight years after publication of the original article. The trial ended with a guilty verdict (five months of prison, suspended; five years probation), but was appealed by the defendant and overturned on a technicality in 1964, some twelve years after it had been initiated. Before it was over, Soltikow had called a number of prominent witnesses, including former State Secretary Gutterer of the Ministry of Propaganda and Chief Prosecutor Lautz. Both testified having seen references to a claim of homosexual relations in the French files (!) and were convinced that a large propaganda trial of Herschel Grynszpan would have been inappropriate and probably counterproductive.

What really grabbed the headlines was the question in the course of the 1960 trial, by a witness who claimed to be a member of the intelligence establishment, about why Grynszpan himself had not been called to testify, since German police had reported him living in Hamburg. Soltikow followed up by testifying that not only was Grynszpan alive, but had been in the courtroom the previous day and was willing to testify if granted immunity. Despite repeated promises, Soltikow failed to produce Herschel or Herschel's fingerprints or, for that matter, any proof that Herschel Grynszpan was still alive. However, his failure to do so was mitigated when the magistrate made the injudicious statement that if Grynszpan did appear as a witness, he would be subject to arrest—not exactly the way to get a reluctant witness to appear.

The other article, by an author given considerably greater credence, was Helmut Heiber's "Der Fall Grünspan." In 1957, this German historian published the first lengthy scholarly article on the assassination of vom Rath and the preparations of a propaganda trial. In the last paragraph, almost as an afterthought, he mentioned that Herschel Grynszpan had been released by U.S. troops from the Magdeburg penitentiary in 1945 and since then had been living under an assumed name in Paris. A year later, in 1958, Dr. Heiber reported that he had provided all materials at his disposal to an Israeli institution representing the interests of the Grynszpan family. Since their investigations had proved unsuccessful, Heiber admitted that his original information may have been in error. He went on to say that "the survival of Grynszpan can be proved on hand of documents only through January 30, 1945."[1]

This last comment by Dr. Heiber was probably based on a report by Walter Hammer, an author and coauthor of several works on the German resistance. Walter Hammer had been sentenced to five years imprisonment by Nazi authorities for preparation of high treason and was liberated from the Brandenburg penitentiary on April 27, 1945. Before that he had been incarcerated for almost two years in the RSHA (Gestapo) prison in Berlin and in the Sachsenhausen concentration camp. Hammer told of coming across Herschel Grynszpan for the first time in August 1940 in Berlin's RSHA prison. He reported that on January 28, 1945, one Otto Schneider, Prisoner No. 35220/44, born March 28, 1921, by profession tailor, had been transferred from the penitentiary at Sonnenburg to Brandenburg, shackled hand and foot. (During the night of January 28/29, 1945, at least 686 political prisoners were reportedly shot at Sonnenburg by an SS execution squad.) According to Hammer, this "Otto Schneider," whose date of birth is identical to that of Herschel Grynszpan, was in fact Herschel Grynszpan. Walter Hammer reported that Schneider/Grynszpan was picked up by the Gestapo two days later, on January 30, and transported to the penitentiary at Magdeburg.

By way of confirmation, Hammer obtained a report of March 30, 1954 from the Allied High Commission's International Tracing Service, established after the war to help trace former concentration or labor camp inmates, that one "Otto Schneider," by profession tailor, born March 28, 1921, had been transferred on January 28, 1945 from Sonnenburg to the penitentiary Görden (Brandenburg). No further information on the inmate was provided.

Harry Naujoks, the longtime inmate of the concentration camp Sachsenhausen, wrote in 1951 that about August or September 1942, Herschel Grynszpan was transported by car from the "bunker" in which he was held, although it was not possible to know his destination. (This probably was the transport of September 26, 1942, to Magdeburg referred to in Chapter 20.) According to Naujoks, it could have been a "fake transport", that is, as in at least one other instance, Herschel could previously have been killed in the "bunker" and the car departed empty to give the impression that the prisoner had been moved to another location. Alternatively, it was equally possible that the car transported him to the "Industriehof," the camp's execution site. In any event, so wrote Naujoks, Grynszpan himself was convinced that the transport would take him to his death. He secretly bade other prisoners farewell with the words, "The time has come, they want to kill me."

In 1976, French television aired a "docudrama" that repeated the rumors of Herschel's survival, conjecturing that he was living in a Paris suburb and working as a garage mechanic under the protection of the French police. However, no evidence of any kind was provided to support this story.

The trail ends on this uncertain note.

It is indeed ironic that the man whose execution by the Nazi regime would have surprised no one may not have shared the fate of his 6 million fellow Jews who were summarily murdered, or at least not until late in the war.

There are several reasons why it is very possible that Herschel survived much of the war. Above all, he was too prominent to be simply eliminated. His trial, after all, was not permanently cancelled but only postponed until such time as the Fuehrer wanted to reopen it. According to a statement in 1955 by Fritz Dahms, a retired ministerial counselor in the Foreign Ministry, the case was never closed and in keeping with the directives of May 1942, it was regularly resubmitted for review until the end of the war. Grynszpan's elimination—except perhaps in the closing weeks of the war—would have had to be initiated from the top, by Hitler himself or someone close to him.

Yet, despite efforts to do so, this author found nothing in German files which would point to the demise of Herschel Grynszpan or the decision to permanently close the case. The last indication that Grynszpan was still alive, or at least that someone at the Foreign Ministry thought him to be alive, was a memorandum of December 7, 1942. On that date, Kruemmer noted in the files that the foreign minister had ordered that the materials prepared by Grimm, demonstrating Jewish participation in the assassination designed to upset the peace of Europe, be made available to the public. The embassy in Paris received instructions to widely disseminate the materials in an appropriate manner "even though, for the time being, the trial does not take place." The pretrial judge in the Soltikow case, van Ginkel, examined the files in the archives of the Foreign Ministry and reported that he also had found no documents about Grynszpan dated later than 1942.

Does this mean that Herschel Grynszpan survived the war? It is unlikely, since Herschel Grynszpan had no reason to remain "underground." Had he survived, he would have known that from a moral or legal point of view, a trial would have been unthinkable. Herschel's parents survived the war, moving from Poland to the Soviet Union in advance of the German onslaught and then to Israel after the war. Sendel Grynszpan, Herschel's father, testified at the Eichmann trial that he had heard nothing from his son since he was turned over to the Nazi authorities.

There is not a single reliable report of a sighting of Herschel in Paris or elsewhere. However, there is at least one plausible explanation for some of the stories circulating about Herschel's postwar presence in Paris. Mordechai Grynszpan, Herschel's older brother, lived in Paris during 1947/48 and at the time actively sought to locate his brother, quite possibly giving rise to various rumors.

What then happened to Herschel Grynszpan? In his deposition, Fritz Dahms reported that "the death of Grynszpan occurred shortly before the end of the war, but I am no longer able to say if he died of natural causes or if he lost his life by violence. At the time, the Foreign Ministry received no precise details on the manner in which he died." Until more definite information becomes available—and it must be out there—we can only conjecture. Chances are that Herschel was not violently put to death, or at least not until toward the waning days of the war. It is equally possible that he died in prison, either through suicide, illness, or Allied action, with this information withheld from Berlin.

While we may never know for sure how and when Herschel Grynszpan died, his saga officially came to an end on June 1, 1960 when the *Amtsgericht* (Lower Court) of Hanover declared Herschel Grynszpan as deceased. The date of death was nominally fixed as May 8, 1945. The decision became official on July 24, 1960.

Notes

INTRODUCTION

1. Composed between 1939 and 1941, *A Child of Our Time* was first performed on March 19, 1944.

CHAPTER 1

1. Friedrich Grimm, *Der Grünspan Prozess* (Nuremberg: F. Willmy, 1942), p. 9.
2. Ibid., p. 10.
3. Wolfgang Diewerge, *Anschlag gegen den Frieden* (Munich: Franz Eher Verlag, 1939), p. 34. Also Grimm, *Der Grünspan Prozess,* p. 10.
4. The first names of the Grynszpan family members underwent changes as its members moved about, using German, Russian, Polish, Hebrew, and Yiddish. Herschel Grynszpan signed himself Hermann when writing to his parents; his father was known as Sendel, Zindel, and Siegmund; his brother went under the names Mordochai, Mardoche, and Marcus; while sister Esther also used Beile and Berta. See "Dramatis Personae" for the various names of key family members.
5. Ministry of Propaganda (MoP) files, Vol. 979, pp. 51–52.
6. MoP files, Vol. 991, p. 98.
7. Ibid., pp. 55–56.

8. Ibid., pp. 54–55.
9. MoP files, Vol. 980, pp. 126–27.

CHAPTER 2

1. The information in this chapter is largely derived from Dr. Alain Cuénot, "The Herschel Grynszpan Case" (unpublished manuscript, edited and privately reproduced by David Rome, Beverly Hills, 1982). Dr. Cuénot's manuscript, in turn, is based largely on Diewerge, *Anschlag gegen den Frieden,* pp. 48–63.
2. Diewerge, *Anschlag gegen den Frieden,* pp. 50–51.
3. Ibid., p. 51.
4. Wilhelm Gustloff was *Landesgruppenleiter* (resident chief) for Switzerland of the Foreign Organization of the NSDAP, that is, the top Nazi Party official in the country. On February 4, 1936, he was shot and killed in Davos by David Frankfurter, a young Jewish student from Yugoslavia, resident in Berne. David Frankfurter received the Swiss court's maximum sentence, sixteen years prison. There were certain superficial similarities, which will be discussed later, between this case and the assassination of vom Rath.

CHAPTER 3

1. Information about Ernst vom Rath was largely derived from Grimm, *Der Grünspan Prozess* and Diewerge, *Anschlag gegen den Frieden,* as well as from information provided to the author by members of the family of the deceased.
2. *Völkischer Beobachter,* January 8, 1939.
3. The comments by Ebeling, Taulin, and Auer are quotes from the French judicial files as reported in Grimm, *Der Grünspan Prozess.*
4. Testimony of Dr. Heinrich Gruber at the trial of Karl Eichmann.

CHAPTER 4

1. For a detailed discussion of the events during and immediately after *Kristallnacht,* see Lionel Kochan, *Pogrom—November 10, 1938* (London: André Deutsch, 1957), and Rita Thalmann and Emmanuel Finermann, *Crystal Night* (New York: Holocaust Library, 1974). For the texts of various Nazi documents and statistical data, see Heinz Lauber, *Judenpogrom: "Reichskristallnacht" November 1938 in Grossdeutschland* (Gerlingen: Bleicher Verlag, 1981). In the preparation of this chapter I am indebted to all three books. A recent addition to the list of books on the events of November 1938 is Anthony Read and David Fisher, *Kristallnacht: The Nazi Night of Terror* (New York: Times Books, 1989), which arrived after the completion of this manuscript.
2. Lauber, *Judenpogrom,* pp. 225–33.

3. Memorandum from the leader of SA Brigade 50 (Starkenburg) to SA Group Electorate Palatinate Mannheim, November 11, 1938. (Doc. 1721-PS, International Military Tribunal, Nuremberg.)

4. Lauber, *Judenpogrom,* p. 80.

5. Ibid., p. 83.

6. Letter to author from Harry Naujoks, February 18, 1951.

7. Statistics by the Arolsen Documentation Center, as quoted in Kochan, *Pogrom.*

8. Lauber, *Judenpogrom,* p. 156.

9. International Military Tribunal (IMT), Nuremberg, Vol. XXVIII, Doc. 1816-PS.

CHAPTER 5

1. H. von Dirksen, *Moskau-Tokio-London* (Stuttgart: Kohlhammer Verlag, 1950), p. 227.

2. Norman L. Zucker and Naomi Flink Zucker, *The Guarded Gate* (New York: Harcourt Brace Jovanovich, 1987), p. 22.

3. *New York Times,* November 17, 1938.

4. Dorothy Thompson, *Let The Record Speak* (Boston: Houghton Mifflin Company, 1939), pp. 256–60.

5. *New York Times* and *New York Herald Tribune,* November 16, 1938.

6. For details on the utilization and disposition of the funds collected, see Chapter 11.

7. Department of State, *Documents on German Foreign Policy,* Series D, Vol. IV (Washington, DC: U.S. Government Printing Office, 1951), pp. 333–34.

8. Ibid., p. 639.

9. Cuénot, *The Herschel Grynszpan Case,* p. 76.

CHAPTER 6

1. Information for this chapter was largely derived from Cuénot, *The Herschel Grynszpan Case*; Kaul, *Der Fall des Herschel Grynszpan* (Berlin: Akademie Verlag, 1965); Grimm, *Der Grünspan Prozess*; and Diewerge, *Anschlag gegen den Frieden.* Also Friedrich Grimm, *Denkschrift über die in Paris im Juni-Juli 1940 von der Deutschen Geheimen Feldpolizei in der Grünspan-Sache beschlagnahmten Akten* [Collection of files concerning the Grynszpan matter confiscated by the German Secret Field Police in Paris in June-July 1940]. This German language collection contains copies and translations of correspondence and Herschel's diary confiscated by German troops in Paris in June 1940. It was also published in French as Friedrich Grimm, [Pierre Dumoulin, pseud.],

L'Affaire Grynspan, Un Attentat Contre La France (Paris: Editions Jean-Renard, 1942).

2. Report to the Ministry of Propaganda of April 17, 1939. MoP files, Vol. 977, p. 182.

3. Report of February 21, 1939. MoP files. Vol. 989, pp. 15–22.

4. Letter to author from Arnold Edber, February 5, 1951.

5. The Maccabees, named after Judas Maccabeus, were a family of Jewish patriots who headed a religious revolt in the reign of Antiochus IV (175–164 B.C.). Maccabeus' wife and seven sons were martyred for refusing to violate the laws of Moses.

6. MoP files, Vol. 989, pp. 23–38.

CHAPTER 7

1. Grimm, *Der Grünspan Prozess,* p. 62.
2. Ibid., p. 63.
3. Ibid., p. 67.
4. Cuénot, *The Herschel Grynszpan Case,* pp. 17–23; Grimm, *Der Grünspan Prozess,* pp. 99–108.
5. Grimm, *Der Grünspan Prozess,* pp. 83–85.
6. Ibid., p. 126.
7. Ibid., p. 28.

CHAPTER 8

1. *Dziennik Ustaw* (The Law Journal), No. 22, Item 191, April 1, 1938.
2. Kaul, *Der Fall des Herschel Grynszpan,* p. 31.
3. MoP files, Vol. 991, p. 100.
4. For the text of the postcard, see Chapter 1.
5. Grimm, Der Grü*nspan Prozess,* pp. 21–22.
6. Cuénot, *The Herschel Grynszpan Case,* pp. 33–34.
7. Diewerge, *Anschlag gegen den Frieden,* pp. 135–38.
8. MoP files, Vol. 982, p. 7.
9. Diewerge, *Anschlag gegen den Frieden,* pp. 139–41.
10. To the reader not conversant with the events in Germany during this period, the story of Sendel Grynszpan's property must sound like the product of someone's vivid imagination, especially since it is based on Nazi sources. But in fact while Nazi Germany passed innumerable laws disenfranchising whole population groups, it often went to great length—at least until the onset of the "Final Solution" a couple of years after the events described here—to meticulously follow existing regulations.
11. Sendel Grynszpan's testimony at the trial of Adolf Eichmann.

CHAPTER 9

1. For a more detailed discussion of this quarrel, and the source of the information provided here, see Chapter 14.
2. Grimm, *Der Grünspan Prozess,* p. 126.
3. Diewerge, *Anschlag gegen den Frieden,* p. 46.
4. Grimm, *Der Grünspan Prozess,* pp. 49–50.
5. Ibid., p. 38.
6. Diewerge, *Anschlag gegen den Frieden,* p. 38.
7. Cuénot, *The Herschel Grynszpan Case,* p. 46.
8. Ibid., p. 46.

CHAPTER 10

1. Cuénot, *The Herschel Grynszpan Case,* p. 91.
2. Serge Weill-Goudchaux, "L'affaire Grynszpan," *L'Arche* (January 1960): 11.
3. Kaul, *Der Fall des Herschel Grynszpan,* pp. 45–48.
4. Friedrich Grimm, *40 Jahre Dienst am Recht, Politische Justiz—die Krankheit unserer Zeit* [40 Years of Service to the Law, Political Justice—the Illness of Our Time] (Bonn: Bonner Universitäts-Buchdruckerei, 1953).

There was yet another side to Grimm. In an affidavit prepared in 1949, shortly before he became the first Chancellor of the German Federal Republic, Konrad Adenauer described how Grimm had defended him in 1933 when, to support his removal from office as mayor of Cologne, the Nazis brought serious disciplinary charges against him. Adenauer wrote that Grimm's actions were not without risk and that Grimm had in private conversations expressed his disagreement with the Nazi methods. Apparently Grimm managed to overcome his reservations in later years.

5. MoP files, Vol. 979, pp. 9–11.
6. Friedrich Grimm, "Ein Dokument zur Zeitgeschichte." *Deutsche Hochschullehrer-Zeitung,* Vol. 5, No. 2, 1957.
7. MoP files, Vol. 985, p. 150.
8. Grimm, *40 Jahre Dienst am Recht.*
9. Letter from Garçon to Dr. Cuénot, September 1, 1961.
10. MoP files, Vol. 977, pp. 84, 139–46 and 155.
11. Ibid., p. 195.
12. Diewerge, *Anschlag gegen den Frieden,* pp. 37–40.
13. Ibid., pp. 113–15.
14. MoP files, Vol. 1009, p. 60.

CHAPTER 11

1. Grimm, *Denkschrift,* p. 11.
2. Ibid., Attachment 4.
3. Ibid., Attachment 5.
4. Kaul, *Der Fall des Herschel Grynszpan,* pp. 56–59.
5. In March 1939, while Herschel Grynszpan was awaiting trial, de Moro-Giafferri defended the German murderer and bandit Eugen Weidmann before a court in Versailles in one of France's more lurid and sensational criminal trials of the period. In his defense arguments, de Moro-Giafferri attributed Weidmann's crimes in part to his having spent 1933 to 1936 in Germany, where he supposedly witnessed untold murders and suicides.
6. MoP files, Vol. 992, pp. 2, 9, 16–17.
7. Excerpt from letter of December 5, 1938, from Dorothy Thompson to Oswald Garrison Villard, a member of the Board of the Journalists' Defense Fund.
8. Grimm, *Denkschrift,* Attachment 6.
9. Ibid., Attachment 11.
10. Ibid., Attachments 21 and 25.
11. Cuénot, *The Herschel Grynszpan Case,* p. 107.
12. Ibid., p. 108.
13. The George Arents Research Library, Syracuse University.
14. Cuénot, *The Herschel Grynszpan Case,* pp. 113–14.
15. Grimm, *Denkschrift,* Attachment 29.
16. Ibid., p. 18.
17. MoP files, Vol. 980, pp. 127–38 and Vol. 991, p. 25.
18. *New York Times,* May 21, 1941.
19. MoP files, Vol. 983, p. 142.

CHAPTER 12

1. This chapter is based in part on Cuénot, *The Herschel Grynszpan Case,* Chapter 15.
2. Grimm, *Der Grünspan Prozess,* pp. 82–83.
3. MoP files, Vol. 986, pp. 2–51.

CHAPTER 13

1.The psychiatric report has not been located. As a result, researchers are dependent on Grimm's 15-page summary report to Diewerge of February 22, 1939 (MoP files, Vol. 989, pp. 23–38) and excerpts quoted by Grimm in *Der Grünspan Prozess.* While Grimm obviously was selective in his choice of quotes, citing only those supporting his viewpoints, there is no evidence that quotes were altered or falsified. Under the circumstances, the use of Grimm's materials for this purpose appears justified in the absence of other sources.

2. Grimm, *Der Grünspan Prozess,* p. 45.
3. Ibid., p. 46.
4. See p. 92.
5. Grimm, *Der Grünspan Prozess,* p. 82.
6. Grimm, *Denkschrift,* p. 13.
7. Grimm, *Der Grünspan Prozess,* p. 81.
8. Cuénot, *The Herschel Grynszpan Case,* p. 115.
9. Ibid., p. 118.
10. *New York Times,* December 28, 1938.

CHAPTER 14

1. MoP files, Vol. 983, p. 13.
2. MoP files, Vol. 979, pp. 75–79.
3. MoP files, Vol. 983, pp. 36–37.
4. Ibid., pp. 19, 39.
5. Ibid., p. 39.
6. MoP files, Vol. 991, pp. 55ff.
7. MoP files, Vol. 983, p. 49.
8. Ibid., pp. 64–71.
9. Ibid., pp. 73–82 (Emphasis added).
10. Ibid., pp. 84–96.
11. Ibid., pp. 114–19.
12. MoP files, Vol. 982, p. 46.
13. Ibid., p. 48.
14. MoP files, Vol. 977, pp. 174–76. Also, Grimm's projected trial testimony, Chapter 18.
15. While Dorothy Thompson's letter mentions marks, all other references speak of French francs.
16. The George Arents Research Library, Syracuse University.
17. Grimm, *Denkschrift,* Attachment 40.
18. Grimm's *Der Grünspan Prozess* was published in French as Gustave vom Rath, *Affaire Grynszpan, Memoire de Monsieur Gustave vom Rath, Parti civile* (Berlin: M. Mueller & fils, 1942).
19. MoP files, Vol. 988, pp. 15–18.
20. Ibid., pp. 38–39.
21. Ibid., pp. 40–58.
22. Grimm, *Denkschrift,* Attachment 42.
23. Ibid., Attachment 45.

CHAPTER 15

1. Memorandum No. R 23317, Foreign Ministry, November 10, 1938 (U.S. Microfilm No. E. 443410–12).
2. Diewerge, *Anschlag gegen den Frieden,* p. 103.
3. Letter from Grimm to Ribbentrop, April 6, 1942.
4. Telegram from Dr. Hellenthal, German Embassy Paris, through the Army High Command to the Foreign Ministry, June 19, 1940 (U.S. Microfilm No. E. 691870).
5. Kaul, *Der Fall des Herschel Grynszpan,* p. 114.
6. Letter from Paul Ribeyre to Dr. Alain Cuénot, March 10, 1961.
7. Varian Fry, *Surrender on Demand* (New York: Random House, 1945), pp. ix-x.
8. Fry, *Surrender on Demand,* p. 52. In response to a query from the author, Mr. Fry in 1951 wrote that he was unable to recall the source of his information, although he thought that it might have come from Konrad Heiden, one of the authors he had assisted.
9. MoP files, Vol. 988, p. 72.
10. Telegram from Ambassador Abetz to the Foreign Ministry (for Albrecht), July 18, 1940 (U.S. Microfilm No. E 691874).
11. MoP files, Vol. 988, p. 64.
12. Letter from Kruemmer, Foreign Ministry, to Thierack, April 16, 1942 (IMT Document NG-1028.).
13. Kaul, *Der Fall des Herschel Grynszpan.*

CHAPTER 16

1. Letters to author of December 14, 1950, and February 18, 1952, from former camp inmates Siegmund Freund and Harry Naujoks.
2. MoP files, Vol. 988, p. 71.
3. Statement of former Chief Prosecutor Lautz to Institut für Zeitgeschichte, Munich, March 28, 1955.
4. Copy of indictment is on file at the Institut für Zeitgeschichte, Munich.
5. MoP files, Vol. 985, pp. 4–5.
6. Wolfgang Diewerge, *Der Fall Gustloff* and *Ein Jude hat Geschossen* (Munich: Franz Eher Nachf., 1937), both dealing with the shooting of Wilhelm Gustloff by David Frankfurter.
7. Friedrich Grimm, "Der Fall Gustloff vor dem Kantonsgericht zu Chur" (mimeographed copy of speech, Hoover Institue and Library, Stanford University).
8. Memorandum from Kruemmer to Luther, December 3, 1941.
9. MoP files, Vol. 985, p. 7.
10. Copy of *Fuehrerinformation,* undated.

11. Not to be confused with Diewerge's *Anschlag gegen den Frieden,* the contents of this pamphlet are largely identical to Grimm, *Denkschrift* and Dumoulin/Grimm, *L'Affaire Grynspan.*

12. Foreign Minister Ribbentrop visited Paris on December 6, 1938, to sign the Franco-German Friendship Declaration.

CHAPTER 17

1. Memorandum for the files by Grimm, December 10, 1941.
2. Telegram No. 378 to Weizsaecker from Foreign Ministry (signed Rintelen), April 5, 1942 (NG-179).
3. Copy of note from Grimm to Albrecht, December 22, 1941.
4. Letter from Diewerge to Kruemmer, December 22, 1941 (NG-971).
5. Copy of memorandum for the files by Platzer (Foreign Ministry), January 6, 1942.
6. Letter from Diewerge to Kruemmer, January 21, 1942.
7. Copy of memorandum for the files by Freisler, January 23, 1942 (NG-973).
8. Otto Georg Thierack was later appointed Minister of Justice.
9. Franz Schlegelberger, State Secretary in the Ministry of Justice, became Acting Minister after the death of Dr. Guertner.
10. MoP files, Vol. 985, p. 75.
11. Ibid., p. 107.
12. Memorandum from Guenther to [Section] Recht (Foreign Ministry) for submission to Ribbentrop, March 28, 1942.
13. MoP files, Vol. 985, p. 107.
14. Ibid., p. 120.
15. Ibid., p. 143.
16. Teletype No. 216 from Weizsaecker to Ribbentrop, April 2, 1942 (NG-179).

CHAPTER 18

1. Memorandum (with attachment) from Kruemmer to Weizsaecker, April 7, 1942, and memorandum for the files by Diewerge, April 11, 1942 (NG-971). Also MoP files, Vol. 985, pp. 150ff.
2. MoP files. Vol. 985, p. 164.
3. Grimm, *40 Jahre Dienst am Recht,* p. 119, and "Ein Dokument zur Zeitgeschichte," *Deutsche Hochschullehrer-Zeitung,* p. 4.
4. Copy of letter from Grimm to Ribbentrop, April 6, 1942.
5. Memorandum from Guenther to Ribbentrop, July 10, 1942, forwarding Grimm's *Testimony in the Grynszpan Trial (Final Draft).*

6. Grimm, *Testimony in the Grynszpan Trial (Final Draft),* p. 3.
7. Grimm, "Der Fall Gustloff."
8. Minutes of meeting prepared by Kruemmer, April 7, 1942, (NG-179). Also MoP files, Vol. 985, p. 140.
9. Affidavits by Drs. Viktor Mueller-Hess, Elisabeth Nau, and Marie Muehlau, February 10, 1947 (documents in author's possession).
10. Memorandum for the files by Guenther, and telegram from Guenther to Abetz, May 8, 1942.
11. Gerhard Ritter, *Carl Goerdeler und die Deutsche Widerstandsbewegung* (Stuttgart: Deutsche Verlags-Anstalt, 1954), p. 417.
12. Memorandum of conversation by Guenther regarding a discussion with Kuenne, April 29, 1942 (NG-1028).
13. Grimm, *Politische Justiz,* p. 119.
14. Copy of report in Hans-Juergen Doescher, *Reichskristallnacht—Die November Pogrome 1938* (Berlin: Ullstein Verlag, 1988), p. 70.
15. Grimm, *Der Grünspan Prozess,* p. 9.
16. MoP files, Vol. 987, pp. 1–3.
17. Memorandum by Diewerge, April 11, 1942 (NG-971).

CHAPTER 19

1. Affidavit by Dr. Mueller-Hess, February 10, 1947.
2. Letter from Grimm to Ribbentrop, April 6, 1942.
3. MoP files, Vol. 985, p. 190.
4. Letter from Diewerge to Kruemmer, April 15, forwarding copy of letter from Schlegelberger to Goebbels, April 10, 1942.
5. Telegram No. 431 from Abetz to Kruemmer, April 14, 1942 (NG-179).
6. Memorandum from Kruemmer to Weizsaecker (reporting on meeting with Goebbels and Diewerge), April 16, 1942.
7. Telegram from Guenther to Paris, April 14, 1942 (NG-1028).
8. Telegram from Paris to Foreign Ministry, April 20, 1942.
9. MoP files, Vol. 985, p. 222.
10. Telegram from Kruemmer to Abetz, April 18, 1942.
11. Memorandum from Guenther to Kruemmer, April 30, 1942. Grimm's belief that U.S. pressure was in part responsible for Bonnet's change of mind may have been due to U.S. Ambassador Leahy being recalled for "consultation" on April 17. The move, according to Leahy's *I Was There* (New York: Whittlesey House, 1950), was meant to demonstrate U.S. displeasure with Laval's appointment to the premiership.
12. Memorandum of conversation by Guenther, April 29, 1942 (NG-1028).

CHAPTER 20

1. Memorandum of conversation by Guenther, April 29, 1942 (NG-1028).

2. Unsigned Foreign Ministry memorandum (probably by Guenther), May 8, 1942.

3. Teletype from Guenther to Abetz (Paris), May 8, 1942. The dates presumably are those on which the individual segments were written. The typed copy of the decoded message contains no punctuation or capital letters and there are a number of grammatical and spelling errors. "Moabich" should presumably read "Moabit."

4. Memorandum for the files by Kruemmer, May 13, 1942, in Doescher, *Reichskristallnacht,* p. 170.

5. Letter from Freisler to Lautz, May 13, 1942 (NG-968).

6. Memorandum for the files by Guenther, May 16, 1942.

7. Dr. Alain Cuénot, *L'Affaire Grynszpan—vom Rath,* p. 254. (This is the French language manuscript edited and translated into English as *The Herschel Grynszpan Case.*)

8. Emphasis in original. According to Guenter vom Rath, the surviving brother, Gustav vom Rath referred to in the "Fuehrer Information" protested his innocence to the end. He died on the Russian front in December 1942 and was subsequently "rehabilitated," which permitted his family to use his old rank (first lieutenant) in the announcement of his death.

9. Grimm/Dumoulin, *L'Affaire Grynszpan.*

CHAPTER 21

1. Letter from Erich Wollenberg to Guenther vom Rath, May 3, 1964, in Cuénot, *The Herschel Grynszpan Case,* p. 100.

2. Helmut Heiber, "Der Fall Grünspan," *Vierteljahrshefte für Zeitgeschichte* (April 1957): 134.

3. On April 17, French General Giraud had escaped from German detention at Castle Königstein; Hitler was under the (mistaken) impression that Giraud had given his word of honor not to escape. The following day, Laval took over a tottering French government from Admiral Darlan against the express wishes of Berlin.

EPILOGUE

1. Letter from Helmut Heiber to Dr. B. Sagalowitz, December 4, 1958.

Dramatis Personae

Abetz, Otto. German ambassador to Paris, 1940–44.

Badin, M. French police official, interrogated Grynszpan.

Bonnet, Georges. French foreign minister at the time of vom Rath's assassination.

Bohle, Ernst-Wilhelm. *Gauleiter,* head of the Foreign Organization of the NSDAP.

Bormann, Martin. Deputy leader of the Nazi Party, head of the party Chancery.

Braeuer, Kurt. Counselor of embassy and deputy to ambassador of German embassy in Paris at time of assassination.

Buch, Walter. *SS Obergruppenfuhrer* (major general), chief of the NSDAP Supreme Party Court, which investigated some of the "excesses" of the pogrom of November 1938.

Carpe, M. Shopkeeper, sold pistol to Herschel Grynszpan.

Diewerge, Wolfgang. Ministerial counselor in the Ministry of Propaganda, responsible for the propaganda utilization of the Grynszpan case and preparations of the trial.

Engert, Karl. Vice president of the People's Court, designated to preside at the projected trial in 1942.

Frankfurter, David. Assassinated Wilhelm Gustloff in Davos, Switzerland, in 1936.

Freisler, Roland. State secretary in the Ministry of Justice, later president of the People's Court (*Volksgerichtshof*).

Garçon, Maurice. French attorney, represented the plaintiff before the French court, 1938–39.

Goebbels, Josef. Minister of propaganda, died by suicide in 1945.

Goering, Hermann. Deputy Fuehrer and plenipotentiary for the Four-Year Plan. Committed suicide at Nuremberg in 1946.

Grimm, Friedrich. Retained by the Ministry of Propaganda and the Foreign Ministry in connection with the Grynszpan case (ostensibly as the representative of the plaintiff).

Guenther, V.L.R. Senior counselor in the Legal Section of the Foreign Ministry.

Guertner, Franz. Minister of justice, 1932–41.

Guinand, Marcel. Swiss attorney, designated to represent plaintiff before French court after outbreak of war.

Gustloff, Wilhelm. *Landesgruppenleiter* (head of Foreign Organization of the NSDAP in Switzerland), assassinated in 1936 by David Frankfurter.

Gutterer, Leopold. State secretary, Ministry of Propaganda.

Jarblum, Marc. Member of Executive Committee, World Jewish Congress.

Kruemmer, Ewald. Minister, the Foreign Ministry's liaison representative with the Ministry of Propaganda.

Kuenne, Dr. Public prosecutor (Reichsanwalt) before the People's Court.

Lammers, Hans Heinrich. Chief of the Reich Chancellery.

Lautz, Ernst. Chief prosecutor of the People's Court.

Lecache, Bernard. President, Ligue international contre l'antisemitism (LICA) in Paris.

Loncle, Maurice. French lawyer, assisted Grimm in representing the plaintiff before the French court, 1939.

Luther, Martin. Under state secretary, German Foreign Ministry.

Monneret, M.J. French police official, interrogated Herschel Grynszpan on day of assassination.

Moro-Giafferri, Maître Vincent de. French defense lawyer for Herschel Grynszpan.

Mueller-Hess, Dr. Victor. German psychiatrist.

Nagorka, A. Embassy receptionist, led Grynszpan to vom Rath.

Pierie, A.R. British journalist.

von Ribbentrop, Joachim. German foreign minister, 1938–45. Sentenced to death by Nuremberg International Tribunal; executed.

Schlegelberger, Franz. Acting minister of justice, 1941–42. Retired August 1942. Sentenced to life imprisonment by court at Nuremberg; released December 1950.

Tesnière, Jean. Examining magistrate, Paris, 1938–39.

Thierack, Otto. President of the People's Court (1940–1942), minister of justice 1942–45. Commited suicide at Nuremberg in 1946.

Weill-Goudchaux, Serge. Associate defense attorney for Herschel Grynszpan.

von Weizsaecker, Ernst. State secretary in the Foreign Ministry.

von Welczeck, Count Johannes. German ambassador, Paris, 1937–1939.

KEY FAMILY MEMBERS—GRYNSZPAN FAMILY

Grynszpan, Sendel (Zindel, Siegmund). Father of Herschel.

Grynszpan, Rivka (Ryfka, Regina; née Silberberg). Mother of Herschel.

Grynszpan, Esther (Beile, Berta). Sister of Herschel. Died 1941 in USSR.

Grynszpan, Mordechai (Marcus, Mardoche). Brother of Herschel.

Grynszpan, Abraham (Albert, Adolf). Uncle of Herschel (brother of Sendel), resident in Paris since 1923.

Grynszpan, Chawa (Chiara, Chana; née Berenbaum). Wife of Abraham.

Grynszpan, Wolf (Willi). Uncle of Herschel (brother of Sendel), resident in Brussels since 1933.

Grynszpan, Lea (née Buch). Wife of Wolf.

Grynszpan, Salomon (Szalama, Schlojma, Saloma). Uncle of Herschel (brother of Sendel), resident in Paris.

Grynszpan, Matka (née Lewkowitz). Wife of Salomon.

Berenbaum, Abraham. Brother of Chawa Grynszpan, French citizen since 1924.

Berenbaum, Esther (née Ankermann). Wife of Abraham.

Berenbaum, Beimis (Bernhard, Bernich). Brother of Chawa Grynszpan, French citizen since 1928.

Berenbaum, Mina (Marie; née Steinhauer). Wife of Beimis.

Wykhodz, Basila. Sister of Chawa Grynszpan.

Wykhodz, Jacques. Husband of Basila, French citizen since 1927.

Bibliography

BOOKS AND ARTICLES

Cuénot, Dr. Alain. "The Herschel Grynszpan Case." Translation of "L'Affaire Grynszpan–vom Rath," an unpublished manuscript. Translated by Mrs. Joan Redmont and edited and privately reproduced in 1982 by Mr. David Rome, Beverly Hills, California.

______."Un crime a l'ambassade d'Allemagne." *Historia*, No. 204 (November 1963): 640-51.

Dick, Lutz Van. *Der Attentäter*. Reinbeck bei Hamburg: Rowohlt Taschenbuch Verlag, 1988.

Diewerge, Wolfgang. *Der Fall Gustloff*. Munich: Franz Eher Nachf., 1936.

______. *Ein Jude hat geschossen*. Munich: Franz Eher Nachf., 1937.

______. *Anschlag gegen den Frieden*. Munich: Franz Eher Nachf., 1939.

Doescher, Hans-Juergen. *Reichskristallnacht—Die November Pogrome 1938*. Berlin: Ullstein Verlag, 1988.

Fry, Varian. *Surrender on Demand*. New York: Random House, 1945.

Graber, Herbert. *Friedrich Grimm, Ein Leben fuer das Recht*. N.p.,N.d.

Graml, Hermann. *Der 9. November 1938 "Reichskristallnacht."* Bonn: Bundeszentrale fuer Heimatdienst, 1955.

______. *Reichskristallnacht, Antisemitismus und Judenverfolgung im Dritten Reich*. Munich: Deutscher Taschenbuch Verlag, 1988.

Grimm, Friedrich. "Der Fall Gustloff vor dem Kantonsgericht zu Chur." 1936. Speech made by Dr. Grimm before the Swiss court trying David Frankfurter for the murder of Wilhelm Gustloff.

______. *Politischer Mord und Heldenverehrung.* Berlin: Deutscher Rechtsverlag, 1938.

______. *Der Neue Europäische Krieg und Seine Historischen Hintergründe.* Berlin: M. Mueller & Sohn, 1939.

______. [Pierre Dumoulin]. *L'Affaire Grynszpan, un attentat contre la France.* Paris: Editions Jean-Renard, 1942. (Documents confiscated by German Secret Police in Paris, June 1940.)

______. *Denkschrift über die in Paris im Juni-Juli 1940 von der Deutschen Feldpolizei in der Grünspan-Sache beschlagnahmten Akten.* (German version of Dumoulin/Grimm's *L'Affaire Grynszpan.*) N.p., n.d.

______. *Der Grünspan Prozess.* Nuernberg: F. Willmy, 1942.

______. *Affaire Grynspan, Memoire de Monsieur Gustave vom Rath, Parti civile.* Berlin SW 68: M. Mueller & fils., 1942. (French translation of Grimm's "Der Grünspan Prozess.")

______. *Politische Justiz.* Bonn: Bonner Universitaets-Buchdruckerei, 1953.

______. "Ein Dokument zur Zeitgeschichte." *Deutsche Hochschullehrer-Zeitung,* Vol. 5, Nos. 2, 3 (1957).

Hausner, Gideon. *Justice in Jerusalem.* New York: Harper & Row, 1966.

Heiber, Helmut. "Der Fall Grünspan." *Vierteljahrshefte fuer Zeitgeschichte* (April 1957): 134-72.

______. *Kristallnacht, Dokumente von Gestern zum Gedenken von Heute.* Stuttgart: Calwer Verlag, 1978.

Kaul, Friedrich Karl. *Der Fall des Herschel Grynszpan.* Berlin: Akademie-Verlag, 1965.

Kochan, Lionel. *Pogrom, November 10, 1938.* London: Andre Deutsch, 1957.

Lauber, Heinz. *Judenpogrom: "Reichskristallnacht" November 1938 in Grossdeutschland.* Gerlingen: Bleicher Verlag, 1981.

Lochner, Louis P., ed. *The Goebbels Diaries.* Garden City, NY: Doubleday & Company, 1948.

Marrus, Michael R. "The Strange Story of Herschel Grynszpan." *The American Scholar* (Winter 1988).

Reynolds, Quentin. "Portrait of a Murderer." *Colliers,* February 25, 1939.

Ritter, Gerhard. *Carl Goerdeler und die Deutsche Widerstandsbewegung.* Stuttgart: Deutsche Verlagsanstalt, 1954.

Roizen, Ron. "Herschel Grynszpan: The Fate of a Forgotten Assassin." *Holocaust and Genocide Studies,* Vol. 1, No. 2 (1986): 217-28.

Sanders, Marion K. *Dorothy Thompson—A Legend in Her Time.* Boston: Houghton Miflin Co., 1973.

Shirer, William L. *The Rise and Fall of the Third Reich.* New York: Simon and Schuster, 1960.

Sington, S., and Weidenfeld, A. *The Goebbels Experiment.* New Haven: Yale University Press, 1943.

Stephan, Werner. *Goebbels, Daemon einer Diktatur*. Stuttgart: Union Deutscher Verlagsgesellschaften, 1949.

Thalmann, Rita, and Feinermann, Emmanuel. *Crystal Night*. New York: Holocaust Library, 1974. (Translated from the French *La Nuit de Crystal*. Paris: Editions Robert Laffont, 1972.)

Thompson, Dorothy. *Let The Record Speak*. Boston: Houghton Mifflin Co., 1939.

Wheeler-Bennett, John. *Munich—Prologue to Tragedy*. New York: Duell, Sloan and Pearce, 1948.

PUBLISHED DOCUMENTS

Office of U.S. Chief of Counsel for Prosecution of Axis Criminality. *Nazi Conspiracy and Aggression*. Vol. IV. Washington, DC: U.S. Government Printing Office, 1946.

U.S. Department of State. *Documents on German Foreign Policy*, Series D, Vol. IV. Washington, DC: U.S. Government Printing Office, 1951.

Woodward, E. L., and Butler, R. *Documents on British Foreign Policy, 1919–1939*. Third Series, Vol. III. London: His Majesty's Stationery Office, 1950.

UNPUBLISHED DOCUMENTS

The book is largely based on official German files. The documents of the Reichs Ministry for Public Enlightenment and Propaganda, commonly known as the Ministry of Propaganda, have been identified in the text as MoP files, with volume and page numbers. These files are located in the Central State Archives of the German Democratic Republic in Potsdam. The documents of the Foreign Ministry and various other German ministries and organizations, to which the author had access in 1946–47, are now located in the Political Archives of Foreign Ministry of the Federal Republic of Germany in Bonn and in the Federal Archives (*Bundesarchiv*) in Koblenz. A microfilm copy of Goebbels' diaries is available at the Library of Congress, Washington, DC.

Index